TEN THOUSAND VOICES

TIMOTHY JARRETT

TEN THOUSAND VOICES

150 YEARS OF THE VIRGINIA GLEE CLUB

Published *for the*
VIRGINIA GLEE CLUB

Distributed by the
UNIVERSITY OF VIRGINIA PRESS

Published for the Virginia Glee Club.
Distributed by the University of Virginia Press.

© 2022 by Tim Jarrett. All rights reserved. Published 2022
Printed in the United States of America
27 26 25 24 23 22 1 2 3 4 5

ISBN-13: 978-1-7374808-0-8

ISBN eBook: 978-1-7374808-1-5

CIP applied for.

CONTENTS

APPENDICES

TEN THOUSAND VOICES

FIGURE 1. Members of the Virginia Glee Club at the University of Virginia Chapel, May 2019.

INTRODUCTION

I joined the Virginia Glee Club in the fall of 1990. I had never sung publicly outside my hometown church before. I didn't realize it was about to become a lifelong habit.

As I walked through the basement of Old Cabell Hall, going to and from rehearsals in room B012, I was conscious that there was a lot of history here that I didn't understand. My curiosity dimmed over the years—we were busy making our own chapters in the history—but never completely diminished. Still, by the time I had relocated to Kirkland, Washington, after graduate school, then moved back to Arlington, Massachusetts, a few years later, my connections to the Glee Club were somewhat diminished.

That changed one day when I discovered Google Books and the newspaper archives in Google News, new at the time, and started uncovering hints of a Glee Club past I could never have imagined. Performances at the Plaza Hotel? A dramatic uproar at Monticello? Performances in the 1910s in women's clothing? None of this was anything that I had imagined. Having become a Wikipedia editor a while before, I started pulling some of what I learned into the official article, but Wikipedia's notability policies meant I had to leave out a lot of what I was learning about concerts, individuals, and other touchstones of the Glee Club's history. So I decided to make my own Virginia Glee Club wiki, where I could collect as much information about the history as I could find. I figured it would take a few years. That was in December 2009.

The last twelve years have been a story of continuous discovery as I created a timeline, sketched out biographies of key members, and learned more about the group and its history than I ever dreamed possible. Along the way, the outline of a narrative around the seasons and events started to form in my mind. I saw the histories of other glee clubs—Cornell, Yale—and decided I could do it too. I started writing this book, which took shape in airplanes and coffeehouses, on porches and in my parents' kitchen, wherever I could grab a few minutes to write between the demands of my day job.

At long last, it's here, and I hope you have half as much fun reading it as I had researching and writing it.

ACKNOWLEDGMENTS

I owe a great deal to many for their support of this project and for their assistance in helping me to locate and catalog the Glee Club's history.

When I joined the executive committee of the Virginia Glee Club as a third year in 1993, one of our jobs was to update the brief history of the group that appeared in every concert program and which was a key communication tool to help explain the group's need for funds. Much of the early history in the statement was deeply mysterious to me at the time: Why 1871? Why the Cabell House Men? How did we know? We ended up leaving much of the early history in, although we hadn't seen the research to back it up. In the main, my skepticism was unmerited, as the history was based on fine early work by James E. Ballowe Jr., whose twenty-plus-page history of the group (as reprinted in the *Glee Club Annual Report* from 1980, a fundraising work) still stands as the most concise and factual summary of its first one hundred years. I owe more than a little to Ballowe for his work, which pointed the way to many fruitful primary and secondary sources.

I am indebted to Jessica Wiseman, who served for nearly ten years as the general manager, institutional memory, and unofficial den mother of the Virginia Glee Club and whose keen eye for treasures helped us to rescue, digitize, and preserve Harry Rogers Pratt's scrapbook of concert programs, photographs, and memorabilia from the 1930s and early 1940s, forming an invaluable record of those pivotal years. That the scrapbook was rescued from almost certain decay in the closet of the Glee Club House still gives me nightmares.

I am appreciative of the written and oral histories, and of the archives of photographs and concert programs, provided by many former members and conductors, including Jeff Slutzky, Dan Roche, John Stanzione, Larry Mueller, Bruce Kothmann, Ellis Butler, Aven Tsai, Jim Tavenner, Donald Loach, John Liepold, Douglass List, Anthony Gal, and Matthew P. Freeman.

I am grateful to Lenox Coffee in Lenox, Massachusetts, the Lenox Public Library, the Days Inn in Pittsfield, Tanglewood, and JetBlue, among others, for the free and paid WiFi that I used while writing this book over many summers at the Tanglewood Music Center and on long flights when there wasn't much else to do but write.

I am also indebted to Catherine Paul, for walking me through the complexity of the book submission process; to Esta M. Jarrett, for being my first and most enthusiastic reader; to Thomas Deal for encouraging my research; to Kevin Ross Davis for his support; to Frank Albinder, Donald Loach, Matt Freeman, Mr. Deal, and Mr. Davis for their review and feedback on the manuscript; and to the Virginia Glee Club Alumni and Friends Association for making the publication of the work possible.

I am deeply in awe of the work of the club's student leaders, especially to Bruce Kothmann and Larry Mueller in 1989 for ensuring the Glee Club's continuity, to Mr. Deal for securing the Glee Club's future by founding the Virginia Glee Club Alumni and Friends Association, and to James Wilusz for forging hope and a virtual Christmas concert from the ashes of the pandemic. Let no one ever say that there is no hope for the future when visionary leaders can arise from among the student members of the club seemingly at need.

Last, I am forever grateful to the more than three thousand known alumni of the Virginia Glee Club, for living this history, bringing life to a 150-year-old fraternity of talent, and continuing to be Virginia's messengers of harmony, love, and brotherhood.

1 1988: GLEE CLUB NO MORE?

Bruce Kothmann, Larry Mueller, Steve Billcheck, and Nick Hoffman looked at each other in the living room of Kothmann's student apartment. It was December 7, 1988, and they had just learned something astonishing: the University of Virginia Glee Club, in existence since 1871, was to be dissolved and combined with the Virginia Women's Chorus in a new mixed-voice ensemble:

> Quite recently, but after close examination, the music depart-
> ment faculty voted for a reorganization of the curricular cho-
> ral music program in the Fall of 1989. The faculty has asked
> . . . to [form] two choruses of mixed voices, one numbering
> 80 or more, the other, 40 or less. It further recommended
> that the large chorus be formed by uniting the Glee Club
> and Women's Chorus and that it be called the University of
> Virginia Glee Club. The faculty also recommended that the
> Chamber Chorus be called the University Singers.
>
> The primary point by far is the desire of the music facul-
> ty to improve its educational mission. . . . It is . . . important
> for capable performers to come to grips with some of the sig-
> nificant works from the vastly superior repertory for mixed
> voices.[1]

How could this be? The Glee Club had been part of the music department since living memory, had been ambassadors for the University abroad since all the officers were toddlers. It seemed unthinkable that its existence was threatened.

Little did they know that this existential crisis was, in reality, more the norm for the Glee Club than an exception. The Glee Club at the University of Virginia had died a thousand deaths before this point. It had faced waning student enthusiasm, small numbers, and outright bankruptcy a dozen times in its first forty years of existence. It was about to enter another period of instability from which it was far from clear it could emerge.

---

1   A report by Donald Loach to the officers of the Virginia Glee Club, as excerpted in a letter from the Glee Club officers to the membership, dated December 27, 1988.

BEFORE 1871, MUSIC AND RIOT

The modern student at the University of Virginia has a wealth of vocal music options to listen to and participate, even without turning on Spotify. There are the Virginia Women's Chorus, the University Singers, Black Voices Gospel Choir, and all the a cappella groups (which at this writing included the Virginia Gentlemen, the Virginia Belles, the Hullabahoos, the Sil'Hooettes, the New Dominions, the Academical Village People, Hoos in Treble, the Harmonious Hoos, and more). And there is the Virginia Glee Club, which with its 150-year history seems the grand old dame of them all, as much a part of the University as red bricks and orange-and-blue-striped bow ties.

And yet, for the first fifty years of the University's existence, there was no such thing as organized student music. Thomas Jefferson had once written: "Music . . . is the favorite passion of my soul," but this passion had no place in the curriculum which he originally designed for the University.[1] There were natural scientists, professors of ancient and modern languages, mathematicians, but no music instructors among the original ten professors. And yet the University was not devoid of music: a spinet is one of the original furnishings remaining in Pavilion VII, and visitors to Mr. Jefferson's home, Monticello, would have found a room devoted to music.

Perhaps it is most accurate to say that the students had no *organized* music. As for disorganized music? It was apparently prevalent enough to be a nuisance. Among the earliest regulations passed to govern the University's ungovernable early students was a prohibition on the playing of instruments except for strictly regulated hours:

In 1835, a disorderly party of performers playing on fiddles and other instruments, and singing very obscene corn-songs, raised a very discordant hubbub in front of Mr. Wertenbaker's house, which was only discontinued when the proctor came upon the ground. . . . It was reported, indeed, that some of these concerts in the dormitories were kept up until two o'clock in the morning; and the effect finally grew to be so distracting that the Faculty restricted all playing to the intervals between two and three o'clock in the afternoon, and four in the afternoon and eight in the evening. It was prohibited altogether now, as formerly, on Sunday. Both rules were constantly broken.[2]

By the early 1840s, the playing of instruments had come to be associated with riot. Calathumps, groups of students who marched making as much noise as possible with their voices and whatever instruments were handy, were common, as were "dykes," which heralded of the departure of an amorous student to visit the object of his affections.[3] But the student population grew, and grew, and the seeds of honor sown in the University's horrified reaction to the shooting of Professor John A. G. Davis in 1840 took root, slowly civilizing the nighttime bands.[4] By 1861 there began to be stirrings of organized musical activity: a glee club had sprung up at the off-Grounds housing near Carr's Hill, performing "serenading songs."[5]

But then came the Civil War. While the University's students greeted the news of the siege of Fort Sumter and the opening of hostilities with initial jubilation—in February 1861 two students broke into the Rotunda to fly a secession flag from the cupola at the top of the dome, the first to fly in Virginia, and about 140 students organized two military companies, the Sons of Liberty and the Southern Guard—the effect of the war on the University was disastrous. Few classes could be held, and the students who remained shared space with soldiers dying of their wounds in makeshift infirmaries. Thanks to the actions of the mayor of Charlottesville and University professor Socrates Maupin in seeking protection for the town and the University, Jefferson's dream was spared outright sacking and destruction, but much around it lay in ruins.

The University and the Commonwealth of Virginia rolled up their sleeves and rebuilt. Both managed their way through five years of Reconstruction; the final removal of the military government following the war did not occur until April 1870. Student memories then as now were mercifully short; five short years after the war's conclusion, they were already writing about the need to form musical groups. In the January 1871 issue of the *Virginia University Magazine*, the student editors complained:

> There is one point on which we are deficient, and that is col-
> lege musical groups. There is no lack of instrumental talent
> among us, as clearly evidenced by the soft, plaintive strains
> of violin music which frequently enter at the back window of
> our sanctum. We are not wanting in vocal powers, as prov-
> en by the deep sounds that rise in sweet cadence from be-
> low us, and also by the sudden outbursts of Shoofly, Upudee
> [sic], Little Brown Jug, and other melodies that occasionally
> startle "the drowsy ear of night." But there seems to be lit-
> tle disposition to collect this scattered talent. We know of
> but one exception to this rule. Those gentlemen rooming
> at the Cabell House, and in that neighborhood, have made
> great efforts, and we understand tolerably successful ones, to
> form a Glee Club. They certainly deserve great credit, and
> they should also command the hearty cooperation and good
> wishes of all who are not fit "for stratagems and spoils." [6]

How had the students at this University under Reconstruction gotten the fever to have a glee club? The answer lies in the pages of the magazine.

The *Virginia University Magazine*, as it was then known, was the product of the University's literary societies, who in the pre– and post–Civil War years did more for the University than practice debate and parliamentary process on Friday nights prior to drinking bourbon in Room 7, West Lawn. They produced a highly visible magazine, with student essays, fiction, poetry, and news of the University, which reached far beyond its borders. It is worth noting that the yearbook, *Corks and Curls*, was first produced in 1888 and the student newspaper, *College Topics* (later the *Cavalier Daily*), was not founded until 1891. In the years before that, anyone wanting to know about the goings on of the student body read about it in the *Magazine*.

The reader of the *Magazine* would find, about six or seven times a session, a section on goings on at the University ("Collegiana") and another on the features of magazines published by *other* universities that month ("Exchanges"). Where there is little evidence that the antebellum University cared much what others thought of it, or what other schools did, the "Exchanges" column is full of notes about different successes and occasional failures of other schools' magazines:

> *The University Reporter*, from the University of Georgia, is one of the best college weeklies that comes to us. It is a spicy and entertaining sheet, containing much to interest its readers, but with all this we must beg our friend to be kind enough to give us credit for our productions. We notice in the last issue a scrap of poetry to which is added the name of the paper from which it was taken, while immediately under this is a piece from us with a slight change of name and no credit given. We trust this was an oversight.[7]

So it was with glee clubs. At Virginia during the 1870s there were frequent editorials noting the absence of a glee club at the University. For example, an editorial in 1878 notes:

> We will venture to say that at the University there are more good voices and less good singing than among an equal number of vocal beings in any part of the world, as far as our geographical knowledge enables us to grope. This may seem like a paradox, but it is the simple truth; for, while individual voices of great superiority are common in all parts of College, yet, it is the rarest thing to hear a collection of fine voices singing with that concert and harmony which can alone result from practise. . . . It is strange, indeed, that while following the time honored example of Colleges in other respects—as boating, &c, we have failed to adopt a custom which is prevalent in every College of the North—from the great institutions like Harvard and Yale, to those of the very lowest grade. And this fact appears stranger still when we consider that Glee Clubs were first started long before the war, by certain Southern students at Yale College. This College music emanated from our own South but the South owns it no more.[8]

So the contagion of glee club fever spread via the pages of the *Magazine*. But what was the germ and how did it arise in the first place?

1   Thomas Jefferson to Giovanni Fabbroni, June 8, 1778, The Avalon Project, Lillian Goldman Law Library, Yale Law School, https://avalon.law.yale.edu/18th_century/letii.asp. This quotation, along with a high-resolution scan of Jefferson's signature, was liberally used by the Virginia Glee Club during the 1992–1993 season, during which it helped the university commemorate Jefferson's 250th birthday. However, the full quotation is somewhat less saccharine: "If there is a gratification which I envy any people in this world, it is to your country its music. This is the favorite passion of my soul, & fortune has cast my lot in a country where it is in a state of deplorable barbarism."

2   Philip Alexander Bruce, *History of the University of Virginia* (New York: MacMillan, 1921), vol. 2, 334–35.

3   In contemporaneous usage, this term referred to the custom of playing musical instruments and noisemakers loudly whenever a University of Virginia student left the Grounds for a date. Virginius Dabney describes the ritual as "a concerted effort on the part of students to embarrass any fellow collegian who was found to be en route to a rendezvous with his fair one. On such occasions, all the noisemaking apparatus that could be assembled, such as drums, horns, whistles, and coal scuttles belabored with pokers, was brought into action. The shouting and screeching crowd surrounded the young man and accompanied him as far as his ladylove's door. If it was at night, the participants in the dyke carried improvised torches. Often the youth was required to make a few brief remarks to the assembled multitude before he was permitted to enter the home of his inamorata. At times the mob lay in wait until he emerged, whereupon it greeted him again with raucous din and ear-splitting cacophony." Virginius Dabney, *Mr. Jefferson's University* (Charlottesville: University of Virginia Press, 1981), 21.

4   Dabney, *Mr. Jefferson's University*, 9–10. Dabney places Davis's shooting in the context of earlier student riots in 1826, 1831, 1836, 1838, and 1839.

5   Paul Brandon Barringer, James Mercer Garnett, and Rosewell Page, eds., *University of Virginia: Its History, Equipment, Influence, and Characteristics* (New York: Lewis Publishing Company, 1904), 199.

6   "Collegiana," *Virginia University Magazine* 9, no. 4 (January 1871): 210–11.

7   "Exchanges," *Virginia University Magazine* 30, no. 7 (April 1887): 541.

8   "Collegiana," *Virginia University Magazine* 16, no. 6 (March 1878): 376–77.

3 THE RISE AND SPREAD OF GLEE CLUBS

Music had been a part of student life in American universities from the earliest days of the republic—and even before—as the Protestant traditions that founded the nation's earliest institutions of higher learning encouraged hymnody, the singing of psalms, and other sacred music as part of the curriculum. At the same time, informal singing was a part of everyday student life. John Quincy Adams's diary on January 3, 1788, notes that he "pass'd the evening at Little's in Newbury. A Mr. Coffin, who graduated two years ago at Harvard, was there. We spent our time in sociable chat and in singing; not such unmeaning, insignificant songs as those with which we killed our time last evening, but good, jovial, expressive songs such as we sang at College, when mirth and jollity prevail'd."[1] Even at this early date, secular music was a popular pastime that promoted bonds of friendship among the singers.

As early as the late eighteenth century, this tradition of secular music was complemented by the rise of the urban musical societies, institutions organized under the leadership of professional musicians to study the new classical music arriving from Europe. In particular, German music made a strong

---

For much of the substance of this chapter I am deeply indebted to J. Lloyd Winstead's *When Colleges Sang: The Story of Singing in American College Life* (Tuscaloosa: University of Alabama Press, 2013).

impact, leading to the formation of musical societies bearing the names of Handel, Haydn, Mendelssohn, and others. This trend of "cultivated" music, as well as the less formalized, "vernacular" or popular music, contributed significantly to the evolution of college singing. Williams College created a Handel and Haydn society that provided sacred music for college functions, and Handel societies sprung up at Dartmouth and Western Reserve College in the late 1820s. Musical groups at Harvard had been established as early as 1810, with the foundation of the Pierian Society. The Harvard Glee Club, dedicated to the art of the "glee" as opposed to the more formal "cultivated" music, was formed out of the Pierian on November 12, 1833, eventually becoming a separate club in 1858.

At Yale, there was the Beethoven Society, founded in 1812 and refounded in 1827 after a hiatus. Hiatuses were the rule in the Beethoven Society's history, as there was no particular honor deriving from membership in the group and rehearsals were poorly attended. Many members of the Beethoven Society were also members of the Yale Glee Club, and concerts were billed as joint affairs, with the Beethoven Society receiving credit for the more artistic works and the glee club for the college songs.

The rise of fraternities in the 1830s and 1840s also sparked student interest in singing. Formed to provide students with nourishment for the "moral, social and intellectual" dimensions of their lives, fraternities helped to institutionalize practices such as singing, as well as card playing, smoking, and drinking.[2] The arrival of fraternities codified these student behaviors as traditions, and their colonization to other schools helped to disseminate these traditions from one institution to another.

The spread of student music was reinforced by the publication of the first student songbooks, helped by the arrival of innovations in printing technology that allowed for easy printing of sheet music. Yale, whose tradition of song was well established, produced the first book devoted to student songs in 1853, *Songs of Yale*. And 1860 saw the first publication of a songbook for multiple colleges, *College Songs*, which drew from Harvard, Yale, Williams, and Dartmouth. Volumes of songs from Williams, Amherst, Hampton University, and others followed.

By the late 1850s and early 1860s, student singing of vernacular music had emerged and been disseminated by the fast-growing fraternity system. Its popularity had encouraged the rise of student groups dedicated to this form of college song. And it had been transformed from a primarily oral art form to one with a printed record, transmitted by books and sheet music from one college to another. Small wonder then that the ten earliest college glee clubs still extant were founded in a few short years between 1858 and 1875, the interruption of the Civil War notwithstanding.

---

1   John Quincy Adams, *Life in a New England Town: 1787, 1788* (Boston: Little, Brown, 1903), 79; quoted in Winstead, *When Colleges Sang.*

2   Talcott Williams, ed., *The Alpha Delta Phi, 1832–1882* (Boston: Alpha Delta Phi, 1882), cited in Winstead, *When Colleges Sang, 63.*

1871 TO 1874: THE CABELL HOUSE MEN AND THE CLARIBEL

Glee Clubs, like football and other hallmarks of college life, spread from school to school along the East Coast and beyond. That they should have found fertile soil at the University of Virginia is unsurprising; though its historical neglect of formal music instruction is well documented, so was the history of avid extracurricular music making, as we have seen.

But that the seed of the Glee Club should have found purchase in this particular soil, in the Cabell House, seems at once odd and oddly fitting.

The Cabell House was a boarding house located on Main Street between the University and downtown Charlottesville. Boarding houses had become a fact of university life in the 1850s, after the enrollment had overrun both the rooms on the Lawn and Range and the newly built row of dormitory dependencies built on Monroe Hill next to the onetime house of the former president. With little support for education from the legislature, boarding houses sprang up in the surrounding Charlottesville community.

The Cabell House had housed many former students of the University in this decade, including a nineteen-year-old third-year student with a keen sense of honor and a remarkable knack for making enemies. John Singleton Mosby, whose nickname during the Civil War as the Gray Ghost, was known in Charlottesville mostly for challenging other students to duel. George R. Turpin, who was described as a bully, threatened Mosby, swearing to eat him "blood raw."[1] On March 29, 1853, Mosby decided to take the offensive, carrying a loaded pepper-box pistol to his tutoring sessions, and returning to his lodgings at the Cabell House. When Turpin found him there, Mosby attacked him, shooting him in the face and wounding him, but not fatally.

The house was considerably more sedate by 1871, when a group of anonymous students started the first Glee Club. But success was far from assured. Little is known of the efforts of that first group of students, and their names are unrecorded. Like the Beethoven Society of Yale, they seem to have faded in and out as students had time and energy.

Why the propitious year of 1871? While we lack a comprehensive history of student activities in the early University, one point is important to remember: Reconstruction in Virginia didn't end until April of 1870. Prior to that, the state was still classified as a rebellious territory and under military rule. Following Virginia's readmission to the Union, the state struggled with the aftermath of the Civil War and the challenges of Reconstruction, but it could also start to rebuild. Small wonder that in the 1870–1871 school year, student attention returned to song.

During the 1873–1874 school year, nascent student interest in college song found new expression in a group calling itself the Claribel. In February 1874, the *Virginia University Magazine* reported:

> Quartette.—Dat Leetle German Band has grown tried of its stock of songs, and not having time to learn more, it is virtually disbanded. We are glad to see, however, that some enthusiasm—perhaps a healthier development of the *cacoethes cantandi* that existed earlier in the session—still manifests itself in the formation of "The Claribel." This organization consists of the gentlemen named below, and includes some of the best voices we have heard in college. Mr. George I. Lyell, first tenor; Mr. R. B. Shephard, second tenor; Mr. Ro. W. Tunstall, first bass; Mr. Budd, second bass.[2]

The Claribel was received with some enthusiasm. A little over a year later, the *Magazine* reported:

> We are glad to see that [the Claribel] still keeps up its old enthusiasm. It was formed last year, and includes this, as well as last session, some of the best voices in college. There is

no recreation that the students can engage in more to be encouraged than the formation of these clubs, for 'tis a source of legitimate amusement to themselves as well as a treat to others. We bespeak for their serenades a kind and hearty reception by the ladies of the University and Charlottesville.[3]

Originally a quartet of singers and growing to a quintet in its second season, the Claribel stuck around for two seasons and is the oldest singing group for whom names have been recorded. Their biographical details tell us a little bit about the University of Virginia singers of the early 1870s.

George I. Lyell. The first tenor of the Claribel and one of the members who spanned both years of its existence, Lyell was a Pi Kappa Alpha brother who also sang in Charlottesville's Mendelssohn Society. A report published February 4, 1874, in the *Jeffersonian Republican* notes: "Mr. George I. Lyell, one of the performers, was loudly called for by the audience to sing the comic song, *Little German Band*, but his extreme modesty prevented his compliance therewith."[4] Nothing is known of Lyell after his University of Virginia career. But his connection to Pi Kappa Alpha is significant; this fraternity (like others) issued songbooks which the pledges were expected to learn but which were rarely performed. The students apparently preferred their "informal songs" and "gross songs" to the "formal songs" of the songbook.[5]

Robert Barnes Shepherd. Hailing from Fredericksburg, where he was born in 1853, Shepherd spent his life after the University in New York—where he earned a Knight of the Order of the Crown of Italy for services to the Italian government—and Nassau, where he died in 1929.

Robert W. Tunstall. Born in 1851 in Norfolk, Virginia, Tunstall sang first bass in the first year of the Claribel. He went into business as a merchant in Baltimore, Maryland.[6]

Samuel W. Budd. Born August 30, 1852, in Petersburg, Virginia, Budd was a medical student at the University of Virginia, having done his undergraduate work at Richmond College. He became a physician in Petersburg but died unexpectedly on May 13, 1899, in Baltimore at Johns Hopkins Hospital, where he had gone for treatment.[7]

William Brooke Tunstall. Born January 9, 1856, in Norfolk, Virginia, Tunstall sang second bass in the second year of the Claribel. After college, he became a merchant in Baltimore, Maryland, with his brother Robert.

William Kimsey Seago. Hailing from Atlanta, Georgia, where he was born on June 10, 1855, Seago became a wholesale merchant in sugar and rice in New Orleans after a lack of funds obliged him to leave the University.

Charles Steele. Probably the most notable member of the Claribel, and a founding rower for the Rives Boat Club, he became a partner in the J. P. Morgan Company in 1889 and later a philanthropist. He donated $5 million to St. Thomas Church in New York City to build a choir school for boys; gave St. Paul's in Charlottesville enough money to allow them to purchase the land where the church now sits; and made multiple bequests to the University. He was probably the only alumnus of a Virginia Glee Club–related organization to boast an Æolian-Skinner organ in his house.

So these were the alums of the Claribel, the earliest known individual students associated with the early Virginia Glee Club. For the most part only in the University for a year or two, then straight into the workforce, these industrious members were a far cry from the alums of the 1840s and 1850s, who would have been principally professionals or members of the gentry. But they weren't wholly consumed with collegiate life in the way that their successors would prove to be. They seem, from the record, to have been most at home with one of the great time-honored traditions of glee clubs: serenading women.

1 From an account by John S. Patton in the *Baltimore Sun,* cited in *The Memoirs of Colonel John S. Mosby* (Boston: Little, Brown, 1917), 7, https://docsouth.unc.edu/fpn/mosby/mosby.html.

2 "Collegiana," *Virginia University Magazine* 12, no. 5 (February 1874): 317.

3 "Collegiana," *Virginia University Magazine* 13, no. 7 (April 1875): 426–27.

4 "Mendelssohn Concert," *Jeffersonian Republican,* February 4, 1874, 2, http://virginiachronicle.com/cgi-bin/virginia?a=d&d=JRP18740204.1.1&e=en=20itxt=txIN=.

5 Winstead, *When Colleges Sang,* 172.

6 "Students of the University of Virginia," University of Virginia Library, http://xtf.lib.virginia.edu/xtf/view?docId=2004_Q1/uvaBook/tei/b006136417.xml;chunk.id=d43;toc.depth=100;brand=default;query=tunstall.

7 Obituary, *Virginia Medical Semi-Monthly* 4, no. 4 (May 26, 1899): 130.

5 | 1879 TO 1880: WOODROW WILSON'S GLEE CLUB

After the Claribel's last season in 1875, the musical students of the University of Virginia appear to have descended into minstrelsy. The *Virginia University Magazine* records that a minstrel show took place, organized by the students, in 1877, 1878, and 1879 for the benefit of the Rives Boat Club.[1] We unfortunately have little record of the performers or the performances, but it is clear that the University was not alone in putting on entertainment in blackface; Mask and Wig, founded in 1889 at the University of Pennsylvania, performed in blackface in their early years, as did student organizations at Princeton beginning in 1886, Columbia University beginning in 1878 or earlier, and even Pomona University in 1907.[2]

While the early roots of blackface performance at Virginia are, perhaps mercifully, scantily documented, we have a little better history on the Glee Club. We pick up the thread of its history on November 1, 1879, when the University Glee Club was formed and the names of the original octet were recorded: first tenors—Woodrow Wilson, Charles William Kent; second tenors—John Duncan Emmet, John W. G. Blackstone; first basses—Alexander Barclay Guigon, George Pierce DuBose; second basses—Sylvanus Stokes, Archibald W. Patterson; leader, John Duncan Emmet.[3]

This octet, like the Claribel, had as its chief pursuit the wooing of women, or "calico" as the men of the University referred to young ladies of the town. This incarnation was noted for its vocal "harmonious sweetness that is peculiarly pleasing to all who are so fortunate as to hear them," and the first account of their performance suggests the impact they had:

> We hear that on moonlight nights they group themselves in a picturesque, romance-suggesting manner around the graceful form of their handsome leader, somewhere on our beautiful Lawn, and pour out entrancing love songs of exquisite sweetness that rouse the slumbering ones for whom the serenade is meant, and a flood of light, a little half-suppressed laughter, a creaking shutter slowly opening, a light footstep among the shadows on the terrace, a bunch of ribbon-tied flowers and a dainty card fluttering to the ground on which is written in delicate feminine tracery:

MANY THANKS

AND

OUR COMPLIMENTS

TO

THE UNIVERSITY GLEE CLUB.[4]

The performance, according to a 1924 biography of Woodrow Wilson, would have included such songs as "Marguerite," "Speed Away," "Over the Banister Leans a Face," and "Forsaken."[5] The latter two songs were collected in the 1906 *Songs of the University of Virginia*, suggesting they stayed in frequent rotation in the repertoire.

The woman-wooing nature of the early Glee Club and proto-Glee Club octets—the *Magazine* once predicted that the Claribel's serenades would win "a kind and hearty reception by the ladies of the University and Charlottesville"—is an interesting through-note in the club's history, and one that does not appear in early histories of the Harvard or Yale Glee Clubs. The earlier groups appeared more focused on the pleasure of brotherly song, at least in official histories, but in the earliest days of the Virginia Glee Club its motivation appears to have been driven by their interest in the fairer sex.

The other thread running through the 1879–1880 group appears to have been power. By percentage, this may have been the most accomplished roster of Glee Club alumni in the group's history. It included two lawyers, Sylvanus Stokes and Alexander Barclay Guigon; two doctors, George Pierce DuBose and John Duncan Emmet; a University of Virginia professor, Charles William Kent; a Virginia state senator and circuit court judge, John W. G. Blackstone; a Commissioner of Chancery for the Richmond Chancery Court, Archibald W. Patterson; and of course Wilson, who was president of Princeton and governor of New Jersey before becoming the twenty-eighth president of the United States.

Sylvanus Stokes. Stokes was born in 1858 in Richmond and studied constitutional and international law at the University of Virginia. A brother in Alpha Tau Omega, he is notable for having helped to extend that fraternity northward by initiating the first brothers in Philadelphia in 1881. He practiced law in Richmond with Harry Marston Smith and died in 1934.

Alexander Barclay Guigon. Also born in Richmond in 1858, Guigon was born into a long-standing Richmond family. His father had served as an ordnance officer during the Civil War and, returning to the practice of law after the war, was elected judge of the Hustings Court of Richmond in 1870. He is credited with having helped substantially to restore Richmond to peacetime standing through his enforcement of criminal law in the days after the war. Upon his father's death, University professor John B. Minor wrote to Guigon, offering him a position in his summer law classes free of charge and stating, "I shall hold your father's services to the state and to the profession an ample remuneration for any benefit you may derive . . . I knew not one man in the commonwealth who might not have been better spared, nor have I ever known one whose death has excited such deep universal and sincere regret." Guigon entered the law himself and practiced in Richmond until his death in 1923.

George Pierce DuBose. DuBose (born 1862 in Sparta, Georgia) appears to have been the least accomplished member of this group, merely becoming a licensed physician. He died in Washington, DC, in 1939.

John Duncan Emmet. Emmet, the group's director, was born in 1857. A member of an old University of Virginia family, Emmet completed his medical degree in 1880 and became the chief gynecologist at St. Vincent's Hospital in New York.[6] He founded the *American Gynæcological and Obstetrical Journal.* Like Guigon, he died in 1923.

Charles William Kent. Kent, born in Louisa, Virginia, in 1860, was also associated with the faculty of the University, albeit more directly. Kent left the University to study at the University of Leipzig, where he received his doctorate in 1887 and became a licentiate instructor of English and modern languages. He subsequently served as a professor in the same subject at the University of Tennessee. When the University of Virginia established a school of English literature (the forerunner of today's English department) in 1892, Kent was elected as its first professor. He remained active in University life, joining the Raven Society and editing the *Alumni Bulletin* in its early years. He died in 1917.

John W. G. Blackstone. Blackstone (1858–1911) was one of the more notable politicians of the 1879–1880 class (Wilson aside), serving in the Virginia State Senate from 1884 to 1896, when he was appointed the county judge for Accomack. He served as a judge on the Eighth and Eleventh Judicial Circuits until his retirement in 1908.

Archibald W. Patterson. Patterson, born in Richmond in 1858, was active in the state's capital all his life. Practicing law in Richmond after graduating from the University in 1882, he was subsequently appointed Commissioner in Chancery for the Chancery Court in Richmond and to the Circuit Court of Henrico County. Patterson served on the board of trustees of Richmond College, overseeing as president its transformation to the University of Richmond. He served on the board until his death in 1940.

Woodrow Wilson. Wilson is undeniably the most famous alumnus of the 1879–1880 Glee Club, if not the most famous Virginia Glee Club alum to date. In addition to his two terms as president of the United States, his work as the president of Princeton University and as the governor of New Jersey rank him the most accomplished. In other ways, he seems very much of a part with his fellows in the Glee Club, though he was the oldest by two years: a Virginia lad, born in Staunton in 1856, he was a law student at the University and was also president of the Jefferson Society before ill health forced him home. He died in 1924.

1 "Collegiana," *Virginia University Magazine* 17, no. 5 (February 1879): 305–6.
2 Jeremy Berman, *A History of Student Theatre at the University of Pennsylvania* (2015, available at https://pennplayersalumniclub.weebly.com/history.html), 23; April C. Armstrong, "The Minstrel Tradition at Princeton University," Princeton and Slavery, https://slavery.princeton.edu/stories/the-minstrel-tradition-at-princeton-university; John Scott Butler, "A Darkened Past: The Role of Blackface Minstrelsy in Forming the Columbia Community," Columbia University and Slavery, https://columbiaand

slavery.columbia.edu/sites/default/files/content/2018%20Papers/Butler%20CU%20
Slavery%20Paper%20.pdf; "Hail, Pomona, Hail!" The Choral Program at Pomona
College, http://choral.pomona.edu/college-songs/hail-pomona/.
3 "Collegiana," *Virginia University Magazine* 19, no. 3 (December 1879): 194–95.
4 "Collegiana," *Virginia University Magazine* 19, no. 3 (December 1879): 194–95.
5 William Allen White, *Woodrow Wilson: The Man, His Times and His Task* (Boston:
Houghton, Mifflin, 1924), 84. White's chronology appears to be a little suspect, since
"Over the Banister" was not written until 1887.
6 Emmet's grandfather John Patten Emmet was one of the first professors at the
University of Virginia, recruited from the practice of medicine in South Carolina to
the faculty after Thomas Jefferson heard him speak in Charleston. He served as professor of chemistry. Emmet Dorm is named in John Patten Emmet's memory.

6 THE 1880S: STRUGGLE FOR TRACTION

I f 1879–1880 was an early triumph for the Glee Club in terms of the caliber of students and their success at their chosen mission, the following years largely went unheralded and unrecorded. At times, indeed, during the 1880s the Glee Club was completely unorganized; there were at least four and possibly six fallow seasons during the period, in which those seeking collegiate song pursued other avenues.[1]

The first solid appearance of a glee club in the 1880s is the 1886–1887 season, though there are hints that they may have organized for the first time in 1885–1886.[2] The members, numbering somewhere between eight and sixteen, included Sterling Galt, the president; T. L. Dabney, vice-president; William P. Brickell, secretary; and G. T. Smith, treasurer. The activities of the club included music for evening chapel services, a benefit performance (sponsored by the Ladies Chapel Aid Society) to raise funds for the continued construction of the Chapel, an April joint concert with other University and community musicians, and even performances away from Grounds.[3]

The association of the Glee Club with the Chapel services and its resurgence in the late 1880s is probably not an accident. The construction of the Chapel in the late 1880s provided the first place on Grounds where religious services could be held, and therefore a place close by that offered a weekly outlet for voices.

One musical outlet does not appear to have been enough. The students also organized a University Minstrel Troupe in 1886–1887, which was also managed and stage directed by Sterling Galt, and which performed a concert of mixed song, minstrel ballads, and even a burlesque of *The Mikado*, in which the boys of the club played all the roles, including the three little maids from school.[4]

All told, this year's Glee Club made so compelling a record of their existence that in the 1930s Harry Rogers Pratt and the Glee Club counted 1886 as their founding year, rather than 1871.

The following season saw a significant development in the history of the University: the advent of *Corks and Curls*. Prior to 1887–1888, there was no yearbook and no student newspaper; virtually all we know about the early Glee Club comes from the scant information given by "Collegiana," a recurring column in the *Magazine* that noted activities on Grounds. But starting with the 1888 volume, *Corks and Curls* provided a consistent and superior record of the activities of the student body. For the first time, we have a picture of the full membership of the Glee Club and the members' other activities, including other singing groups such as the West Range Sextette.

The 1887–1888 group was conducted and led by J. R. A. Hobson, who was both music director and president; E. M. Stires was secretary and treasurer. The group numbered sixteen, including at least one repeating member (Brickell) from the previous season. Little information is available regarding the group's activities this season, though a note in the *Magazine* in February 1888 indicated that they were rehearsing for a concert in "a room above the post-office":

> There are numerous speculations as to what will be done
> with the proceeds of this concert. Some think that the club
> will give the Ladies' Chapel Aid Society enough to complete
> the chapel, and that all the rest, excepting probably a small
> amount which will be given to purchase four or five boats for
> the boat club, will be used to construct a Glee Club building.
> The building will be located at the foot of the Lawn.[5]

While the "Collegiana" writer's tongue was firmly in cheek, he unwittingly anticipated the coming of the Glee Club's eventual performance space, though it would be almost ten years before ground was broken for Cabell Hall in the aftermath of the 1895 Rotunda fire.

The following season saw a late organization of the Glee Club; apparently the group did not re-form until after November 1888, when "Collegiana" asked, "Why doesn't the Glee-Club organize? There is evidently no lack of material in college, and enough of last year's club are back to start it up again, and set it going."[6] That the Club did re-form is indicated by *Corks and Curls*, which again lists sixteen members, though no officers or directors. Of the sixteen, notably, seven were returning members, including Hobson, who may again have directed the group. Other returning members included M. Andre Burthé, who would return forty-eight years later as an alumnus to support the group's fiftieth anniversary concerts in 1936.

The 1888–1889 season also saw the formation of a smaller, less formal group that competed with the main club. Calling itself the Holmes Glee Club, the group, like many others around the University, came and went over the years, showing unusual longevity and even existing for a few years when the Glee Club itself did not.

The following season saw an important milestone with the Glee Club's first confirmed appearances outside the University and Charlottesville community. One reason that the 1889–1890 season yields the first firm evidence of outside concerts is the arrival of another important historical source—the student newspaper, *College Topics*. Later renamed the *Cavalier Daily* in the 1940s, the newspaper provided yet more coverage of student activities, including performances of the Glee Club in the Public Hall in the Rotunda annex, as well as in Richmond and Lynchburg; the latter concerts were fundraisers for the Confederate Soldiers Cemetery. According to the editorial, "No other [glee] club has ever ventured to lift its voice outside of the walls of our beloved alma mater or its immediate vicinity. The club of '90, however, emboldened by the favorable criticisms of those who have heard them sing, both friends and strangers, are about to pioneer the way in the State for future clubs."[7]

The Glee Club was more formally organized alongside the Banjo Club, with C. Shirley Carter the president of both organizations and Z. W. Coombs directing the Glee Club. William Stringfellow was the business manager. Though there was again a double octet, only two members from the prior season, M. B. Corse and R. F. Williams, returned.

So went the 1880s. Though there was little activity in the first half of the decade, the second half saw the establishment of two cornerstones that just a few years later would underpin some of the young Glee Club's earliest successes. The first was the combination of the vocal Glee Club with the University's emerging instrumental clubs, in particular the Banjo Club and Mandolin Club. By themselves each of these groups could produce engaging music; put them together and you had *a show*. The second cornerstone was a less likely factor, but one that became ubiquitous in Virginia—and American life—in the 1880s, with a squeal of iron wheels and a belch of smoke and steam: the arrival of the railroad in Charlottesville.

---

1 Nothing is written of the Glee Club in the years from the 1882–1883 to the 1885–1886 season. For the two seasons before there were cursory notes in the *Magazine* about the group organizing, but no roster and no further evidence of activity. See "Collegiana," *Virginia University Magazine* 20, no. 1 (October 1880): 59; "Collegiana," *Virginia University Magazine,* 21, no. 2 (November 1881); and "Collegiana," *University of Virginia Magazine* 22, no. 2 (October 1882).

2 "The Glee Club has been organized. . . . The success of the entertainment given by this organization last session leads us to hope that it has come to stay, and to be a prominent feature of student life in the University"; "Collegiana," *Virginia University Magazine* 30, no. 2 (November 1886): 112–13.

3 "The Glee Club promised to provide music for Sunday evening services in the chapel; but, up to this time, its performances in that elegant building have been few, and we have been entirely without music during the last six weeks, while the Glee Club has been giving concerts in the North"; "Collegiana," *Virginia University Magazine* 30, no. 5 (February 1887): 365.

4 "University Minstrel Troupe," University of Virginia Library Online Exhibits, http://explore.lib.virginia.edu/items/show/5460, accessed October 21, 2015. The report is undated, but performance would have been held in 1886 or 1887, based on the performers listed and the evidence of the University of Virginia Catalogue.

5 "Collegiana," *Virginia University Magazine* 31, no. 6 (February 1888): 403–4.

6 "Voices," *Virginia University Magazine* (November 1888): 136–37.

7 "Glee and Banjo Concert," *College Topics,* March 26, 1890.

7 1890S: ON TOUR WITH THE GLEE CLUB

That the Glee Club's early history should be bound to the Grounds of the University is unsurprising, if one considers both the fragile civil life and convalescing infrastructure of post-Reconstruction Virginia. That just twenty-two years after its founding it would be touring major southern cities in four states staggers the mind until one thinks about one aspect of that badly injured infrastructure: the railroad.

Prior to the Civil War, the railroad did not enjoy the same rise to prominence in the South as in the North. In Virginia particularly, the spread of the railroad was hampered by the political power of the planters, who were suspicious of transportation initiatives that did not directly help get their goods to market faster, and of the elite in Richmond, who, starting with George Washington, had championed river transportation for goods with an eye to keeping commerce in Virginia ports rather than sending it down the Mississippi River to the port of New Orleans (under Spanish control until the Louisiana Purchase).[1] In this spirit, the canal-building enterprise that created the still visible Chesapeake and Ohio Canal between Georgetown and Cumberland, Maryland, and the James River and Kanawha Canal in Richmond sought to create water links from major plantations to ports. When railroads first started to be built in a significant way in Virginia, they were likewise viewed as ways to market for the planters; there was no vision of a network of rails that could assist with transit of goods over land and across state lines, much less comparable carriage of passengers.

After the Civil War, this began to change. The railroad company eventually known as the Chesapeake and Ohio Railway bought smaller rail companies and began to connect the lines to out-of-state networks. Following Reconstruction, the C&O was purchased by northern rail barons and expanded still further. Passenger trains then became more widely available. In 1885, the Charlottesville Union Station, a passenger depot serving the C&O, the Virginia Midland Railway, and the Charlottesville and Rapidan Railroad, opened on West Main Street, where it still sits (serving Amtrak) today. Before the advent of the railroad, distance travel relied on horse power; afterward, students could—and did—ride the rails.

So it was that the Glee Clubs of 1889–1890, 1891–1892, and 1892–1893 mounted their first performances outside Charlottesville—albeit in the relatively close-to-hand locales of Staunton, Norfolk, Richmond, and Petersburg. As we have seen, the Glee Club of 1889–1890 had held a concert in the Public Hall in the Rotunda Annex, on April 11, 1890, and followed it that same weekend with performances in Lynchburg and Staunton. Two years later the Glee Club returned to the Public Hall on December 17, 1891, with a program that featured song in less than half the performance's fifteen numbers, the balance being devoted to banjo, guitar, and mandolin works; the following night found them in Staunton, and a performance in Norfolk followed on April 20. The 1892–1893 club broadened its horizons still further, with a performance in town at the Levy Opera House in January, and a three-city tour with appearances in the Richmond Theatre, the Norfolk Opera House, and the Academy of Music in Petersburg in February.[2]

Let's take a minute to meet a few of the faces in these Glee Clubs, as some of them figure later in the successful touring of the 1890s, and one in the history of the group for many years after.

As with our 1879–1880 alumni, quite a few of the Glee Club's alumni in the early 1890s were there for the law school. William Barnfeather Eagles (1869–1928) practiced in Louisiana and Kentucky after his law school graduation. Arthur Peter (1872–1960) was another Kentucky lawyer, also serving as a county judge in Louisville. William S. Stuart (1870–1917) was a law student as well, though we don't know what happened to him after graduation.

The other professional school at Virginia was also well represented by Hugh Ferguson Parrish (1872–1935), who practiced medicine in Portsmouth, Virginia; Herbert Old (1871–1957), who interned in New York and practiced in Norfolk as well as serving in World War I; James Stuart Doubleday (1870–1918), who passed his New York boards in 1897 but died of pneumonia in 1918; and Alfred Leftwich Gray (1873–1932), who served on the faculty and as dean at the Medical College of Virginia.

A few of the Glee Club men of the early 1890s ended up peripherally involved in music after graduation, though none professionally. Gustave Aurelian Breaux Jr. (1869–1953) worked in sales for Ballard and Ballard Mills for thirty-five years but was also president and board member of the Louisville Symphony.[3] And William Hanna Sweeney, who worked for Duquesne Power and Light in Pittsburgh, apparently directed an orchestra there.[4]

A few of the early 1890s alums made it big in business. Charles Behan Thorn (1872–1955) worked for numerous brokerages in New Orleans, including his own Thorn and McGinnis, then later became a vice president of the New Orleans Cotton Exchange and at the Interstate Trust and Banking Company; he established the New Orleans Council of Boy Scouts.[5]

One of the most notable Glee Club alums of the period was Harrison Randolph. Born December 8, 1871, the same year the Glee Club was founded, Randolph was one of the few Glee Club directors in the nineteenth century to lead the group musically for more than a single season, directing from the 1892–1893 season through the 1894–1895 season. He was also the chapel organist, but he was not destined to be a lifelong professional musician. He took a post as chair of the mathematics department of the University of Arkansas in 1895, then two years later was elected president of the College of Charleston, South Carolina, where he remained until 1945.[6] He died in 1954.[7]

The most famous alumnus of this group was Edward Addison Craighill, born in 1873 in Lynchburg, Virginia. His uncle and namesake, surgeon Edward Addison Craighill, had been at age seventeen the youngest doctor to serve in the Medical Department of the Confederate Army, and he wrote a memoir of his experiences.[8] Craighill entered the University of Virginia to study law in 1892 and was there to greet the football team in the fall of 1893 as they returned triumphant from a victory. Out of the crowd came what is now the first verse of "The Good Old Song." Craighill subsequently wrote a second verse and, for an alumni banquet in 1910, a third verse for the song.[9] But in a 1922 article in the *University of Virginia Magazine*, he disclaimed authorship of the first stanza, noting that "no one man should be credited with the authorship."[10] During his time at Virginia he was a member of the Virginia Glee Club and participated in the 1894 tour.

Craighill graduated in 1895 from the Academic Department and finished his law degree in 1896, gaining employment as a writer for a law encyclopedia before joining the firm of Fletcher, McCutcheon, and Brown in New York. He died in 1948.[11]

After 1892–1893, the group decided to travel much more ambitiously. Led by Bernard W. Moore and with help from a few graduating alumni, including George Ainslie, the group mounted its first major tour outside the state of Virginia. The 1894 *Corks and Curls* dramatically illustrates the growth of the group's accomplishments, with the modest touring of 1891 through 1893 together taking up less than the space allotted to 1894.

Before the tour proper, the Glee Club held performances in the Levy Opera House and the Staunton Opera House in mid-January 1894. The tour proper kicked off with a performance in Fayerweather Gymnasium on Tuesday, January 30, and was off to the Mozart Academy in Richmond the next day. Thursday saw the group in the Lexington (Kentucky) Opera House, and they continued in Kentucky with an engagement in the Louisville Masonic Temple on Friday. Saturday was the Grand Opera House in Nashville. The group took a day off for travel (and the Sabbath) but performed in DeGive's Grand Opera House in Atlanta on Monday, February 5. Turning north again, they ended the tour the next day in Chattanooga's New Opera House. A performance in the Lynchburg Opera House on March 29 concluded the season.

How was such an elaborate and lengthy tour possible? Again, the railroad not only facilitated but was the only conceivable way to travel the miles from state to state so rapidly. Here the group had the assistance of the general passenger agent of the Chesapeake and Ohio Railway, John D. Potts. Apparently having no University of Virginia connection, Potts nevertheless worked closely with the group through the 1890s, to the point of being named business manager in 1895–1896.

But Potts was not the only force supporting the 1894 tour. Club president Moore's detailed narrative of the tour in the *Virginia University Magazine* also credits alumni in each town, including Ainslie in Richmond and Breaux in Louisville, with ensuring that the group had good houses for the performances. And the back of the program in each town featured a list of patronesses who ensured the group's support. Among them in Charlottesville were the wives of many of the University faculty, including Barringer, Cocke, Davis, Humphreys, Lile, Mallet, Minor, Nelson, Peters, Thornton, and Venable.

One might ask how it was that the club was permitted to tour in the first place. Leaves of absence were in fact granted. According to a note from William Wood Glass Jr. to Ada Bantz (later Beardsworth) scrawled in pencil, with underlining for emphasis, on a program from the February 12 Levy Opera House concert, the faculty stipulated that "every member of the club who is *under age* must secure permission from their *parents* before they grant leave of absence from the Univ."

The tour appears to have been highly successful. Press in the *Atlanta Constitution* hailed the arrival of "the Virginia boys," noting the growing success of southern colleges in sports and declaring:

> Having proved her equality thus on so many occasions, the
> Virginia university decided to send out her musical club over
> an extended tour through the south, and the encouraging let-
> ters and notices they have received all along their trip indi-
> cate that the southern people are going to give them an even
> more enthusiastic reception, if it were possible, than they
> have given Yale, Princeton and Harvard on their numerous
> trips through the south.[12]

Moore also wrote about the tour for the newly established *Alumni Bulletin* that the tour was a "financial success," though an article in the *University of Virginia Magazine* noted that the tour merely met its expenses of around $2700 "without the smallest deficit."[13] It went on to note "that no funds were brought back is not remarkable" and praised the advertising for the University that the tour accomplished.

So we see that the first major tour undertaken by the Virginia Glee Club was a success. It's interesting, though, to note one major way in which this tour differed from those later undertaken: the repertoire, as shown in a program for the club's post-tour performance at the Levy Opera House in Charlottesville. While subsequent tours could include a large number of University of Virginia songs, this tour included a single Virginia song, "Here's to Old Virginia." Only a dozen years later, there were enough songs to fill a songbook—*Songs of the University of Virginia*. We turn our attention next to the evolution of Virginia songs and their inextricable ties to the evolution of Virginia sports.

---

1   "Railroads of Virginia," Virginia Places, http://www.virginiaplaces.org/rail/, accessed January 7, 2016.

2   *Corks and Curls* 7 (1894): 147.

3   "Editor's Page: Gustave A. Breaux, Vice-President of the Filson Club," *The Filson Club Historical Society,* 293ff.

4   "William H. Sweeney," Ancestry, https://www.ancestry.com/.

5   Ray L. Bellande, "Lovers Lane: The Fort Point Peninsula," December 21, 2005, https://oceanspringsarchives.net/book/export/html/142.

6   "A Brief History of the College," College of Charleston, https://cofc.edu/about/historyandtraditions/briefhistory.php.

7   "Harrison Randolph," Find-a-Grave, https://www.findagrave.com/memorial/50203206/ran.

8   "Confederate Hospitals in Lynchburg, Virginia," Gravegarden, https://www.gravegarden.org/confederate-hospitals-in-lynchburg/; Jimmy Price, "'A Bloody Battle Is a Dreadful Experience': Edward Craighill and the Aftermath of First Manassas" (blog post), Emerging Civil War, July 29, 2015.

9   "Finals Week: June 12–15, 1910," *Alumni Bulletin* 3, no. 4 (August 1910): 346–47.

10   Virginius Dabney, *Mr. Jefferson's University* (Charlottesville: University of Virginia Press, 1981), 37.

11   "Edward A. Craighill, Jr.," Find-a-Grave, https://www.findagrave.com/memorial/109164308/edward-addison-craighill.

12   "The Virginia Boys," *Atlanta Constitution,* January 28, 1894, 24.

13   Bernard W. Moore, "The Glee, Banjo, and Mandolin Club," *Alumni Bulletin* 1, no. 2 (July 1894): 45–46; "Editorial," *University of Virginia Magazine* 33, no. 5 (February 1894): 229–30.

"THE GOOD OLD SONG" AND EARLY FOOTBALL SONGS

The balance of the Glee Club's repertoire in its earliest days came from the minstrel and ballad tradition. The earliest songs that we have a record of the Glee Club performing, "Upidee" and "Shoo Fly, Don't Bother Me," were popularized during the Civil War as soldiers' songs. The repertoire of the 1894 Glee, Banjo, and Mandolin Clubs was almost entirely marches, with an occasional waltz thrown in.

And then there was "Here's to Old Virginia." While the 1906 *Songs of the University of Virginia* records no authorship for it, the song has features common to other student songs, namely, melody and even text borrowed from other songs. The original melody appears, uncredited, in an 1870 Yale song book under the title "Drink Her Down," and the second part of the song quotes melody and text from "Balm of Gilead."[1] The work appears to have become a common college song, as variants appeared at Yale University ("Here's to Good Old Yale"), University of Chicago (where it is called "Bingo"), Milwaukee-Downer College ("Here's to College Hall"), and Smith College ("Balm of Gilead").[2] The song appears other places, including as a sorority song for Alpha Omicron Pi.[3] It bears one other important feature placing it in the college folk song tradition: lyrics celebrating drinking ("Here's to old Virginia, drink her down").

Portions of this chapter were originally published on the Virginia Glee Club Wiki and on the author's blog at Jarrett House North.

"Here's to Old Virginia" is a prototype of one important category of University of Virginia song, the borrowed drinking song. We'll see other common types as well, including the football song and the original alma mater composition. But one of the most celebrated of all Virginia songs, while sharing a folk origin, functions less as a drinking song and more as a pure alma mater song, designed to build comradeship and still sung at sporting events.

The authorship of the words to "The Good Old Song," which is set to the old Scottish melody "Auld Lang Syne," is disputed. It is traditionally ascribed to Edward A. Craighill Jr., but as we have noted, he can only properly be credited with authorship of the rarely sung second and third verses. In 1922, he wrote of the introduction of the song:

> the names of those individuals who contributed from their golden stores to the making of that majestic first stanza can never be ascertained with any approach to accuracy. Certainly no one man should be credited with its authorship. It sprang spontaneously from hundreds of glowing hearts and should be allowed to stand, in its Homeric splendor, a perpetual monument to the collective genius of the student body of '93.[4]

There's further evidence for the date of the spontaneous origin of the song in the lyrics of its first printed version, in the 1894 *Corks and Curls*, which render the last four lines as:

> We come from old Virginia
> Where all is mirth and glee
> Let's all join hands and give a yell
> For the team of '93. (Here give the yell.)[5]

That "The Good Old Song" is so unique is in some ways an accident of its authorship, the common use of its melody sung in New Year's celebrations, and its birth in the late nineteenth century when optimism about the school was at its highest and when the focus was still on creating a positive image of the school, rather than on football competition.

During this period, other songs were being written that were more purely football songs, such as "Oh, Carolina." Sung to the tune of "Oh My Darling, Clementine," it was written by William Roane Aylett Jr., who graduated from the University in 1895 with his medical degree and would have been in his first autumn on Grounds in 1892 when the first match in the South's Oldest Rivalry was played. Eleven years later, "Oh, Carolina" was still in circulation, as evidenced by its presence in A. Frederick Wilson's collected *Songs of the University of Virginia* (published 1906). It also appears in a 1911 football program book along with other song texts, but after that, nothing until the Glee Club's 2008 *Songs of Virginia* recording.

There's no evidence that "Oh, Carolina" was ever performed in a Glee Club concert, though there would have been lots of opportunities. University of North Carolina has been the Virginia Glee Club's oldest partner in its annual fall opening concerts (later called "kickoff concerts"), with joint performances with the UNC Glee Club in 1953, 1954, 1955, 1956, and 1977 and with the UNC Women's Chorus in 1988 (from the records we have handy); none of the programs mention anything about "the smell of pine" or "running / Turpentine from every pore," to cite two of the anti–Tar Heel song's more provocative lyrics.

But the song is handy as a reminder: not only did (do) University of Virginia students take this hundred-plus-year rivalry with the UNC Tar Heels seriously, they also sang about it. In the bleachers. At football games.

One student song functioning both as a folk song with a borrowed melody and as a football song is "The Orange and the Blue." Dating at least to 1896, when it is documented in *Corks and Curls*, the song bears no author, but it is presented with an elaborately notated four-part harmonization of the original borrowed tune, "Grand Old Rag." The lyrics celebrate drinking, the school colors, and football ("where there is sport about we're sure to be there to take a lead in the game").

After the 1895 period, there's a slowdown in the creation and documentation of new Virginia songs. The next significant moment in Virginia songbook history is the publication of *Songs of the University of Virginia,* edited by Wilson with assistance from Charles S. McVeigh and Albert Frederic Chandler. Though published in a fallow period for the Glee Club (Wilson was a member of the Holmes Glee Club, a singing group whose membership was not open across the University), it's a critical book for the history of the group as the only source for a great many University songs, and the only publication to provide sheet music and attribution for many others, though some also appear in football "songbook" pamphlets.

New songs appearing in *Songs* included "Glory to Virginia," "Hike, Virginia," "The Boys Who Wear the V," and a surprisingly large number of sentimental college songs such as the "Rotunda Song" and "Virginia Chapel Bell." The first three survived to become part of the Glee Club's later repertoire.

"Hike, Virginia" was written by McVeigh with assistance from Lewis D. Crenshaw; other sources credit a Williamson as a coauthor. McVeigh (1883–1962) was King of the Hot Feet, the predecessor to the IMP Society, as well as associate editor of the *University of Virginia Magazine*, vice president of the athletic association, and president of his law class; he later went on to become senior partner in the New York law firm of Morris and McVeigh. He may have been fabulously wealthy; it is reported that he administered the sale of his aunt's home, Knollwood, in Syosset, on Long Island, to the former King Zog of Albania and received "a bucket of diamonds and rubies" in payment.[6] Crenshaw (died 1947) is known as the first secretary of the University of Virginia Alumni Association, in which capacity he headed up the European bureau of the University in Paris during World War I. He instituted the first significant modern reunions at the University in 1914.

"Hike, Virginia" appears to be that rarity, a University of Virginia football song with a wholly original melody—or at least one not originating at another university. A 1911 football songbook, though, gives away the secret: the song is to be sung to the tune for "Hot Feet." While lyrics to this tune don't survive, both McVeigh and Crenshaw were in the Hot Feet, a secret society, and it can be supposed that the song was associated with the society. The song can tentatively be dated to between 1902, when the Hot Feet were founded, and 1906, when the songbook was published.

"The Boys Who Wear the V," also known as "Just Another Touchdown for U-Va," was written by Stephen Mazyck O'Brien (born 1878), a 1902 graduate of the University who served in the Kentucky House of Representatives in 1914. The tune is "Just a Little Bit Off the Top," also known as "When Johnny Comes Marching Home." Like many football songs of the period, the song has variable lyrics according to the opponent, with second and third verses that go "They stop the bucks, they block the kicks, Carolina's [or Georgetown's] 'on the roll' . . . We'll gather in Carolina's [or old Georgetown's] tin, Virginia's sure to win." "Just Another Touchdown" is still performed on occasion as a historical football song by the Glee Club.

Last, "Glory to Virginia" and "Fill Up Your Silver Goblet" are best known for being performed in combination with the notorious "From Rugby Road to Vinegar Hill," but both were originally complete stand-alone songs. "Fill Up Your Silver Goblet" is set to the tune of the 1909 song "Put On Your Old Grey Bonnet" and parodies the text of the original as a college drinking song: "Fill up your silver goblet with Virginia written on it / And we'll all have another glass of beer, / For we all came to college, but we didn't come for knowledge / So we'll raise hell while we're here!" Other universities record similar settings, including Canadian universities in Montreal and British Columbia, both of whom sing "Put on your old red sweater / 'Cause there isn't better / And we'll open up another keg of beer," as well as other, more morally questionable lyrics.

"Glory to Virginia" is a three-verse football song with words by the as-yet-unknown "W.A. '05," featuring an opponent verse originally referring to Yale ("We've wrestled with old Eli's sons—perhaps you know the score; we've pulled the Tiger's striped tail—no doubt you've heard him roar").[7] "Glory to Virginia" takes as its tune the "Battle Hymn of the Republic."

Both songs reuse existing tunes, which provides useful illustration of the practice of adapting tunes for different songs throughout the nineteenth century. Julia Ward Howe set her patriotic text to the tune of "John Brown's Body," which featured words collectively written by the members of the Second Infantry Battalion of the Massachusetts militia as a marching tune. The "Tiger" battalion, in turn, had used a tune for their words that had originated as a camp meeting song in the late eighteenth and early nineteenth centuries, "Say, Brothers, Won't You Meet Us," with the earliest printed version of the tune appearing from 1806 to 1808 in camp meeting song compilations. Beyond that, credit for the inspiration of the tune is given to an African American wedding song from Georgia or a British sea shanty that originated as a Swedish drinking song. "Glory to Virginia" and "Fill Up Your Silver Goblet" therefore illuminate a useful principle of college songs: they participate in a long tradition of adaptive reuse that also includes hymn tunes and marching songs.

Last, let's look at another song that adapted an existing tune and was associated with the University through performances by the Glee Club and the Pep Band, among others. "From Rugby Road to Vinegar Hill" recycles a tune used for many other college songs, most notably "Ramblin' Wreck from Georgia Tech." But the tune itself is older, coming from the folk song "A Son of a Gambolier," which was memorialized by Charles Ives in an 1895 arrangement, and possibly even earlier from the Confederate marching song "The Bonnie Blue Flag," published in 1861.

Then there are the lyrics, and here the similarity to transmitted ballad songs is even more apparent. While the first verse is highly topical to Virginia, with echoes of the shot that killed John A. G. Davis on the Lawn in 1841 ringing through the lines, "The faculty are afraid of us, they know we're in the right," and the traditional poles of Grounds ("Rugby Road") and downtown

Charlottesville ("Vinegar Hill") serving as the site of the revels, the second traditional verse is rather more timeless. It begins:

> All you girls from Mary Washington and R. M. W. C.,
> Don't ever let a Virginia man an inch above your knee.

Far from being a waggish invention of some Wahoo or other, this line is practically a lock-stock-and-barrel lift from "The Dundee Weaver," a bawdy Glaswegian street song:

> Come aa ye Dundee weavers an tak this advise fae me,
> Never let a fellae an inch abune yer knee.[8]

The same sentiment appears in the Irish song "Home Boys Home" and the Yorkshire song "The Oak and the Ash," both of which feature variations on the lyric:

> Oh come all of you fair maidens, a warning take by me,
> And never let a sailor lad an inch above your knee,
> For I trusted one and he beguiled me.
> He left me with a pair of twins to dangle on me knee.[9]

Just when "Rugby Road" entered the student repertoire is unclear. Though the earliest Glee Club recording is on *Songs of the University of Virginia*, featuring a well-practiced band and chorus arrangement suggesting familiarity, a recurring feature entitled "From Rugby Road to Vinegar Hill" first appeared in the *University of Virginia Magazine* in 1936. The first edition of the feature credited "the first line of the song" for the feature's title and gave the lyrics as:

> From Rugby Road to Vinegar Hill,
> We'll rule this town tonight.
> The Faculty's afraid of us
> Because we're in the right.
> So, fill up a cup, a loving cup
> As full as full can be.[10]

There are also references to the song having been sung in the precincts of the Eighth Evacuation Hospital (the University of Virginia hospital unit) in the Italian countryside during World War II alongside other songs like "Someone's in the Kitchen with Dinah."[11]

So "Rugby Road," like other University of Virginia songs, grew from and was embedded in an oral folk song tradition. As with other songs of the times, it's clear from its presence on the first two Glee Club recordings that it was viewed as a humorous folk song. That perspective was to change substantially, but it would happen over a hundred years later.

1 *Minstrel Songs, Old and New: A Collection of World-wide Famous Minstrel and Plantation Songs* (Oliver Ditson Company, 1882), 109–11.

2 Donn Barber, *Yale Songs Illustrated* (Press of J. J. Little, 1893), 12–13; "Chicago Songs," University of Chicago, http://web.archive.org/web/20140810105304/http://home.uchicago.edu/~ahkissel/cgosongs.html, accessed December 12, 2013; *Cumtux: Milwaukee Downer Annual* (1903), 104; Katherine M. Sewall, *Smith College Songs* (C. W. Thompson, 1909), 24–25.

3 "Songs," *To Dragma of Alpha Omicron Pi Fraternity,* 1 no. 1 (January 1905): 31–32.

4 Edward A. Craighill Jr., "'The Good Old Song' in the Making," *University of Virginia Magazine* 83, no. 1 (October 1922): 1–4.

5 *Corks and Curls* 7 (1894): 200.

6 Richard Jay Hutto, *Their Gilded Cage: The Jekyll Island Club Members* (Macon, GA: Henchard Press Ltd., 2006), 108.

7 The authors of *College Fight Songs II* believe A. W. to be A. Frederick Wilson, though he could just as easily be William Aylett; William E. Studwell and Bruce R. Schueneman, *College Fight Songs II: A Supplemental Anthology* (Binghamton, NY: Haworth Press, 2001), 36.

8 "The Dundee Weaver," *Dick Gaughan's Song Archive,* archived from the original on April 1, 2016. "Wahoo" as a nickname for a University of Virginia student has been present since the 1890s based on the "Wahoowa" yell and may actually precede "The Good Old Song."

9 "Home Boys Home," Collection of Irish Song Lyrics, Donal O'Shaughnessy, https://www.irishsongs.com/lyrics.php?Action=view&Song_id=499. The lyrics to "The Oak and the Ash" are similar, warning "servant girls" not to trust a "sailor boy" who will "reward" the listener with a pair of twins.

10 "From Rugby Road to Vinegar Hill," *University of Virginia Magazine* 95, no. 3 (December 1936), 7.

11 Byrd Stuart Leavell, *The 8th Evac: A History of the University of Virginia Hospital Unit in World War II* (Petersburg, VA: Dietz Press, 1970), 137.

1895 TO 1912: THE TIDE OF YEARS MAY PASS

Following the tour of 1893–1894, the Glee Club carried on as a unit with the Banjo and Mandolin Clubs but lacked the same attention from the University community it had previously enjoyed.

Harrison Randolph stayed to direct in 1894–1895, with Micajah W. Pope as president. The group sought to repeat their success with another tour, traveling to Staunton, Roanoke, and Lynchburg in Virginia; Lexington and Frankfort, Kentucky; Cincinnati; Memphis; St. Louis, Missouri; and back to Virginia, stopping in Norfolk and Richmond. The tour lasted almost two months, with breaks, from December 17, 1894, to February 25, 1895, and ventured further west than any Glee Club tour ever had, but it was not as successful. The *Magazine* noted:

> The Glee Club, too, was a great success in every way except financially. Our musicians were well received and most hospitably entertained nearly everywhere they went, and they did our University and their trainer much credit. They may wear their parsley wreath with as good a grace as the athlete his laurels.[1]

In 1895–1896 there was no mention of a tour. The club was under new musical leadership with the arrival of Frederick G. Rathbun, beginning a revolving door that would continue for many years, and with McLane Tilton Jr. serving as president. An article in the *Magazine* laid the blame for the club's lack of financial success when touring at the feet of the club itself:

> The recent lack of interest on the part of the societies of Alumni in behalf of the Glee Club was, in a measure, just and excusable. Deeper than love for alma mater in every heart is love for self—though there be those who would not confess it—and the average play-goer feels that he is treated too contemptuously when the performers stroll around through the audience, appear carelessly indifferent, and, in every way, make it appear that it is a great condescension on their part to appear before this audience of inferior beings. The beautiful young ladies in the boxes may forgive the disregard of propriety and the airs of superiority on the part of the stalwart youths—because it's romantic you know—but not the papas and the bachelor uncles, and they are the ones who have the money. Until the Glee Club men can learn to regard their performances as a business transaction and endeavor to perform their part of it in a businesslike way, with the good taste of high class stage rules, we venture to say that the same lack of encouragement will be found, as was the case this year, and the financial result will be the same as it has been for many years.[2]

Despite the criticism and the pause in touring, the Glee Club continued organizing for the next several years. In 1896–1897, the club's president, Rockwell Smith Brank (1875–1947, a future lawyer and minister), and manager, Eugene Lanier Sykes (1873–1965, a New York lawyer who became president of the First National Bank of Aberdeen, the Monroe County Cotton Oil Company, and Sykes Plantations), led a group of eighteen singers, continuing collaborations with the Banjo and Mandolin Clubs. The following year saw the Glee Club grow to twenty-one singers under the leadership of president John Lawrence Vick Bonney (1875–1934, an industrial leader who became a victim of the Great Depression, fatally shooting himself in his own basement) and manager Elbert Lee Trinkle (1876–1939, to date the only Glee Club member to become governor of Virginia, from 1922 to 1926).

The last season to end in the nineteenth century, the 1898–1899 season, had as musical director a student, Francis Harris Abbot (1877–1933, later a well-beloved and eccentric professor of French at the University), alongside Edmund Bradford Burwell (1877–1949), president. But though the caliber of leader was high, musical standards had fallen off; the *Magazine* reported:

> the Glee Club's speciality was college songs, and so they tried a song that they had heard sung on the "bleachers" when the "rooters" wished to encourage the team. Five of them knew most of the words; three of them knew the tune; and all of them were able to come in on the chorus; so between them, with Langdon leading manfully on the piano and filling up the breaks with beautiful dashes of chords and scales, "The Good Old Song of Wah-Who-Wah" was sung with much feeling and much original interpretation. . . . This song was followed by others, not always in tune, and not always in time.[3]

It appears that charm alone was insufficient to save the organization from incompetence. The 1899–1900 Glee Club was only a quartet that performed with the Mandolin and Guitar Club, including future music directors Nevil Gratiot Henshaw (1880–1936) and Burnley Lankford (1879–1926). The following year there was no Glee Club, and no Mandolin Club either. The only organized musical outlet on Grounds was the University Choir, later called the Chapel Choir.

What caused this disappearance? Partly it appears to be the effect of negative word of mouth about the club breeding indifference to its performances by students and alumni alike. But partly the world was changing. There had been a resurgence in religious interest at the University at the end of the nineteenth century, with sufficient membership and activity to support the building of Madison Hall in Madison Bowl on Rugby Road in 1901. The new building offered both religious and social activities and became the de facto student center, and its central organization supported and encouraged the formation of a permanent chapel choir that seems to have temporarily sated the student body's interest in singing.

The club's hiatus lasted from 1900 to 1902, when it re-formed together with the Mandolin and Guitar Club. Under the direction of Lankford and the leadership of president Albert L. Roper (1879–1966, four-term mayor of

Norfolk) and Nathan Lynn Bachman (1878–1937, associate Tennessee supreme court justice and United States senator), the group numbered some twenty-one singers. The period seems to have been a significant year for student activity in general; the Raven Society was founded the following year, and three members of the Glee Club of 1902–1903 were numbered in the founding twelve of the Ravens.

The Glee Club's revival continued in 1903–1904 under the leadership of director Robert B. Crawford (1875–1919, who married wealthy heiress Lizzie Florence Olney and built Villa Crawford, which later grew into Keswick Hall, before separating from his wife—who would go on to marry fellow Glee Club alum Henry Waldo Greenough—and dying under suspicious circumstances in a hotel room in Baltimore).[4] The group was active, giving a concert at Randolph-Macon Woman's College, but numbered only enough members to form an octet.

The following year saw the formation of a Glee Club closer to full size under the musical direction of Crawford and the leadership of president Thomas Pinckney Bryan (1882–1920, later a naval lawyer) and secretary William McCulley James (1880–1942, a colleague of Walter Reed, who led the Panama Hospital). The club's financial status, after three years of renewed vigor, allowed it to tour again, performing in Richmond, Baltimore, and Alexandria and receiving press coverage. Members included Frank Morse Rummel, grandson of telegraph inventor Samuel Morse, son of German concert pianist Franz Rummel, and a painter and printmaker whose works are in the collection of the British Museum; John Jennings Luck, a member of the Hot Feet and IMPs and later on the University mathematics faculty; William McCulley James, another Hot Foot, a foremost authority on malaria and other tropical diseases and the chief of the medical service of the Panama Hospital; and Charles S. McVeigh. James was the founder of the Raven Society, and fellow 1904–1905 Glee Club members James Tappan Hornor, John Beverly Pollard, Irving Miller Walker, and Thomas Pinckney Bryan were all charter members.[5]

The momentum continued into 1905–1906, with Crawford again directing. Under the presidency of Hornor (1885–1957, who was also a Hot Foot) the club carried out a tour of neighboring cities, including Lynchburg, earning a mention in the *Alumni Bulletin*, which called that year's Glee and Mandolin Clubs "the best musical clubs the University has had for years."[6] The program even featured one of the first known concert performances of "The Good Old Song."

And then . . . nothing. The sudden disappearance of the University Glee Club in 1906–1907 leaves no explanation for why, after a four-year renewal, the group would suddenly disband. Part of it may have been lack of leadership; Crawford graduated from the University in 1906.

And part of it may have been a reaction to the success of the group, as some members stepped back from the increased time commitments required for wide touring. It was during these years that the Holmes Glee Club, originally founded as a residential octet in 1887–1888, flourished, to the point of causing confusion about whether they were in fact the University Glee Club. A. Frederick Wilson, who organized the group in the fall of 1906 on the heels of the publication of *Songs of the University of Virginia*, felt compelled to write a letter to *College Topics* explaining how the group had come about:

> The Holmes Glee Club was organized during the latter part of October 1906. Its purpose was to form a club at the University, using the material that was not available for the Varsity clubs. There were half a dozen men in College who did not feel that they had the time to sing with the larger organizations, and from such material as this the Holmes Glee Club was formed. The question has continually been put to candidates for the clubs: 'Will this, in any way, interfere with your duty towards the Varsity clubs, should they be organized during the present season?' Some very good material has been dropped for fear of interfering with the larger University interests. . . . The Holmes club has not advertised or represented itself as in any way connected with the University of Virginia Musical clubs.[7]

So the Holmes appears to have been formed as a conscious alternative to the touring clubs but may perhaps have contributed to the main University Glee Club's failure to form during the first season, as it included among its octet two who had sung in the University club in 1905–1906.

Ironically, given the concern over lack of time, the 1907 *Corks and Curls* indicates that the Holmes performed in eleven venues around the state, more than the 1905–1906 Glee Club managed. Wilson graduated in 1907, and the Holmes does not appear to have performed the following season.

Just as both glee clubs vanished, the Arcadians were reaching their apex.

This early dramatic troupe at the University at first mounted plays but turned to musical entertainment, and the fully staged productions may well have consumed the time and attention of the musically inclined students. Certainly there was overlap; there were seven Arcadians who also sang in either the University Glee Club, the Holmes, or both. In fact, Cyril Dadswell, the director of the Arcadians, apparently held at least one rehearsal to organize the Glee Club in November 1906, but nothing more came of it.

The Arcadians produced five light operas between 1904 and 1910. The first two, *Khan of Kathan* and *The Conspirators*, both productions borrowed from Columbia University, were more expensive than the group could afford.[8] It managed better with *The Visiting Girl* and *La Serena*, and *The King of Kong* did well enough to tour. The last, *Turvyland*, was composed by a law student and performed in Old Cabell Hall, but the business manager of the group was apparently asleep at the wheel:

> the expense which it entailed was so heavy that no money
> was left to be carried over to the following year. Such a
> comedy required the vigilant service of an expert coach; and
> the number of actors indispensable was so great, and the
> equipment in costume and scenery so voluminous, that the
> costs, on these various scores, ate up all the pecuniary profit.
> In consequence, no play was offered in 1910–11. This fact led
> to the revival of the Glee Club.[9]

So it was that the bankruptcy of the Arcadians led musically minded Virginians to revive the Glee Club. According to Philip Alexander Bruce, "a mass-meeting of all the students interested in music was held; a new vocal and instrumental club organized; and rehearsals at once began."[10]

One of the motivating forces behind the re-forming of the Glee Club in 1910 was its director. Martin S. Remsberg (1887–1947) was the new director of music at Christ Church in Charlottesville and was eager to engage musically at the University of Virginia. He issued a call for members in the spring of 1910 but did not get things going in earnest until the fall, when he took charge of musical activities at the YMCA in Madison Hall. At that time, he issued the general call for musicians that led to the formation of the Glee Club.

In 1910–1911 this new group, under the presidency of Malcolm W. Gannaway (1889–1967), performed widely both within the University precincts and beyond. It gave two performances on University Grounds, including a fall performance that included "specialties, solos, quartettes" and "Mr. G. P. Waller, in a female impersonation, and Mr. J. W. Hamilton, as a black-faced musician."[11] George Platt Waller (1889–1962) survived this ignominious performance to enter the American consular service, where he is noted for having helped lead and support the resistance to the Nazi occupation of Luxembourg (where he was American consul from 1931 to 1948), as well as for singing Virginia songs in the Panhellion Café in Athens in 1915.[12] Less is known about the fate of John Waddie Hamilton (1885–1962) aside from his participation in the blackface performance tradition.

This group, still under the directorship of Remsberg and under the presidency of Arthur F. Triplett (1891–1958), continued in 1911–1912 with a membership of twenty-four (including future Glee Club president and University of Virginia medical school faculty Robert V. Funsten) and grand plans for a tour of the South, including stops in Greensboro, Charlotte, Atlanta, Macon, Montgomery, and Birmingham.[13] It is unknown whether the tour ever took place.

What does survive is a record of one of the oddest brushes with history that the early Glee Club experienced, when its April 26, 1912, concert at the Columbia Theatre in Washington, DC, was interrupted by a public baiting of United States Representative Jefferson Monroe Levy, owner of Jefferson's Monticello, by socialite Maud Littleton of New York. The encounter, memorialized in the *New York Times*, was a public continuation of a long argument over whether Levy should donate the house to the American people. Levy, and his uncle, Uriah P. Levy, who was the first Jewish commodore in the United States Navy, had devoted considerable amounts of money to the upkeep and preservation of Monticello, including recovering the house after its seizure by the Confederate Army during the Civil War. Littleton was not persuaded by their stewardship and mounted a national campaign during this year to get Levy to donate the house to the federal government.[14]

In retrospect, there was a clear subtext of antisemitism in Littleton's efforts, as she called out "themes of greed, selfishness, and lack of patriotism" in Levy and called him an "Oriental potentate."[15] Littleton's crusade took advantage of an opportunity during the Glee Club's concert to address Levy directly, as reported in the *New York Times*:

> The controversy over Monticello, the home of Thomas Jefferson, which Mrs. Martin W. Littleton of New York thinks

should be turned over to the Nation by its owner, Representative Jefferson M. Levy of New York, unexpectedly found a place on the programme of the University of Virginia Glee Club to-night, with the result that Mr. Levy was forced to listen to rather pointed criticism of himself by Mrs. Littleton before a large audience in the Columbia Theatre. He heard her out, but when she concluded he left the building. Mrs. Littleton was one of the patronesses of the entertainment, and was on the programme to deliver a short lecture on "Historic Shrines." Mr. Levy went to the concert as the guest of a friend, and occupied a box. Mrs. Littleton was brought on the stage during the intermission, and glancing occasionally toward her adversary, she told the audience his ancestors had willed Monticello to the American people and how, in spite of that fact, Mr. Levy, simply because a court had found a way to break Commodore Levy's will, persisted in holding on to it.

"Uriah Levy," said she, "willed Monticello to the United States, but his heirs brought a lawsuit and the court decided that the Commodore's wish and will should go for naught, and thus Monticello came into the possession of its present owners.

"Uriah P. Levy," accenting the Uriah so nobody could think she was referring to Jefferson Levy, "found that there were certain things he could do. He could serve his country on his ship; he could offer his sword to Lincoln; he could leave his fortune to his family, and he could crown his life of unselfishness and patriotism by leaving to the people of the United States things that they would regard as precious. Monticello, holding in its bosom this precious and consecrated thing"— she referred to the ashes of Jefferson—"should belong to all the people. And as we revere and respect Uriah Levy"—again accenting the Uriah—"for the gift he gave us, so we should respect and immortalize Jefferson Levy if he would make it possible for us to accept that gift."

Mrs. Littleton was asked to-night if she enjoyed the proceedings as much as the audience seemed to have done.

She laughed merrily and said: "I was most happy that he was there, because I could not say to him in private conversation what I could say in public."[16]

After this excitement, the Glee Club's season ended in uncertainty. The club tried to organize in the fall of 1912 but was forced to disband; Remsberg moved on and no conductor was to be found. There was no organized musical activity in 1912–1913. Again the Glee Club was fallow.

Thus ended a run from 1887 to 1912 that was marked by high success and complete disintegration, in which the club was organized for seventeen years and fallow for eight. Lack of consistent access to talented directors (most only staying for a season or two) and changing student interests appear to have been the principal culprits and led to a pattern in which the group could not be sure in any given year of successful organization and performances, no matter how strong the showing the prior season. But it was at this unpromising time that the club would restart in earnest and stay restarted, thanks to musical leadership from an unlikely source.

---

1 "Collegiana," *University of Virginia Magazine* 38, no. 3 (December 1894): 126.
2 "Editorial," *University of Virginia Magazine* 39, no. 3 (Christmas 1895): 199.
3 Morris Palmer Tilley, "A Dawson's Row Strategem," *University of Virginia Magazine,* November 1898, 61ff.
4 Chris Gosnell, "The Barrows Family," www.ocotilloroad.com/geneal/barrows1 .html, accessed April 15, 2018; David Maurer, "Author Documents Keswick Hall's History," *Daily Progress,* August 14, 2011, www.dailyprogress.com/entertainment/ author-documents-keswick-hall-s-history/article_2f5b93b1-aaf5-515d-a323 -2647968bd8ce.html.
5 Dave Wolcott, "Raven Society Celebrates Centennial Anniversary," *University of Virginia News,* March 11, 2004, web.archive.org/web/20121014131328/http://www .virginia.edu/topnews/releases2004/raven-march-11-2004.html.
6 *University of Virginia Bulletins,* vol. 5, no. 4 (January 1906), 243–44.
7 "Editorial," *College Topics,* April 3, 1907, 4–5.
8 "Items of Interest: The Arcadians," *Alumni Bulletin,* vol. 7, no. 2 (April 1907): 212–13.

9 Bruce, *History of the University of Virginia*, vol. 5, 287–88.

10 Ibid., 288.

11 "Glee Club Gave Final Performance," *College Topics*, November 23, 1910, 8.

12 Willard Allen Fletcher and Jean Tucker Fletcher, *Defiant Diplomat George Platt Waller: American Consul in Nazi-Occupied Luxembourg, 1939–1941* (Newark: University of Delaware Press, 2012), 178.

13 "Southern Trip Planned," *College Topics*, October 7, 1911, 8.

14 Uriah P. Levy purchased Monticello in 1834 from James Turner Barclay, a local apothecary. Jefferson's daughter Martha Jefferson Randolph had sold it to Barclay in 1831, seeking to address some of the estate's debt and her own financial problems. Levy was a great admirer of Jefferson and used his own funds to restore and preserve the house.

15 Michael Beschloss, "The Near Death, and Revival, of Monticello" (blog post), The Upshot, *New York Times,* February 7, 2015; "Jefferson Monroe Levy," Jefferson Foundation, https://www.monticello.org/site/research-and-collections/jefferson-monroe-levy, accessed April 29, 2016.

16 "Mrs. Littleton Baits Levy: Owner of Monticello Forced to Listen to Criticisms at Concert," *New York Times,* April 27, 1912, 6. The Levy family sold Monticello eleven years later to the Thomas Jefferson Foundation, who continue to maintain it today.

10 | 1914 TO 1917: UPS, DOWNS, AND ALFRED LAWRENCE HALL-QUEST

O n the heels of such a run of intermittent existence, it is hard to imagine the Virginia Glee Club forming again, much less entering an age of excellence. Yet that is exactly what happened, thanks to the arrival of a new professor at the University with "scientific" ideas.

Alfred Lawrence Hall-Quest was young, energetic, and (most importantly for the Glee Club) trained as a musician. Having just completed a master's degree at Princeton University, where he conducted the Princeton Glee Club, he put out a call for members in the fall of 1914 and "undertook to reorganize the old association and train it scientifically."[1] Hall-Quest's arrival was significant for two additional reasons: like Remsberg he was a trained musician, but he was also the first member of the faculty (albeit the summer faculty) to direct the Glee Club since assistant professor Harrison Randolph almost twenty years before. Though Hall-Quest was not engaged by the University to teach music (there was still no music department), his arrival presented the closest thing to professional, stable musical leadership that the group had seen in its forty-two years of existence. Great things began to happen.

The membership in 1914–1915 consisted of twenty-four students, including an accompanist who may or may not have been a singing member. The following year the membership had swelled to thirty-two; Holsinger Studios' photo for the 1916 *Corks and Curls* barely manages to get everyone into the frame.

More importantly for the vocal and musical development of the group, some of the nearly constant turnover of members that had bedeviled the club since the 1890s began to abate. Some measure of continuity had been preserved from the older Glee Clubs into the 1914–1915 one, thanks to the continued presence of Malcolm Gannaway and Robert Funsten.

Another helpful factor was that undergrads were staying longer. In the nineteenth century, it was not uncommon for students to attend for anywhere from one semester to four or more; there were no set required courses, and originally Jefferson envisioned the school offering no degrees. The medical and law students, committed by their professional curricula to attend for several sessions, had provided some of the only year-to-year continuity of members. But the University's first president, Edwin Alderman, was an education innovator (he would have said "reformer"), and under his leadership the University began to evolve toward the four-year curriculum model.

Whatever the reason, whether Alderman's influence or Hall-Quest's, the Glee Club in 1914–1915 had only one repeat member (down from four in 1911–1912), while in 1915–1916 it had six. The group had begun to build some musical and organizational continuity.

That continuity paid off in renewed touring in 1916–1917. While numbers were back down to twenty-five members, the group undertook a large-scale tour for the first time since 1911–1912 (if the tour of the South indeed took place as planned) or 1905–1906 (if it didn't).

The 1916–1917 tour is infamous for providing photographic evidence of the Glee Club's early blackface performance, thanks to surviving photos of the cast of *Oh, Julius!* Though there had been minstrel numbers performed before, this performance coincided with the skilled use of cameras by photographers from the Holsinger Studio, who took photographs of the performers in costume (including dresses) and burnt cork. The photographs survive in the University's Special Collections, providing irrefutable and accessible witness to this chapter in the Glee Club's—and the University's—history.

By any measure, Hall-Quest's tenure was successful. But it was not long lasting; he only conducted the Glee Club in 1914–1915, 1915–1916, and 1916–1917. His early years appear to be wandering years. Born in 1879, he was ordained in the Presbyterian ministry in 1903, after receiving his master of arts and bachelor of divinity degrees from Princeton Theological Seminary. Bruce reports that for the six years he was there, he had been in charge of the Princeton Glee Club.[2] He appears to have rambled a bit; between ordination and 1914 he was associate pastor at one church and pastor at three, professor in philosophy and education in Westminster College in Fulton, Missouri, and an "assistant in education" at the University of Illinois. He is listed as teaching the summer session at Illinois in 1914, then teaching the summer session at Virginia in 1915. He remained an associate faculty member at the University of Virginia until 1917, when he left to join the faculty of the University of Cincinnati, where he was professor of secondary education and director of the School of Affiliation.[3] In the early 1920s he moved on to the University of Pittsburgh.

In Pittsburgh, his personal life temporarily derailed his academic career. His wife ran off with his friend, Frederick William Hart, a former major in the British army.[4] Hall-Quest decided to grant his wife a divorce. As professors were expected to set a high moral example for their students, this was grounds for dismissal from his post at the university in October 1924.[5] He moved on to Milwaukee University, where he resigned his position in 1927 after disagreement with the trustees.[6] He eventually landed at New York University, where he was employed at least until 1941.[7] He died in 1971.

The intersection of Hall-Quest's life with the Glee Club seems odd, given his educational track; the best guess is that he leveraged his combined background in education and ministry into a job at the University of Virginia YMCA, which, as we have seen, nurtured the remnant of the Glee Club during the lean years of the early twentieth century. He had an institutional connection to the YMCA, where he was director of the chancel choir in 1916.

So the Glee Club's rescue from obscurity and subsequent training in scientific principles appears to have been a happy accident. Hall-Quest had ambition and drive and did much to move the group forward, but in the end his influence, like his tenure at Virginia, was brief. Though he refounded the group, he did not provide the stability the group needed to move beyond its year-to-year existence.

1 Bruce, *History of the University of Virginia,* vol. 5, 289.
2 Ibid.
3 "Famous Educators for the Institute," *Union County Journal,* August 13, 1920, 1.
4 "Mrs. Hart Divorced in Hall-Quest Case," *New York Times,* October 13, 1924.
5 "Hall-Quest Goes from Pittsburg," *Los Angeles Times,* October 29, 1924.
6 "City Teachers at Institute," *Reading Eagle,* October 10, 1931, 6.
7 "US, World War II Draft Registration Cards, Alfred Lawrence Hall-Quest," Ancestry.com, https://www.ancestry.com/, accessed August 1, 2016.

11 THE GLEE CLUB IN WORLD WAR I AND AFTER

The Glee Club swiftly reverted to type following Alfred Lawrence Hall-Quest's departure. The 1917–1918 season saw the group hiring a director who was unaffiliated with the University, Kirk Otey Payne, and making one concert trip to Staunton. But wider events were about to sweep the club up in their grasp: on April 6, 1917, the United States formally entered World War I. The Great War, though only lasting another nineteen months, had a profound effect on the University of Virginia, and on the Virginia Glee Club.

The war had, of course, been well under way prior to the United States' entry. The most notable early participant in the war was James Rogers McConnell, king of the Hot Feet, member of the Seven Society, ambulance driver, aviator, and Icarus-like martyr. McConnell was at once the last and first of his kind: first because he was the first University of Virginia student to be killed in the Great War; last because he was the last American airman killed before the United States officially entered the war April 6, 1917, just eighteen days after his death. He was also effectively the last American warrior-as-adventurer, in the model of Teddy Roosevelt and other early twentieth-century military leaders who held greater fame in civilian life. Indeed, his decision to head to France, and later to join the Escadrille after serving as an ambulance driver, is best read through the lens of Roosevelt as a role model. As he is quoted in the introduction to his memoir *Flying for France*, "these Sand Hills will be here forever, but the war won't; and so I'm going."[1] He was converted to the belief of the absolute rightness of the French cause, and so he entered his combat role.

But while McConnell and others joined the fight early, for many at the University it was business as usual. Indeed, the 1916–1917 season was a full one for the University Glee Club under president Robert Gilliam Butcher, vice president DeLos Thomas Jr., and secretary Arthur Kyle Davis Jr. During the season they staged the musical *Oh, Julius!*, with its troupe of actors in blackface and doing female impersonation, and they toured Virginia, with stops in Lynchburg, Roanoke, Staunton, Petersburg, and Danville, under the direction of Hall-Quest. But shortly after the conclusion of the tour war broke out, and so the officers and other members of the club had to decide whether to proceed.

It seems they did, according to a note in the *Alumni Bulletin*: "The [Glee and Mandolin Clubs'] program consists of a Musical Comedy as a vehicle for Glee Club singing, Mandolin music and dramatics. On account of war economy, no special scenery is employed this year, and costumes have been greatly simplified. . . . Performances will be given in Charlottesville and nearby

FIGURE 2. Thomas Claude Durham Jr. (right), Glee Club member, shown in the musical revue *O Susie Behave* with the Virginia Theatrical Club, ca. 1918. Photo by Holsinger Studios circa 1918. Photo courtesy Small Special Collections Library, University of Virginia.

cities. Like all other student activities, the club feels the effects of the war, but its standard is as high as ever, and a successful season awaits it."[2]

The University was indeed feeling the effects of the war. The Great War had originally drawn dashing volunteers like McConnell; it now affected students on a massive scale. The University approved a proposal to establish its first Reserve Officer Training Corps (ROTC) on March 15, 1917, just three weeks before the United States officially joined the war. In general, the University's policy was as follows: the school's resources (men and equipment) were to be put at the disposal of the national government; its "normal functions and activities" were not to be interrupted; students under twenty-one, who were ineligible for military commissions, were to continue in their classes but were to avail themselves of the military training offered on Grounds; and college athletics were suspended. By the end of the 1916–1917 season, 334 alumni were actively involved in the hostilities and 784 students and professors were registered in the ROTC.

The following season felt the effects of the war more dramatically. At the beginning of the 1917–1918 season, enrollment had been 1,064 students, but by January 1918 it had fallen to seven hundred. The Glee Club indeed still performed, winning praise from its audience at Sweet Briar for a program that was "unusually attractive," but the writing was on the wall. The 1918–1919 session of the University was even more reduced, with enrollment falling below six hundred; and the Glee Club suspended all activities during that season.

Many of the Virginia men who passed through France stopped in the University's European Bureau, a small suite in Paris established by alumni secretary Lewis D. Crenshaw (coauthor of "Hike, Virginia"). He reported: "It is almost uncanny the way Tom from Flanders, or Dick from Alsace, or Henry from southern France, will land here the same day—all attracted by the old orange and blue banner—and fall on each other's necks, in a regular grizzly bear." Crenshaw published *The University of Virginia Overseas Song Book* from Paris, featuring "La belle chanson de 'wah-hoo-wah.'"

Among the Glee Club men who left to fight in the war were its officers. Robert Gilliam Butcher joined the United States Navy Reserve, graduated from the officers' training program, and participated in the Aisne-Marne offensive in 1918, where he was shot through the arm and lung. Recuperating, he returned to the University, and the Glee Club, after the armistice and had a long career in law. (His son, Robert G. Butcher Jr., served on the Board of

Visitors of the University in the late 1980s and 1990s.) DeLos Thomas Jr. became a naval aviator and participated in an aerial bombing test that sought to establish whether airplanes could be an effective anti-submarine defense; he perished in 1923, after leaving the navy, when a plane he was flying from Bimini to Florida disappeared without a trace. Arthur Kyle Davis Jr. served as a second lieutenant, returning to the University to complete his studies after the armistice, then enrolled at Oxford University as a Rhodes Scholar. He taught for years afterward at the University and is remembered for writing the lyrics that Glee Club music director Donald Loach set to a tune by Handel as "Vir-ir-gin-i-a," as well as for his tireless work collecting and publishing folk ballads from the Virginia countryside.

All told, sixty-four Glee Club members or alums are known to have served in World War I in some capacity, and no doubt many more did whose stories have faded from memory. They included two known war fatalities: Mortimer Park Crane joined the British Royal Air Force after serving in the Canadian army as a gunner in the field artillery and died in a training accident when he turned the wrong way while flying in formation and clipped the wing of another plane. Frank Nelson Lewis was a captain in Company M in the Fourth Infantry and died of wounds received on October 5 or 6, 1918, while his company advanced on Cunel, France, for which he received the Distinguished Service Cross.

Those who could returned to the University after the armistice, but there were no performances in 1918–1919. The following season all was back to normal: Payne returned in 1919–1920 and directed performances in Lynchburg and Roanoke and undertook a tour in April 1920 through the Homestead Resort at Hot Springs, Virginia, and in West Virginia to the Greenbrier at White Sulfur Springs, Charleston, and Huntington. The tour was based on the musical *Nothing*, which brought back banjos, mandolins, and musical comedy.[3] Membership was up, to more than thirty-four members.

Musical comedy continued to be the theme of the 1921–1922 season, but with considerably less acclaim. The director, Nevil Henshaw, was the author of that year's show, *The Visiting Girl*, a revival of a work created for the Arcadians in 1907. The work drew a blistering critique, at least in the pages of the University's anonymous humor newspaper, the *Yellow Journal*. Coverage began with a small house ad—"To-Night: University Glee Club in a Musical Comedy. (Suggestion: Why not cut out the 'musical'?) (Suggestion: They might cut out the 'comedy' too.)"—and continued with a detailed, withering review:

The Visiting Girl *presented by the University of Virginia Glee Club, John Koch, president, director and chief actor. Jefferson Theatre as an April Fool joke, April 1, 1921.*

We saw this show in December and later we saw it in Richmond during February. If it hasn't improved, and we doubt whether it has improved, we advise you not to go to see it. Go to the movies at the Lafayette instead. The chief attraction of the show is Jack Parrott as a girl and John Koch as a rube. Jack plays his girl's part very well, though he is a bit awkward. The girls' chorus looks about as much like a bunch of girls as a litter of pups does. Several of them are very nicely built and should please first nighters.

The songs are rotten and those who sing them very ably get through with the same impression. There is but one voice in connection with the show—the voice of disapproval. We know of fewer groups in college which are less significant than the Glee Club. Half of them have never been heard of, and most of the other half could never be heard of and the college would not suffer.

How Jere Willis and Frank Cox were ever persuaded to be in this show is a mystery. Shake Westcott plays the role of the baseball hero, who wins the game and the fair damsel. Shake is fair as an actor, being at his best in long hikes to Washington. Thomas Jefferson would turn over in his grave if he knew that Nicholson was playing the part of Jefferson in the show. This bird Akeley impresses us as being the wrong end of the candle.

The social end of the club's activities is well taken care of by "Gentleman Jim" Hennelly and a few others. Rudolph Carroll is electrician, and Harry McKee is stage manager. Allan Gibbons is supposed to be business manager, but the president of the club says he does all the work. In the men's chorus we have such celebrities as Willis Carey and Bobbie Taylor. Need we say more? The *Yellow Journal* doesn't like to knock. We like to praise, but we feel forced to criticize this show. It is rotten, but go to see it![4]

The show was neither a critical nor a popular success, as evidenced by a review for the following season's show, *I.O.U*, which began with the comment, "The Glee Club's show this year was called 'I.O.U.,' and from the debts which last year's performance left to it, its name was very appropriate."[5]

The reviews for *The Visiting Girl*, and its poor receipts, appear to have taken the wind out of the Glee Club's sails. Though the membership in 1921–1922 was strong, there were no recorded tours. The musical *I.O.U.* appears to have been more of the same, with guitars, banjos, and mandolins abounding, though we see a note of things to come, as the group closed the performance with "The Good Old Song."

The musical director for the season, Francis Harris Abbot (1877–1933), was one of the more colorful figures from this period of Glee Club history, having been a member and assistant conductor in 1898–1899 before returning as a University professor to conduct the group in 1921. An instructor in French, he was known occasionally to sing an aria in class. He was also known to complain about the accommodations for his classes:

> Three hours a week I teach in P.H.B. 2, not a classroom at all, but a cellar, of which the ceiling is supported by pillars that shut off the students' view of the blackboard (one blackboard). . . . Part of this room has been enclosed to make somebody an office (a beaverboard office), and this professor has the privilege of passing in and out during my class. You enter this room through a dark limbo, stacked with old desks and chairs and lumber piled in confusion. . . . I can neither leave a book, nor hang a map nor send a student to the board in this room. Why they learn what they do is a mystery.[6]

He apparently told his colleagues, "If I don't arrive in class some morning, you just come over to my house and you will probably find me dead." One morning in 1933, he felt faint while teaching his French class, went to lay down in his office, and quietly passed away.[7]

Whatever Abbot's influence on the group during this season, it apparently did not extend to regulating their behavior. George Saunders, a first-year student, reported:

The season of 1921–22 was a most haphazard affair. There was no faculty supervision. . . . We had a wonderful time on tour, but I doubt if our audiences enjoyed it as much as I did. Things were, to put it mildly, sometimes out of hand. I still cherish the gold watch charm showing four drunks engraved on a Mason jar.[8]

The academic year 1921–22 marked a turning point for the Glee Club. With the shows that had been their mainstay running out of gas (and apparently producing little or no profit), the following season abandoned the musical comedy format entirely. It also shifted away from amateur leadership with the coming of the Glee Club's first director who was a professor of music. And on the musical front, two significant works were added to the Glee Club's repertoire.

---

1 James R. McConnell, *Flying for France: With the American Escadrille at Verdun* (Doubleday, Page and Co., 1916), xi.

2 James Bardin, "Fifteenth Annual Letter to the Alumni," *Alumni Bulletin of the University of Virginia* 11, no. 3 (July 1918): 306–7.

3 "Glee Club Scores in 'Nothing,'" *University of Virginia Alumni News*, March 1920, 180.

4 "C.Y.J. Goes to the Show: 'The Visiting Girl,'" *Yellow Journal*, April 1, 1921.

5 *Corks and Curls*, 35 (1922): 312.

6 Dabney, *Mr. Jefferson's University*, 191.

7 Joseph L. Vaughan, *Rotunda Tales* (Charlottesville: University of Virginia Alumni Association, 1991), 44–45.

8 George Saunders, letter to Donald C. Loach, 1972; cited in James Ballowe, "A History of the University Glee Club," 1977 (published in the *Glee Club 1980 Annual Report*).

12

"VIRGINIA, HAIL, ALL HAIL" AND "THE CAVALIER SONG"

The most famous musical conductor for the 1921–1922 season was the assistant conductor, John Albert Morrow (1883–1949). He completed his undergraduate degree at Emory and Henry College and then enrolled in graduate studies in mathematics, philosophy, and physics at the University of Virginia around 1916. A member of the YMCA and the Washington Literary Society, he sang in the Chapel Choir under the direction of A. L. Hall-Quest in 1916 and 1917. *Madison Hall Notes* reported in 1917 that Morrow's solos in chapel had "added much to the attractiveness of the Chapel music this session. . . . As soon as he had begun, there was a perceptible change in the attitude of the congregation and faculty, students and visitors listened with keen pleasure as each verse closed and the thrilling chorus repeated."[1] World War I found him volunteering to join the Allied Expeditionary Forces. He later received his PhD from the University of Florida and taught chemistry at Ward-Belmont College in Nashville, Tennessee. But in 1921 he was a newly minted master of arts and teaching fellow in chemistry in the engineering department, and assistant to Francis Harris Abbot in conducting the Glee Club. It was during that season that he made his most famous contribution to the University.

Sometime during the fall of 1921, Morrow wrote the words and music for "Virginia, Hail, All Hail." His manuscript of the work has not survived—the earliest extant version is a mid-1920s handwritten arrangement of the work by Arthur Fickénscher—but he did write both the melody and words of the song, submitting it as an original composition in a contest run by the *College Topics* student newspaper. The melody is simple enough—the tune spans a relatively narrow range of a major sixth—and the words are well known to modern Glee Club members:

> Ten thousand voices sing thy acclaim
> Ten thousand hearts beat high at thy name
> All unafraid and girded with good
> Mother of men, a queen thou has stood
> Children of thine a true brotherhood:
> Virginia, hail, all hail!

The song does not appear to have immediately caught on; there are no recorded performances prior to 1923. Indeed, it might have languished unsung except for a contest sponsored by the alumni association and publicized in

FIG 3. John Albert Morrow, author of "Virginia, Hail, All Hail." Photo by Holsinger Studios circa 1918. Photo courtesy Small Special Collections Library, University of Virginia.

College Topics, which sought to inspire the creation of more official songs of the University. Up until that time, most of the University's songs were either football songs or new words to familiar tunes; the ambitions of the *College Topics* editors were for the creation of more songs of the University with both original words and music.

By February 16, 1923, the editors had made their selections. The alma mater song was to be Morrow's "Virginia, Hail, All Hail," and the fight song honors went to "The Cavalier Song" by Lawrence Lee and Fulton Lewis Jr. Two other songs set to familiar tunes, by G. G. Crawford and Harter F. Wright, placed second. The announcement of the prizes in *College Topics* suggests that the committee was not entirely satisfied with the outcome of the contest:

> The Committee desires to thank those who submitted songs and to congratulate the winners. It is hoped that the contest will stimulate the student body and alumni to greater effort to give Virginia a still better group of songs with original music.[2]

"Virginia, Hail, All Hail" received its first public performance by the Glee Club on April 6, 1923, in the Cabell Hall auditorium and was shortly afterward performed on tour in Richmond, Washington, DC, and Baltimore.[3] It was subsequently performed in concert in 1925 in Staunton, was included in a 1938 student songbook, and appeared on the Glee Club's first recording and on concert programs through the 1950s. But it never truly attained the status of a beloved alma mater song for the rest of the student body, who continued to sing "The Good Old Song." Glee Club performance practice for many years has been to combine the official and de facto alma mater songs by introducing "The Good Old Song" with one verse of "Virginia, Hail, All Hail."

The other award winner in 1923 fared better for continuity of performance thanks to its adoption by the University's marching and athletic bands. "The Cavalier Song" is generally heard only as an instrumental performance of the tune written for the song by Lawrence Lee, an instructor in English at the University, but it also has words which were written for it by Glee Club member Fulton Lewis Jr. (1903–1966).

Lewis is one of the Glee Club's more colorful alumni. Born in Washington, DC, his family appears to have been wealthy—their summer home stood on land now occupied by Washington National Cathedral. Withdrawing from the

University in 1923 after three years of study, and completing only a portion of his studies at George Washington University School of Law, he ultimately settled in journalism, reporting for the *Washington Herald* and shortly becoming the city editor. He met his future wife, the daughter of the former chairman of the Republican National Committee, while working at the newspaper; President Herbert Hoover attended their wedding.[4]

He left the *Herald* for Universal News Service, where he at first wrote a syndicated news column, but his career picked up in earnest when he filled in for a vacationing news reporter at the Washington radio station WOL, impressing the station with his "on the spot" reporting. His fifteen-minute weekday news commentary program was soon picked up and syndicated; at its peak he could be heard on more than five hundred radio stations and reached a weekly audience of sixteen million. His influence encouraged the United States Congress to begin allowing radio broadcasting of congressional activities.

Lewis was highly conservative, first making his mark by opposing Franklin Delano Roosevelt's New Deal programs. Later in life, he was a Barry Goldwater supporter and opponent of John F. Kennedy and Lyndon B. Johnson and their policies. He was also a strong supporter of the America First Committee, which sought to keep the United States out of World War II in the late 1930s as the Nazis rose to power. Most notably, he was avidly anticommunist and a vocal backer of Senator Joseph McCarthy. He continued to advocate for McCarthy even after the senator's nationwide disgrace, ultimately diminishing his own audience and appeal. Nevertheless, he continued to broadcast until his death in 1966.

Lewis is remembered today largely for "his complete lack of objectivity" and as "one of the most unprincipled journalists ever to practice the trade."[5] But he also wrote one of the great enduring fight songs of the University, even if we chiefly remember the song for its tune. And his words were responsible for giving the team its official name. From the song's final chorus:

> Once more our might has won the fight;
> We gain the victor's due.
> And all men raise their voice to praise
> The orange and blue.

So, through the years, like Cavaliers,
We'll shout Virginia's name!
It e'er shall be on land and sea
A sign of might and fame.

1 "Morrow's Solo Pleases," *Madison Hall Notes,* March 3, 1917, 1.
2 "Results Announced in Alumni Song Contest," *College Topics,* February 16, 1923, 1.
3 "Glee Club Concert Lets New Standard," *College Topics,* April 10, 1923; "University Glee Club Scores Successfully in Neighboring Cities," *College Topics,* May 11, 1923.
4 "Fulton Lewis, Jr.," Radio Days, https://www.otr.com/lewis.html, accessed September 1, 2010.
5 Eric Boehlert, "'Fair and Balanced'—The McCarthy Way," *Salon,* May 26, 2005, https://www.salon.com/2005/05/26/fulton_lewis_connection/.

13 | 1922 TO 1931: PROFESSOR FICKÉNSCHER AND THE MCINTIRE DEPARTMENT OF MUSIC

U p until the early 1920s, the University of Virginia had little formal instruction in music. While Jefferson had reserved a room in the Rotunda for instruction in the arts, and the faculty had advertised for a music teacher beginning in 1825, it was not until 1828 that a Mr. Bigelow began giving lessons for fees, followed by Mr. Deems and then, in 1853, by Mr. Robinson, who for the first time instructed students in singing; however, these were not University professors and there was no music in the published curriculum. There was no dedicated performance space until the Public Hall was built in the Rotunda Annex in 1853. But in Edwin Alderman's years as the first president of the University, this gap was redressed, thanks to a generous alumnus.

Paul Goodloe McIntire (1860–1952) attended the University during the 1878–1879 session, then left, as he said, "since I had to make a living."[1] Entering the coffee trade in Chicago and purchasing a seat on the Chicago Stock Exchange, he subsequently moved to the New York Stock Exchange in 1901, where he made his fortune. He retired in 1918 and returned to Charlottesville. The town, and the University, would benefit handsomely from his largesse, which was so great that by 1942 he was reduced to a fixed income and "was struggling to live within his annuity of $6,000" (about $100,000 in today's money).[2]

The donations he made to the University were substantial, and in 1921 alone included a donation of $200,000 to establish a school of commerce and economics, which the University named for him, and $120,000 to build the McIntire Amphitheatre as an outdoor performance space. He later gave $50,000 for a new building for the University hospital, $75,000 to establish the study of psychiatry at the University, $100,000 toward cancer research, and $47,500 to purchase Pantops Farm. He contributed much to fine arts at the University as well, including financing a concert series in Cabell Hall and donating a rare books collection to the library and nearly five hundred works of art to the University's museum. In Charlottesville at large, he helped finance the sculptures of George Rogers Clark, Thomas Jonathan Jackson, Robert Edward Lee, and Meriwether Lewis and William Clark through the National Sculpture Society.

His philanthropy indirectly benefited the Virginia Glee Club via one of his earliest gifts, the 1919 gift of $155,000 to endow the chair of fine arts. He wrote to University president Edwin Alderman that he hoped "the University will see its way clear to offer many lectures upon the subject of art and music, so that the people will appreciate more than ever before that the University belongs to them; and that it exists for them."[3] The donation was the impetus behind the creation of both the McIntire Department of Music and the McIntire Department of Art.

In the fall of 1922, one year after the donation for the music department, the first occupant of the chair arrived at Virginia. Arthur Fickénscher was as old as the Virginia Glee Club, born March 9, 1871, in Aurora, Illinois. He studied music in Munich under Joseph Rheinberger, then taught in Berlin and in Oakland, California. His appointment at the University of Virginia under Alderman marked the arrival of the first formally trained musician to the faculty. And somehow he became director of the Glee Club as well. History does not record how or why a group that just a few years before was doing musical theater performances would have come under the wing of this European-trained musician, but it may have had to do with the state of the group's coffers. One suspects that, after years of unsteady income from touring, a music director whose salary was paid by the University may have looked highly attractive.

He appears to have had serious contemporary musical inclinations—he invented the Polytone, an instrument capable of producing sixty distinct tones within an octave, and is credited as an early twentieth-century innovator in microtonal music—but he did not bring these to bear on the Glee Club's performances.

Their appearances in neighboring cities continued, with planned stops in the first season including Washington, Baltimore, Sweet Briar, Lynchburg, Newport News, and the resorts at White Sulphur Springs (the Greenbrier) and Hot Springs (the Homestead), according to Glee Club president Harry Glenn Kaminer—and they did mount a tour in Baltimore, Richmond, and Washington.

But there were two significant changes that occurred during the first year. One was the return of the Glee Club's annual (and apparently only) University concert to Cabell Hall, rather than the Jefferson Theater in downtown Charlottesville, where they had performed for the preceding few seasons. Cabell Hall has remained the group's performing home, with brief exceptions for renovations and the occasional schedule conflict, until the present day.

The second change had to do with the quality of performance. "Glee Club Concert Lets New Standard" read the front-page headline of the concert review on April 10, 1923, and (typo notwithstanding) the reviewer found that the standard had indeed been raised:

> Setting a new standard of excellence that displayed neither the absence of talent nor the over-ambition that frequently characterizes college musical organizations, the University of Virginia Glee Club last Friday night drew round after round of well merited applause from the large audience that completely filled Cabell Hall. This year's performance was not a show. It was advertised and put on as a concert.[4]

That said, the concert did not correspond to our modern notion of a choral performance. While there were choral numbers, they were interspersed with solo songs, a banjo duet, and a xylophone duet. But the choral numbers were significant: the first public performance of "Virginia, Hail, All Hail" was featured, as were Thomas Morley's "Now Is the Month of Maying" and works by Palestrina, Edward Elgar, and Jules Massenet. For the first time, recognizable classical chorus repertoire had entered the Glee Club's sphere.

The club, under the leadership of president Kaminer, vice-president Fred N. Ogden, manager John Dismukes Green, and publicity manager Robert Lee Hinds, took this program on tour to Richmond, Washington, DC, and Baltimore, where audiences agreed with the home assessment of the new regime. The *Richmond Times Dispatch* wrote, "In decidedly favorable contrast to the performances of the last few years of the University of Virginia Glee

Club, the concert Thursday night at the Women's Club offered an evening of real music."[5] It also noted the solo performance of Fulton Lewis Jr., who "sang songs of his own composition in a delightfully charming manner."[6] Only the *Baltimore Sun* disagreed, noting that while "the ensemble showed the productive training of Prof. Fickénscher," the first few songs featured "a few discordant notes and a noticeable lack of confidence"; this apparently "wore away" by the time the club got to the third number on the program.[7] George Saunders, now a second-year student, wrote, "The season of 1922–23 was a great success, and no longer did I feel sorry for our audiences."[8]

The changes wrought by Fickénscher seem to have been well received by the membership, though they reflected the change in work ethic. Herbert L. Morgenroth wrote, "We met in a room at the tip end of West Range (near the Amphitheatre) and were under the direction of a delightful little ferrety man, Professor Arthur Fickénscher—a good musician and quite a taskmaster."[9]

The momentum continued into the following season. The 1923–1924 season, under the leadership of president Randolph Conroy, saw performances in Washington, DC, Roanoke, the Greenbrier resort at White Sulfur Springs, and Baltimore, as well as the Glee Club's first known radio broadcast performance. The Glee Club had begun to build a regional reputation. In an article dated February 21, 1924, an Alabama newspaper held up the Vanderbilt College Glee Club to the Virginia Glee, calling the latter "the best club of the sort in the South today."[10]

Fickénscher and the club leadership also innovated the organization of the club: the group was divided into general membership, consisting of all those who auditioned and then made a final cut based in part on attendance, and touring membership, consisting of selected singers. The touring group represented the Glee Club in competitions, such as the *Richmond News* Leader Glee Club Competition of 1928 (where they were defeated by the University of North Carolina Glee Club).[11]

The successful reception for the Glee Club for these early seasons appears to have revitalized the group, at least for a while. The membership, which numbered thirty-six in 1921–1922, was fifty-three in 1924–1925, with Conroy repeating as president from the prior season. Conroy even led a Glee Club Orchestra, which lent a big band sound to concert performances and allowed the Glee Club to sponsor dances. The Glee Club also began an annual tradition of performing at the Greenbrier and the Homestead around Easter weekend, pairing a concert with dances and receptions.[12]

The most notable event happened in the fall of 1928, with the Glee Club's appearance on the newly launched Fox *Movietone News* newsreel. The *Virginia Reel*, normally a humor magazine, noted in its November 1928 issue:

> During the past few years, the University in general has accorded the Glee Club hardly more than a mild smile of derision. The smile was partially wiped off last year when the Glee Club went on a number of good trips, and now this year the smile has been totally banished. The leap of the vocalists from obscurity into the publicity of the movie-tone screen has placed them in a position of importance among the student activities.[13]

But the happy times did not last. If once Fickénscher's Glee Club had captured the imagination and respect of *College Topics'* critic, by the early 1930s the group no longer was drawing crowds. The planned 1932–1933 tour of the South had to be canceled for lack of funds.[14] *College Topics* noted that an April performance was lightly attended, while poking fun at the group generally:

> Out of the odd 600 seats in Cabell Hall, this reporter could count only 595 empties.... At the conclusion of the program, the audience surged on stage and carried away with it such souvenirs as it was able to obtain—bits of the piano, autographs of the singers, Dr. Fickénscher's baton, and finally, as has been mentioned, the Doctor himself.[15]

Something had to change. Fickénscher continued to teach music on the faculty of the University, but he left the conducting of the Glee Club to a new face: Harry Rogers Pratt.

---

1 Dabney, *Mr. Jefferson's University,* 123.
2 Ibid.
3 Bruce, *History of the University of Virginia,* vol. 5, 152.

4 "Glee Club Concert Lets New Standard," *College Topics,* April 10, 1923.

5 "University Glee Club Scores Successfully in Neighboring Cities," *College Topics,* May 11, 1923. This was a collection of reviews from various newspapers of the tour.

6 Ibid.

7 Ibid.

8 George M. Saunders, personal letter to Donald Loach, 1972, quoted in Ballowe, "A History," 6.

9 Herbert L. Morgenroth, letter to the University Glee Club, 1970, quoted in Ballowe, "A History," 6.

10 "Vanderbilt's Glee Club Has Experts," *Florence (AL) Tribune,* February 21, 1924, 1.

11 "News Leader Glee Club Concert Is Won by Renowned Tarheel Singers," *Collegian* (University of Richmond), May 11, 1928, 1.

12 The Glee Club performed at the Homestead in 1932, 1933, 1934, and 1935, with the performances often covered by the society pages of the *New York Times.* An article on April 23, 1934, noted: "A concert by the University of Virginia Glee Club in the Homestead Theatre last evening attracted a large audience. There was a striking display of evening gowns." The Greenbrier was on the list for 1932 as well, though no evidence survives of return engagements.

13 "A Growth in Power," *Virginia Reel* 9, no. 77 (November 1928): 12.

14 "Glee Club Prepares New Concert Work," *College Topics,* February 10, 1933, 4.

15 "Throng Greets Glee Clubbers," *College Topics,* April 21, 1933, 1.

14 1933 TO 1935: PRATT'S BOYS

Harry Rogers Pratt was a far cry from Arthur Fickénscher. Where Fickénscher learned music in European schools, Pratt studied at Harvard. Fickénscher was single-mindedly devoted to music—composing, teaching, and even inventing instruments. Pratt was more of a showman. Indeed, his first teaching role at the University of Virginia was as a professor of drama, and he founded the Virginia Players, the University's longest-lasting dramatic club.[1] Fickénscher studied in Germany; Pratt favored the French tradition.[2] Physically, too, they were different, with Fickénscher's narrow, unfortunately rodent-like face a marked contrast to Pratt's handsome visage.

Born in Wellesley, Massachusetts, in 1884, Pratt studied music at Harvard University for two years before leaving school.[3] Though listed in alumni reports with the class of 1906, he is listed in a 1906 alumni report as "not heard from." Interestingly, he is also listed as Henry Fearing, apparently his stage name.[4] After Harvard, he is next attested (in his *New York Times* obituary) as joining the Ben Greet Players on a tour of the South, then Charles Coburn's theatrical company, which performed in the old Empire Theatre in New York. He then moved into music and was musical director of the Lake Placid Foundation when he was hired away by Alderman to join the music faculty.[5]

Pratt took over the Glee Club in the 1933–1934 season. There was no concert in the fall, though the Glee Club did sponsor a dance, with music provided by 1932–1933 Glee Club president Charlie Gasque and his Royal Virginians. Behind the scenes, though, Pratt was hard at work recruiting and building a group of singers.[6] In spring of 1932–1933, the membership of the Glee Club stood at thirty-two; by the time the members were listed in the 1933–1934 *Corks and Curls*, the club had grown to fifty-seven.

The first concert, a benefit for the Hospital Circle and Hospital League, was held February 15, 1934. Pratt left nothing to chance; he sent a letter with the concert program to members of the University community ten days before the concert, writing:

> Last Fall Mr. Fickénscher asked me to take over the leadership of the University of Virginia GLEE CLUB. Since that time I have been training sixty young men for our first concert together, to be given THURSDAY EVENING, FEBRUARY 15 at 8:30.
>
> It is the combined hope of Mr. Fickénscher, the members of the Glee Club and myself to regain for this organization the popularity it has held in past years and to win back its traditional prestige as the leading musical organization of the student body.[7]

The program was a departure from what we know of Fickénscher's standard fare, which featured skits, quartet performances, and "speciality" numbers, usually instrumental solos, but which had added jazz performances from Gasque's orchestra.[8] In their place, Pratt's program featured spirituals, works by Palestrina, and the first appearance of Russian choral works in the Glee Club's repertoire, the *Hospodi Pomiloi*.

The combined effect of the training, larger-sized group, and new repertoire was apparently electric. In an article titled "Demon Gleemen Score Triumph," *College Topics* wrote the day after the concert:

> Some six hundred people in Cabell Hall last evening were awakened in a startling manner to the fact that this University has a substantial start towards an organization of which any university could well be proud—Mr. Pratt's Glee Club. Rumor has been current for some time concerning the high musical standards and unusual ability of the group, and rumor was fully and splendidly confirmed last night.
>
> From the first note of the "Netherlands Prayer of Thanks-

giving," the eyes and ears of the audience were opened. After this number, the first group continued with three "spirituals," as the program blithely commented, lumping together "Deep River" and a Motet each by Praetorius and Palestrina. Outstanding in this group was the magnificent "Adoramus Te" of Palestrina, which was repeated in response to the enthusiastic applause....

The climax of the program came with the last number of the third group, a well-nigh perfect rendition of "Hospodi Pomiloi," the Russian version of the Kyrie Eleison. This chant, which consists of the constant repetition of this phrase in first descending and decreasing tones, and then ascending and increasing tones, was greeted by an outburst of applause that could only be stopped by an encore.[9]

Pratt's Glee Club followed their first concert with performances at women's colleges at Sweet Briar and St. Catherine's, at the resort at Hot Springs, Virginia, and in Richmond. The Glee Club had first sung with Sweet Briar's glee club in the spring of 1933, a collaboration that continued until the 1980s.

The student leadership of the Glee Club this year was especially strong, particularly the junior leaders. Little is known of the 1933–1934 president James McKenney Barry aside from his twenty years of army service after graduating from the University of Virginia, but manager Guy Hope was one of two brothers who would play a significant role in the club's trajectory over the next decade, as would assistant manager Rial Rose. The accompanist for this season, James S. Constantine, served in this capacity through 1935 and then returned as assistant director from 1939 to 1941, before eventually becoming a classics professor at the University; the Constantine Library and Constantine Lecture Series are named in his memory.

But the 1933–1934 season was only the beginning. Pratt's next big innovation with the group was the first formal outreach to its alumni, beginning in 1934–1935. The first concert that season that we know about, on February 26 in Cabell Hall, billed as the "Annual Concert," advertised that the next season would highlight the group's fiftieth anniversary (presumably counting the 1886–1887 season as the starting point).

More importantly, the program listed a newly formed alumni advisory board for the Glee Club, including composer (and white supremacist) John

Powell as honorary member as well as alumni including M. André Burthe (class of 1889), Lawrence Thomas Royster (1897), John Jennings Luck (1908), ten alumni from the 1910s (including Malcolm W. Gannaway), and three from the 1920s. The concert even featured a performance by an alumni quartet, consisting of professors Robert V. Funsten, Arthur Kyle Davis, and Oscar Swineford and 1919 alum Edward Gamble. This was the first time a concentrated effort had been made by the group to enumerate its alumni, much less include them in concert proceedings.

The February 1935 concert also featured the first known performance of the Glee Club Quartet. Unlike other small groups from the Glee Club who performed a handful of songs during concerts of the larger group, this quartet (also called the Tin Can Quartet) seemed to have an independent life of its own, much like the group known as the Virginia Gentlemen nearly twenty years later. The quartet appeared in radio performances, at gigs away from the University, and also in concerts. The first known members in 1934–1935 were Vincent Tramonte, Guy Hope, his brother Winston Hope, and Rial Rose.

The following season, 1935–1936, was a high-water mark for the Virginia Glee Club. Not only was it celebrated as an anniversary season, but the Glee Club performed in New York City and on national radio, and it held its first Concert on the Lawn. Under the leadership of Rial Rose (now president) and Robert Carter Wellford Jones, manager, as well as the assistant conductorship of Guy Hope, the group executed eight known concerts, including several stops on the New York City tour.

The season began in September 1935 with an article by Rial Rose in the *University of Virginia Magazine*, in which he exhorted men to try out for the Glee Club, noting, "There are just two things that are absolutely required of a man who wishes to join the University of Virginia Glee Club. He must be enrolled at the University, and he must be able to carry a tune." Rose pointed out that the nature of Glee Club singing had evolved:

> It is almost certain that by this time forty-nine of every fif-
> ty men just entering college will want to ask, "Just what is
> a college Glee Club, anyway?" It's the question I asked on
> entering school, and it's a hard one to answer, for, you see,
> Glee Clubs change from year to year, even from month to
> month. One used to think of mandolins and nasal quartets
> "rend-ering" Sweetheart of Sigma Chi. Fortunately it's some-
> thing else now.

In answering the question, I want, in the first place, to talk about male choruses. Have you ever heard the Don Cossacks, or the male section of the Metropolitan Opera Chorus, or Fred Waring's Glee Club, or the Hampton Institute singers? I know you've heard one of them—you must have—and maybe all. When you heard the wonderful effects the voices made, you said to yourself, "That's surely the greatest music in the world!" You were right. It was the plain truth. Men's choruses do make the greatest music. Orchestras, whether jazz or symphonic, can't touch them, for, after all, the instruments in an orchestra only imitate human voices. They may do it well, but still they aren't the real thing.

Now, a College Glee Club, in these days, is a very ambitious organization. It attempts to combine the best of all these various kinds of music. The religious and folk music of the negroes and Cossacks appear on the same programs with the popular and "pretty" music of the "Pennsylvanians," and with the strong, soul-stirring music of the great composers. In 1934–35, for instance, the University Glee Club sang music of America, England, Germany, Russia, Finland, the Netherlands, and the Latin Church, while a quartet sang negro songs, on a typically arranged program. And, not content with merely singing the music, we attempted to perform it nearly as possible in the various styles of the peoples it represented.[10]

The drive apparently paid off; twenty-three new names appear in the roster of members in the 1936 *Corks and Curls*, compared to the prior season. Among the new members was Daniel A. Jenkins, who wrote in the early 1990s about his audition:

Walking along University Avenue one evening during my first week in Charlottesville I heard singing coming from the steps of a boarding house. Good close harmony. Edging my way up the sidewalk, I contributed a few notes and soon was asked to join in. The rest of the evening consisted of beer, cigarettes and singing, at the end of which it was suggested that I attend the Glee Club tryouts the following day. Next morning, badly hung over and hardly in the best of voice, I presented myself to Prof. Harry Rogers Pratt, distinguished director of the Glee Club, as a second tenor. About five notes into it he stared at me and said, "Try the bass." Given the beer and the cigarettes and the non-stop singing the previous evening, bass it was. "Eureka!" cried Prof. Pratt. Seventeen-year-old basses did not grown on trees.

For four years thereafter I had to retire to The Corner the night before every concert for remedial drinking, smoking and singing in order to turn myself into a proper bass for the following evening's performance.[11]

In keeping with the practice of the time, Jenkins and the other new recruits spent the fall rehearsing; there were no official concert performances on the schedule, though doubtless its members sang at football games and other informal performances. The first official Glee Club appearance was of the quartet (Tramonte, Hope, Hope, and Rose), which performed at an alumni dinner in Washington, DC. The first known public performance of the full Glee Club for the season came February 21, 1936, in Cabell Hall and was billed as the "50th Anniversary Concert." No program survives of the concert, but *College Topics* wrote both a preview and review of the concert, declaring, "After listening to last night's performance we feel that the Glee Club is quite prepared for its northern tour next week."[12]

The next week was indeed a momentous trip: the Virginia Glee Club was headed to New York City for the first time.

---

1 Vaughn, *Rotunda Tales,* 144–46.
2 "Insidious propaganda in behalf of the Italian school, intended to discourage native ambition and felt in every great capital, had been emboldened by the residence in Paris and the monstrous popularity of Rossini and Meyerbeer, the two most picturesque prostitutors of the art of music—one an Italian, the other a German characteristically living where business was good.

"The bright, pure flame of French musical art, lighted by Couperin and Rameau early in the eighteenth century, had been snuffed out by the indifference of the Parisian public, busily idolizing their imported gods." Harry Rogers Pratt, "The Rebirth of French Music," *Virginia Quarterly Review* (Spring 1925): par. 2–3.

3 "Harry Rogers Pratt, Massachusetts Town and Vital Records, 1620–1988," Ancestry.com, https://www.ancestry.com/, accessed February 12, 2017.

4 *Harvard College Class of 1906, Secretary's Third Report* (Crimson Printing Co., 1906), 134.

5 "Harry R. Pratt, 72, Educator, Ex-Actor," *New York Times,* May 7, 1956, 27.

6 In addition to his other talents, Pratt was apparently much better organized than his predecessors. His is one of the best documented of almost any Glee Club directorship, thanks to his habit of keeping not only concert programs but also news clippings, photographs, telegrams, and letters in a series of scrapbooks that survived the ignominy of being stored at the Glee Club House. They are now in the Special Collections of the University of Virginia Library.

7 Letter from Harry Rogers Pratt, February 5, 1934, courtesy Special Collections, University of Virginia Library. The custom at the University of Virginia has been to address professors, regardless of academic degree, as "Mr.," perhaps inspired by the Enactments of 1825, which limited the diplomas of the University to awarding only the degrees of graduate and doctor, and the latter only in the medical school (Bruce, *History of the University of Virginia,* vol. 3, 385).

8 "Glee Club Prepares New Concert Work," *College Topics,* February 10, 1933, 4.

9 "Demon Gleemen Score Triumph," *College Topics,* February 16, 1934.

10 Rial Rose, "Yo Ho! Yo Ho! We'll Blow the Man Doowwn!" *University of Virginia Magazine* 44, no. 1 (September 19, 1935): 12ff.

11 Daniel A. Jenkins, "Of Camels and Camels®," *Virginia Glee Club Newsletter* 20, no. 1 (Fall 1993): 2.

12 Howard Bailey, "Previews and Reviews: Glee Club Concert," *College Topics,* February 22, 1936, 2.

15 | 1936: NEW YORK AND AFTER

Most of the Glee Club's tour dates until this time had been southward bound. When it ventured outside the Commonwealth of Virginia, it tended to head south and west, with Atlanta representing its farthest foray afield; Baltimore had been its farthest northern excursion. But nothing less than a visit to the Big Apple would be an acceptable marking of the fiftieth anniversary of the Glee Club. Pratt, perhaps leveraging connections made when he worked on Broadway, arranged a joint performance with the Barnard College Glee Club of Columbia University and a concert at the famed Plaza Hotel. The events on the day of the Plaza Hotel concert included a Columbia radio broadcast, marking another first for the Glee Club.

Pratt and his officers left nothing to chance, distributing a one-page memo of tour logistics. The boys were to board the train on February 26 at Union Station (the 12:25 p.m. from Southern Railway). They were lodged at the Hotel Taft, just north of Times Square. Thursday's performance was at Barnard, complete with instructions on how to take the Seventh Avenue Local to 116th Street. On Friday would be the radio broadcast in the afternoon followed by the Plaza Hotel concert in the evening ("Every man must be there for seating rehearsal by 7:45 p.m."). Sunday they were to return home (Penn Station, 2:30 p.m.). At the bottom of the memo, Pratt wrote: "While in New York please bear in mind that we are under contract to give three top-form concerts. Don't eat too much before a concert and don't get hoarse singing and talking."

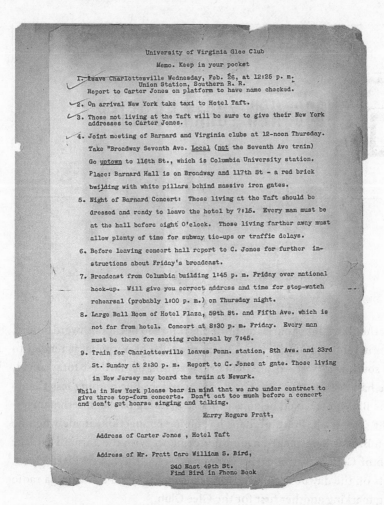

FIGURE 4. Checklist from the 1936 New York tour. From the Glee Club scrapbook.

It was an ambitious agenda, with unprecedented levels of exposure. But the club by all accounts performed spectacularly. The Barnard concert had in its audience Daniel Gregory Mason, Columbia professor, critic, and composer of the "Ode to Big Business," which the club had been performing on the tour; he expressed "extreme satisfaction" with the performance. The Glee Club scrapbook saved congratulatory telegrams and letters from Hamilton College professor Edward N. Main, University of Virginia president John

Lloyd Newcomb and his wife, and tour manager R. C. W. Jones's mother. Press coverage included photos at the Associated Press and a front-page photo in the *Washington Post*.

The Glee Club being the Glee Club, there was, perhaps inevitably, some degree of foolery, and even some minor crises. It is reported that the club members compared purity test scores with the Barnard girls on Thursday, and that the alumni who attended Friday night's concert and the subsequent supper dance "brought their young and attractive daughters with them ... (but the daughters didn't stay with their parents for very long)."[1] One unfortunate singer fell sick in the Hotel Taft Thursday morning and stayed after the rest of the group departed, nursing a high fever. Another missed the train in New York; a third left his suitcase in a subway station locker. And Daniel Jenkins reported being "asked to leave (that is, thrown out of) the Taft Hotel bar late one evening during a New York trip. Nobody is perfect."[2]

Calamities aside, it was clear that the Glee Club had acquitted themselves exceptionally during their four nights in New York. And the season wasn't over. There was a concert in Richmond at the Woman's Club, with proceeds donated to the restoration of the Adam Craig House, where Edgar Allan Poe wrote "To Helen."[3] There was a return to Sweet Briar on April 25. On the next day, Sunday, there was a concert in the McIntire Amphitheatre, featuring Pratt himself on the "MIGHTY Wurlitzer Organ, the University Band, audience participation singalong, and audience response from University mascot dog Beta":

> No session in the amphitheater is complete without little boys wrestling on the grassy banks and Beta presiding over all. When the little boys weren't yelling and Beta wasn't busy barking at the boys who insist on bicycling around being a menace to spectators, one could hear the band "swinging" the good old-time marches and concert pieces. . . . Beta went to sleep during this interlude except for one election called "The Whistler and His Dog." The piece ends with the band whistling and barking, all of which nearly upset Beta's equilibrium until he was set right.[4]

The account of this outdoor concert concluded with a "last minute flash": Pratt swung by the *College Topics'* offices to announce that this first "song-fest" had gone so well that he planned to repeat the experience the following Sunday.[5]

Originally planning to return to the Rotunda, the concert was relocated to the Rotunda steps. Pratt told *College Topics* in a follow-up article, "Ability to sing is not a pre-requisite. Those who think they can sing are wanted especially. Tenors will be protected by Beta and Captain Mack. Baying, bellowing, and booing will be allowed. 'Sweet Adeline' will be sung as often as demand warrants."[6]

Perhaps fortuitously (and perhaps not), the May 4 concert followed the club's annual beer party at which its officers were elected. That concert was the very first Concert on the Lawn. *College Topics* wrote:

> With beer in front of them, beer in back of them, beer inside of them, "Pratt's Boys" went to town last night and lifted the skies from the steps of the Rotunda. Some say the interlude was caused by a shortage of foaming brew, but whatever it was, either the Lure of the Lawn or the Radiance of the Rotunda, it was good!
>
> The flitting ghostly figures that came running out of the nowhere to see what had happened to the quiet solitude showed conclusively by their applause that it was good. Whistles, cheers and stamping in between songs was sufficient proof to the Glee Club that their final gathering was their greatest success. It further showed that informal "step-singing" (and it was informal) has a great future.
>
> Beerly dampened steps may have been the cause for the stimulating effect of the Gleemen, but it's doubtful, for spontaneous song cannot be dampened even by "soft" drink. With Mr. Pratt leading and Guy Hope substituting here and there, the "Boys" started off with "Swanee River." Before it was finished, the Rotunda steps started filling up with astonished, but highly pleased onlookers. The concert was on! Between gulps of beer (carried from the party in Dixie cups) "Ten Thousand Voices" and "Massa's in Da Cold, Cold Ground" were heard. In the interlude (while Mr. Pratt sounded pitch) cries and shouts for "Hospodi" were heard. Finally the mob ruled and "Hospodi Pomilui" got under way. We didn't know quite what it was either, but when the final rendition was done (we say final for a few "beer soured notes" first held

sway) we knew that we had heard some first-class singing. If you've never heard "Hospodi," a Russian anthem, get "Pratt's Boys" to sing it.

"Old Harry Pratt, he ain't what he use to be" was the next unexpected offering and it continued until all the members of the retiring staff had received their "song of recognition." By this time, the Gleemen thought that perhaps "the other keg" had arrived and they were anxious to get "Bock." So, with a fitting climax to a very extemporaneous concert (and probably their best) "The Good Old Song" rang out loud and clear. Then singing, humming, whistling and harmonizing, "Pratt's Boys" wandered down the lawn and to those on the steps, strains of "Good Night Ladies" and "One Keg of Beer" drifted back through the night. Once again the dignity, silence and [unintelligible] of the Lawn held sway![7]

Jenkins recalled in an article for the *Virginia Spectator* two years later:

Under a shimmering moon and mingling with the proverbial purple shadows of the Lawn, the sweet lusty tones of "Sweet Adeline" resounded from pillar to pillar and rolled majestically down the moon-lit greensward in an ever-increasing swell of tenor and bass. The doors along the Lawn were flung open and little clusters of figures merged together in the dusk to listen. Students who had been cramming for exams in the Library laid down their books and joined the small crowd of onlookers who were slowly gathering around the steps. The Glee Club, inspired by this unexpected audience, went through almost its entire repertoire and for over an hour the merry sound of song broke into the sombre atmosphere of study and provided a delightful respite to exam-worried students.[8]

So the 1936 season ended. Only three seasons into his tenure as director, Pratt had brought the group to new heights: its first New York tour, first radio performance, first Concert on the Lawn, a substantially revived and enlarged membership, and an unprecedented level of alumni engagement and outreach.

Pratt's 1936–1937 season, with McDonald Wellford as president, featured less touring and a slightly different program approach. There was an appearance in Washington, DC, with the full club and the quartet, an Easter week concert in Cabell Hall, and a late season performance in Norfolk. All three performances featured alternating songs from the full Glee Club, from the quartet, and piano solos by a new member of the Glee Club, Ernest Mead. Mead performed with the Glee Club during his first year but would remain close to the Glee Club and the University, returning in 1953 as a professor of music and remaining in the McIntire Department of Music until his retirement in 1996.

FIGURE 5. Glee Club, 1936. From left: McDonald Wellford, Glee Club president; Chester Harris Robbins; Harry Rogers Pratt; Ernest Mead; Kenneth Seaman Giniger. Photo courtesy Small Special Collections Library, University of Virginia Library.

According to Jenkins in a 1938 article for the *Virginia Spectator*, the end of the 1936–1937 season found a return to public singing, led by members of the Glee Club, this time during reunions:

> On Saturday nights of Finals, however, a minor miracle took place. Gathered in and around a certain room on East Lawn were a goodly number of dark conspirators; six members of the class of 1912 had slipped away from their comrades, bearing with them a huge Mason jar containing a mint julep, and were on their way to join the group lurking in the shadows of East Lawn. Three members of the Tin Can Quartet, a dozen members of the Glee Club, past and present, and an odd assortment of dates waited expectantly as the six alumni approached. And then, a short five minutes later— ah, shades of the mighty Caruso!—it had been a long year— the soft, harmonious tones of "Sweet Adeline" once again rolled up and down the Lawn. The same moon shimmered through the trees and the same purple shadows mingled with the ghostly figures that stood grouped beneath a stately oak. A prominent and dignified New York attorney gazed up at the stars and hit notes of which he had never before believed himself capable. A notorious "big business man" drowned the sorrows of a troubled world in his Mason jar and gazed down at the green sod beneath his feet, rumbling a potent bass that seemed to mingle with the very roots of the mighty oak which towered above him.
>
> For three hours the singing continued. They sang every song that ever graced a barbershop of old. Juleps were plentiful and so were first tenors—happy coincidence. But finally, at four o'clock in the morning, and when voices were so hoarse that anything above a whisper was an effort, the small crowd began to break up. The six alumni, their eyes tired but shining, stumbled wearily across the Lawn, speaking in reverent tones of the song-fests that used to be so common and now are so rare. The others, lingering for a brief moment over the dregs, said good-night and went their separate ways. The Lawn was once again cloaked in silence.[9]

During the late 1930s, the Glee Club only had one episode that garnered the publicity it had earned during the anniversary year, and it was for an entirely different reason. During the 1938–1939 season, Pratt expanded the repertoire of the group substantially, introducing opera for the first time and performing excerpts from Wagner's *Die Meistersinger* jointly with the Virginia Symphony. It was during the run-up to this concert that Pratt issued a statement that was syndicated by the Associated Press and appeared in the *Washington Post*:

> Prof. H. R. Pratt, director of the University of Virginia Glee Club, said today members of the glee club had refused to sing praise to "German masters" even though set to Wagner's immortal music. Prof. Pratt said members of the club demanded a revision of the wording of a line of the finale to the Wagnerian opera, "Die Meistersinger," before they would agree to sing it with the Virginia symphony orchestra in a joint concert at Cabell Hall tomorrow night. The line objected to, translated, reads: "Honor your German masters," and the score requires all 80 voices to sing it in crescendo. The club director said he had rewritten the line to read "honor your master singers."[10]

The following year, Pratt touched again on international issues when he invited the Don Cossack Choir under the direction of Serge Jaroff to perform at Old Cabell Hall on January 30, 1940. Jaroff had formed the chorus from exiled Cossacks who had been defeated by the Red Army and were interned in the Çilingur camp near Istanbul. The chorus had emigrated to the United States in 1930, becoming US citizens in New York City in 1936. Meanwhile, under Pratt's leadership the Glee Club had been singing Dmitri Lvovsky's Russian devotional "Hospodi Pomilui" since at least the 1933–1934 season. Bringing Jaroff's chorus of exiles to the University provided an opportunity to hear the "Hospodi" sung by native singers, and perhaps to make an unsubtle political point; by this time the Soviets had signed the Molotov-Ribbentrop Pact and were busy invading Poland, Finland, Estonia, Latvia, and Bessarabia.

Pratt's boys, under the leadership of Thomas P. Bryan as president and Marvin Perry as manager, returned in 1940 to the Plaza Hotel and also took the program on the road to Randolph-Macon College.[11] The Plaza Hotel program featured some of Pratt's signature works, including the "Hospodi Pomilui," and some newly added arrangements of spirituals by Marshall Bartholomew, including "De Animals A'Comin'" (last performed by the Glee Club in 1925) and "Steal Away." The concert opened with "Virginia, Hail, All Hail" (by now bearing its alternative title of "Ten Thousand Voices") and closed with "The Good Old Song."

The membership of the Glee Club stood at forty-six this season, including Hollis Chenery (1918–1994) of Richmond, who would go on to teach economics at Stanford, win a Guggenheim Fellowship in Economics in 1961, serve as vice president for economic development at the World Bank, and lead Secretariat, who was owned by his family, to the winner's circle at the Triple Crown.[12]

The following 1940–1941 season was a busy one for the Glee Club under the leadership of president Albert Kirven Cocke. Although war continued to brew overseas—prompting the Glee Club to donate their services to two benefit concerts for Queen Charlotte's Hospital in London, on February 24 and May 9, 1941—the United States was still neutral and college life continued apace. Including the benefit concerts, the Glee Club performed no fewer than eleven concerts that season, including appearances at Woodberry Forest, Gunston Hall, Mary Washington College, Madison College (now James Madison University), Hollins College, and Averett College; a return engagement at the Plaza Hotel; performances at the University's 1941 Music Festival in honor of the retirement of Arthur Fickénscher; and a special quartet performance at the Southeastern Folklore Society meeting of folk songs arranged by Arthur Kyle Davis Jr., the Folklore Society's president. Supporting all this concert activity was perhaps the largest roster the Glee Club had ever seen, weighing in at 130 members.

But the writing was on the wall that things were about to change. The benefit concerts sought to raise funds for victims of the German Blitz, which by May 1941 had considerably intensified. The United States could not stay out of the war for much longer, and this would change the Glee Club, its director, and the University forever.

1   Howard A. Bailey, "Gleemen Return to University after Successful N.Y. Trip," *College Topics,* March 3, 1936.

2   Jenkins, "Of Camels and Camels®," *Virginia Glee Club Newsletter* 20, no. 1 (Fall 1993): 2.

3   "Richmond Junior League Hosts to Virginia Gleemen," *College Topics,* March 28, 1936, 9.

4   "Glee Club, Band and Pratt with Students and Beta Have Concert," *College Topics,* April 28, 1936, 1.

5   Ibid.

6   "Rotunda Step-Singing to Be Inaugurated This Coming Sunday," *College Topics,* April 30, 1936.

7   F. Robert Strauss, "Happy Beer-Filled Gleemen Render Own 'Step-Singing,'" *College Topics,* May 5, 1936, 1.

8   Daniel A. Jenkins, "Sing, Brother, Sing," *Virginia Spectator* 1, no. 8 (April 1938): 15ff.

9   Ibid.

10   "Glee Club Balks at Song Lauding German Masters," *Washington Post*, January 17, 1939, 28.

11   Bryan was the son of Thomas Pinckney Bryan Sr., who was a soloist with the Glee Club in 1903–1904. Marvin Perry would go on to serve as a professor of English at the University of Virginia and became dean of admissions, in which role he persuaded a young John Casteen to enroll at the University. Perry subsequently was president of Goucher College from 1967 to 1973 and of Agnes Scott College from 1973 to 1982.

12   Eric Page, "Obituary: Hollis B. Chenery Dies at 77; Economist for the World Bank," *New York Times,* September 5, 1994.

16 1941 TO 1951: RANDALL, *THE TESTAMENT OF FREEDOM*, AND A RECORDING

The 1941–1942 Glee Club season started with a round of second tryouts for new members scheduled for early November and serious fall rehearsals devoted to a new addition to the repertoire. The tryouts weren't unusual, but the piece was; it was a work called *Tarantella*, and it was written by the new chair of the McIntire Department of Music, a scholar named Randall Thompson.

Thompson had come to the University from the Curtis Institute of Music to fill the vacancy left by the retirement of Arthur Fickénscher at the behest of University president John Lloyd Newcomb, who had taken over the presidency in 1931 after the sudden death of Edwin Alderman. Thompson brought with him, in addition to a considerable reputation (one local article, at the time of his appointment, called him "one of America's foremost composers"), several works for men's voices, including *Tarantella*, which had been composed for the Harvard Glee Club in 1937.[1] Harry Rogers Pratt took up the challenge, beginning rehearsals of the work in the fall, alongside several Finnish folk songs. The plan was to have "at least one concert by the end of January."[2]

Then came Pearl Harbor. Amid the confusion, many things were lost, including any record of a significant first for the season—the first Glee Club Christmas concert. Glee Club tradition holds that the first Christmas concert was held in 1941 and the numbering of the concerts is given on that basis (for example, the fortieth anniversary concerts held in 1990), but the first documentary evidence for a Christmas concert comes with an October 26, 1942, article in *College Topics* about an upcoming Christmas concert.[3]

Almost immediately, the impact on the Glee Club's season began to be felt. In early January it was announced that the club would cancel a series of out-of-town engagements, including performances at Gunston Hall, Hollins College, Chevy Chase Junior College, and others, due to one of the first wartime shortages: tires. Pratt announced that the club would continue its local performances, including "its annual concert in Cabell Hall, concerts in Charlottesville, and several radio broadcasts," and would "sponsor mass singing for the whole student body in Cabell Hall." The latter was apparently an initiative of Pratt's, who "had experience in that line during the last war directing large movie audiences singing the popular songs." The new slogan of the Glee Club was announced as "Keep 'Em Singing!" It can be inferred that Pratt saw his responsibility as primarily keeping up morale among the students who were beginning to be drafted.[4]

But signs were not good for the morale of Pratt himself. It was announced prior to the April 1942 annual concert that Thompson himself, rather than Pratt, would take the podium to direct his own *Tarantella*. For a showman like Pratt, yielding the baton so another man could conduct "his boys" must have been challenging. Unfortunately, no correspondence between the two survives to cast light on their relationship or why this occurred.

Whatever the relationship between the two men, Pratt continued as director through the fall of 1942. Under the leadership of Charles Edwin Butterworth Jr., Paul Webb Bourjaily, Thomas Conlon, and Ralph van Sickler Chamblin, the Glee Club remained a going concern even with the outbreak of the new European war, though the group's activities were constrained not only by wartime limits on supplies and travel but also by the availability of men to sing.[5] Pratt stated in an interview in *College Topics* in October 1942:

> This will be the most important year in the long history of the Glee Club. We will sing not once, but many times in Cabell Hall, and the public will be invited. We will probably make several broadcasts, the most important one being on next April 13th, the two hundredth anniversary of Thomas Jefferson's birth. Our manager, Tom Conlon is seeking engagements to sing at nearby army camps for which we are authorized to charter a bus. It has been the experience of Europe that the worse the times the greater is the demand for music and plays presented by local amateurs. It should be the Glee Club's pleasant duty to fill this demand and take the

initiative in organizing mass singing in Cabell Hall. If you like to sing and are not tone deaf, I can assure you of a hearty welcome.[6]

Indeed, the group not only actively performed, but it quietly confirmed a tradition apparently begun the prior year (though no document of the 1941 concert remains): it held the second annual Christmas concert. According to *College Topics*, the concert was to have commenced with a "caroling procession down the Lawn" prior to performances of sacred Christmas songs and "several merry Wassail songs."[7] This announcement is the first historical record of a tradition that has continued otherwise uninterrupted to the Glee Club's present day.

Given the challenges of performing with no certainty of maintaining membership for an entire season, to say nothing of the other limits imposed by the war, there is something in Pratt's carrying on with the Christmas concert that feels like an act of affirmation, if not outright defiance. It was to be his last hurrah. In January 1943, just halfway through his tenth season as Glee Club director, he announced that, in light of new responsibilities teaching navigation as part of the navy's preflight preparatory program, he was taking a leave of absence from directing the club.

It was a leave from which he would not return, citing the demands not only of his teaching but also a return to directing the Virginia Players. So ended one of the most dramatically dynamic periods in Glee Club history. Much of what we associate with the modern Glee Club and its practices, including the combination of classical repertoire and spirituals, high-profile tours outside the Commonwealth of Virginia, the Concert on the Lawn and the Christmas Concerts, and the dramatic growth in the Glee Club's overall size, dates to his leadership. As does a certain swagger: "Pratt's Boys" had a combination of popular repertoire, solid performances, and beery camaraderie that will be familiar to many late twentieth- and early twenty-first-century Glee Club "fossils."[8]

Pratt initially left the Glee Club's legacy in Thompson's hands, but by the time he made his retirement from directing official in the summer of 1943, a new faculty member had stepped up to lead the group: Stephen Davidson Tuttle.[9]

The second half of the 1942–1943 season was an appropriate exclamation point on the Glee Club's legacy. There had never been substantial original music composed for the Virginia Glee Club beyond the odd football song. But with Thompson at the head of the music department and wartime morale to lift, the club debuted a work that was subsequently performed on the radio and in symphonic halls and would enter the repertoire of men's choral works well beyond the group that premiered it. The conductor who premiered the work went on to cement the Glee Club's legacy as a significant force in men's choral performance. The work was *The Testament of Freedom*, written by Thompson to texts from Thomas Jefferson's writings, conducted by Tuttle.

The planning for *Testament* was well underway in the fall of 1942. Pratt noted that the Glee Club would undertake a significant performance and radio broadcast for Founder's Day 1943, marking the 200th anniversary of Thomas Jefferson's birth. Newcomb commissioned the work from Thompson to mark the Jefferson bicentennial. The work was ready for rehearsals in late January 1943; a *College Topics* article noted that the new composition was "now in rehearsal by the Glee Club every Tuesday and Thursday night."[10]

The work was uncharacteristically consuming for the club; no record survives of a performance prior to Founder's Day. This is likely due to the ambitions of both *Testament*, which was performed with the University Band and the composer at the piano, and the program as a whole, which paired the new setting of Jefferson's words with new arrangements of music from his personal library, including works by Daniel Purcell, Carl Maria von Weber, Thomas Augustine Arne, Maria Conway, and Charles Dibdin, as well as band performances of marches dating from Jefferson's presidency. Complicating the endeavor, there were two conductors: Thompson, who directed from the piano, and Tuttle, listed as the assistant director and as "conducting."

Tuttle had been at the University since 1941, joining from the Harvard faculty alongside James E. Berdahl, who was later the director of the Cal Marching Band at the University of California at Berkeley, and Thompson, who was a mentor for Tuttle.[11] He had had an unusual path to the faculty. The son of Baptist missionaries, his childhood was spent in the family home in Parkersburg, West Virginia, but also in India.[12] He studied music at Denison University and at Harvard, where he roomed with Elliott Carter; their acquaintance resulted in Carter's composition "To Music."[13] He therefore arrived at the University with a good deal more formal education in music than the debonair showman Pratt. And with several years of undergraduate music instruction at both Harvard and Virginia under his belt, he was a more natural director for the Glee Club than the more famous Thompson.

Tuttle soon graduated from assistant director to full director. By the end of the 1942–1943 season he was the solo director of the Glee Club in back-to-back performances at Camp Lee (now Fort Lee, located near Petersburg,

Virginia) and Randolph-Macon College. Both concerts featured *Testament*, presumably in piano reduction, and other works from the Founder's Day program.

The performance seems to have met or exceeded expectations for celebrating Jefferson; indeed, it put *Testament* on the symphonic repertoire map, thanks to a nationwide radio broadcast of the performance on CBS and shortwave rebroadcast to the Armed Forces overseas. Performances of *Testament* in the original piano version and with the 1944 orchestration followed, with none other than Serge Koussevitzky leading the Boston Symphony Orchestra and the Harvard Glee Club in a performance of the orchestral version in April 1945.[14] Koussevitzky, who had previously commissioned Thompson's *Alleluia* for the opening of the Berkshire Music Center (now Tanglewood) in 1940, programmed *Testament* again with the BSO in August 1946 in the Shed at Tanglewood, and in June 1947 with the Princeton University Glee Club and Chapel Choirs at Princeton; it has been performed twice more by the BSO since then, in 1966 and 1976.[15]

The Glee Club ended 1943 covered in laurels from the *Testament* premiere and with a new director at their helm. But the group was also diminished by the war effort. The membership stood at forty-four as of April 13, down from ninety-six in 1941–1942. Among those who had not returned for 1942–1943 were Frank Hereford, future president of the University of Virginia, and Lawrence Snoddy (later Snowden). Snoddy had graduated in 1942 and joined the US Marines, where he served as a company commander on Iwo Jima and in Guam.[16] University of Virginia graduates recalled not knowing from day to day who might be called up.

The trend continued into 1943–1944. Only twenty-five men were listed on the Glee Club page in the 1944 *Corks and Curls*, but an additional thirteen had performed in the 1943 Christmas concert. Among those who did not complete the season were future Curry School professor James Havens Bash. Glee Club president Daniel Wheeler (later a charter member and minister at University Baptist Church) and manager Ridgely Miller had their hands full with the shifting membership, but they somehow eked out a respectable season, performing not only at Christmas but also in a fall concert, a spring concert, and a performance at Sweet Briar.

After the 1942–1943 season, Tuttle had become the full conductor of the Glee Club, with Thompson appearing as accompanist in the fall concert. Tuttle's choices of repertoire swerved dramatically toward more highbrow material. Tuttle's scholarship, and his Harvard roots, showed in the programming;

gone were the spirituals and Russian chants that had characterized Pratt's programs, and in their place were works by Palestrina, Josquin, Bach, and Brahms. His fall 1943 program opened with "Glorious Apollo," a traditional English glee dating to 1787 which had become a theme song for the Harvard Glee Club. The spring concert added Tuttle's arrangements of Child ballads like "The Place Where My Love Johnny Dwells" and works by Gilbert and Sullivan. There were no performances of "The Good Old Song" or "Virginia, Hail, All Hail" on record for the 1943–1944 programs.

During this season, Tuttle also organized the Madrigal Group, a women's chorus numbering between thirteen and forty-nine with membership open to women students in all the schools of the University. While such an undertaking would have failed in earlier years, the population of women at the University in all the schools save the College of Arts and Sciences had grown steadily. The Madrigal Group performed with the Glee Club in the 1943 Christmas concert and the 1944 spring concert, and it continued joint appearances through Christmas 1945. With the end of World War II and the return of many male students to the University, the Madrigal Group apparently faded away. There was no women's chorus at the University until the advent of full coeducation in the early 1970s.

By the fall of 1944, the tide of the war had shifted, with D-Day dramatically marking the arrival of the Allies in Europe in June. Membership continued steady but low, with thirty-two members performing under the baton of Tuttle and the student leadership of Walter H. Beaman Jr., Ralph O'Dette, Stuart Hanckel, and Charles E. Hamm.[17]

The 1944 Christmas concert begins to show some of the features familiar to contemporary audiences. According to a *College Topics* review, the Glee Club and Madrigal Group played to a standing room only crowd from a stage "gaily bedecked with green shrubs and fronds in keeping with the Christmas atmosphere." One concession to the ongoing wartime: "members of the Glee Club wore tuxedoes and Navy dress uniforms." The program was a collection of carols from various nations, including audience participation.[18]

In addition to Christmas, the group mounted fall and spring concerts, and performances at both Sweet Briar and Randolph-Macon rounded out the season in May of 1945.

While the season carried on, however reduced, the war was levying a substantial toll on the University and its students. The memorial plaque on the wall of the Rotunda lists several hundred students and alumni, of which thirteen were Virginia Glee Club members. Edwin Robson Nelson died a prisoner aboard a Japanese ship in the Philippines. Bruce H. Bode died a hero when his small plane suffered engine failure while taking off in France; he changed course to avoid crashing into a backyard occupied by children playing, knowing that he would destabilize his aircraft and almost certainly die as a result. William Noland Berkeley Jr. landed in France six weeks after D-Day and was killed in action in an ambush a month later. Mason Williams was shot down over Munich at the end of 1944. John McCown died fighting in the mountains near Florence and is buried there. John Gordon died serving in the cavalry in Europe. Moss Plunkett was killed in action in New Guinea in 1943. Louis Smith died two months before V-J Day, somewhere in the Pacific theater. Robert Gamble, Edmund Van Valkenburg, and Alfred Marshall Luttrell were killed in action, though we know nothing further about their deaths. Ralph Chandler's plane disappeared while on a flight to the US Marine Corps base at El Toro, California, and Fielding Mercer died while stateside in Pensacola, Florida. In addition to the casualties, another 192 Glee Club alumni are known to have served in the war.

The next season, Tuttle's third, opened as if in an entirely new world. V-E Day in April 1945 had begun to put an end to the war; the atomic bombs dropped at Hiroshima and Nagasaki decisively finished it. Students, freshly discharged from service, began to return to University of Virginia en masse. Helping the numbers was the GI Bill, passed in 1944 and offering tuition and living expenses to veterans who had been in service for at least ninety days. Nationwide, 2.2 million veterans used the program for college tuition in the twelve years following the bill's passage. The arrivals crowded the limited housing available at the University, leading to the rapid construction of housing to accommodate the larger student population—and their families. The number of married students grew as men returned from combat and were reunited with their sweethearts. University of Virginia student Arthur Hyde Buell returned from a twenty-one month deployment with the Air Force to marry Miss Joyeuse Lennig Sweet in February 1946; Glee Club librarian Chamblin was an usher at their wedding, having returned from naval service in the Central and South Pacific.[19]

Tuttle and the Glee Club benefited from the return to normalcy. New executives Charles S. Russell (a future Virginia Supreme Court justice) and Steven N. Root (who would later teach at the University of Hartford) presided over a Glee Club composed of twenty-five tenors and, if *Corks and Curls* is to be believed, a staggering eighty-two basses.

Among the crowd of basses was Robert R. Fair, a future Darden School professor who had returned from the European front. Fair was only seventeen when the war broke out, and he spent several months working on the Alaska Highway project before he finally received his orders to report. His convoy was the first to land at Marseille, and he fought on the front lines in France and Germany until he was wounded on April 11, 1945. Fair was a member of the 100th Division, also known as the "Sons of Bitche" for their role in retaking the heavily defended French town of Bitche. Fair would occasionally afterward hand a card to generals or other senior officers in formal occasions, declaring them an "official Son-of-Bitche."[20]

With the much larger Glee Club, ranks swelled by returning soldiers, came larger ambitions. The following season saw the first Virginia Music Festival, a three-day outdoor event in which "Scott Stadium [was] transformed from a football field to an open-air concert hall."[21] Anchored by the National Symphony Orchestra, the Glee Club joined the first program, accompanying Metropolitan Opera mezzo-soprano Mona Paulee in Brahms's *Alto Rhapsody*. The second program featured John Powell, who continued a close association with the music department of the University, as piano soloist. The audience included alumni Admiral William F. "Bull" Halsey and Edward R. Stettinius Jr., newly minted Secretary of State; Stettinius chaired the festival's advisory committee.

The following season continued the trend of a supersized Glee Club, with membership at twenty-seven tenors and seventy-seven basses. J. Robert Winstead Jr. served as 1947–1948 president and John D. Haxall as manager. Rehearsals were crowded; a photo shows Tuttle crammed against the piano with the massive group before him in one of the first-floor classroom spaces in Old Cabell Hall. The year's collaborations included events with the Mary Baldwin and Sweet Briar Glee Clubs.

After five seasons of Glee Club directorship, Tuttle must have been somewhat relieved to take a sabbatical year, thanks to a Guggenheim Fellowship. In his absence, the reins were handed to Henry Morgan, who directed a slightly smaller group (thirty-one tenors, forty-four basses) through 1948–1949. Morgan was a University of Virginia music professor who had studied under Thompson. George A. Van Pelt was president and Bash (since returned from his military service) was the manager. As in previous years, the club performed at Christmas and collaborated with two women's college glee clubs, Madison College (now James Madison University) and the redoubtable Sweet Briar.

As the 1940s drew to a close, the Glee Club was utterly transformed. Larger in number (though smaller than the peak postwar seasons) and focused on

FIGURE 6. Stephen Tuttle conducting a Virginia Glee Club rehearsal in Old Cabell Hall, 1947–1948. Courtesy *Corks and Curls* 1948.

far more sophisticated repertoire, the club had shed itself of most of the signatures of the Pratt years. Along with the move away from spirituals, Russian liturgical music, and Pratt's showmanship, the club had ceased touring out of state. If its numbers were larger, its impact was now smaller. This may explain Tuttle's embarkation, upon his return, on a major project: the first ever commercial recording of the Glee Club.

That there had been no commercially published recording of the Glee Club prior to Tuttle's time is perhaps unsurprising. Even the mighty Yale and Harvard Glee Clubs did not release their first commercial recordings until 1941 and 1943.[22] But by the late 1940s it was becoming more common for college glee clubs to release albums of university songs, at least judging from the 1948 effort by Virginia Tech.[23] By the late 1940s University enrollment had boomed, and there was a market for such an album.

The result, *Songs of the University of Virginia*, was recorded sometime around 1950.[24] The recording was a collaborative effort between the Glee Club, under Tuttle's direction, and the University of Virginia Band, conducted by a young M. Douglas MacInnis, who joined the University of Virginia music faculty in 1950 after completing his graduate work at Princeton. The program included Virginia football songs ("The Cavalier Song," "The Good Old Song," "Hike,

Virginia," and "Yell Song"), songs of secret societies ("Eli Banana, the Starry Banner" and "Come Fill Your Glasses Up for T.I.L.K.A."), drinking songs ("From Rugby Road to Vinegar Hill / Glory, Glory to Virginia / Fill Up Your Silver Goblet,") and even one of Tuttle's Jeffersonian discoveries, the Daniel Purcell setting of Psalm 15 that was performed in the centennial Founder's Day concert in 1943 at the premiere of *The Testament of Freedom*. "Virginia, Hail, All Hail" closes the set.

The performance, as captured on the recording, is interesting. Like the *Testament* recording, it is slightly underpowered vocally, at least by modern standards, belying the ninety-member strength claimed by that year's *Corks and Curls* entry. Part of this was no doubt due to the logistics of the recording, which featured both the Glee Club and the University Band on stage in Old Cabell Hall at the same time, with only a handful of microphones to capture the performance (figure 7).

FIGURE 7. The Glee Club recording *Songs of the University of Virginia* in Old Cabell Hall.

The recording was released as an album of three ten-inch 78 rpm records, just in time for the 1951 Easter dances. The album featured aerial photography of the University and liner notes by Marvin B. Perry, by now a professor at

FIGURE 8. Original release, *Songs of the University of Virginia* (78 rpm three-disc album)

the University.[25] It was to be the Glee Club's most enduring record and went through at least three different pressings, including two re-pressings to twelve-inch 33⅓ rpm discs (figure 8).

Tuttle led one more season of the Glee Club before being hired away in March 1952 by Harvard University. He tragically died of heart failure just two years later, leaving behind a reputation as a scholar of Renaissance music, editing editions of Thomas Tomkins and William Byrd.

Several notable alumni sang with the Glee Club during Tuttle's tenure, including John Archer Carter (1931–2009), a member in 1950–1951 and a chair of the English department at Wake Forest; Derwood S. Chase, member from 1949 to 1951 and founder of the Chase Investment Corporation;[26] Herbert A. Donovan (b. 1931), a bishop in the Episcopal Church who served as bishop of the Diocese of Arkansas and assisting bishop of the Diocese of New York; Owen Jander (1930–2015), member from 1947 to 1950 and a professor of music at Wellesley College, where he founded the Wellesley Collegium Musicum; Evans Jessee (1930–2004), Glee Club member from 1949 to 1951 and University of Virginia Board of Visitors member; Donald J. Kenneweg (1933–2015), a club member in 1950–1951 and a professor of clinical radiology at the University of Virginia Medical School; Kermit Lowry Jr. (1935–2006), Glee Club member from 1952 to 1956 and a doctor in East Tennessee who helped to establish the Bristol Surgical Center and the medical school at East Tennessee State University; William Courtney Spence (1926–2002), a member from 1947 to 1952 and corporate counsel at Gulf Oil Company and Columbia Gulf Transmission Company; John A. Warwick Jr. (1928–2002), president in 1951–1952 and general manager of the Army and Air Force Exchange Service; and Edward Earle Zehmer (1931–1996), a club member from 1949 to 1951 and chief justice of the First District Court of Appeal in Florida.

The Glee Club, meanwhile, carried on under the baton of Tuttle's codirector on *Songs of the University of Virginia*, M. Donald MacInnis. MacInnis would see them through much of the rest of the 1950s.

---

1 "Randall Thompson on University of Virginia Faculty," *Danville Bee*, May 19, 1941, 20.

2 "Glee Club Roster to Be Determined by Second Tryouts," *College Topics*, November 12, 1941, 1.

3 "Glee Club Plans December Concert as First Offering," *College Topics*, October 26, 1942, 1.

4 "Glee Club Votes to Cancel Future Journeys by Car," *College Topics*, January, 23, 1942, 1.

5 The leaders of the club had diverse fates. Butterworth, who was a member of the Tin Can Quartet, served in Korea before joining the faculty of the University of Alabama. Conlon was president of Kappa Alpha and went on to a career in public school education. Chamblin saw action with the US Navy in the South Pacific; after the war, he taught in schools in Delaware and New Jersey for thirty-three years before joining the Peace Corps. Bourjaily served as business manager of the Glee Club in the fall of 1942, but after that nothing is known.

6 "Glee Club to Hold First Rehearsal Tomorrow Night," *College Topics*, October 19, 1942, 1.

7 "Glee Club Plans December Concert as First Offering," *College Topics*, October 26, 1942, 1.

8 Graduated Glee Club members have been called "fossils" at least since the early 1990s when the author was a member of the group, and possibly since before then.

9 "Randall Thompson to Direct Glee Club for Rest of Season," *College Topics*, January 18, 1943, 4; "University Glee Club Director Pratt Resigns after Leading Singers for Nearly 15 Years," *College Topics*, July 15, 1943, 1.

10 "Glee Club Begins Rehearsals on New Composition," *College Topics*, February 1, 1943, 4.

11 "Virginia Broadens Its Musical Program," *New York Times*, August 31, 1941, D4.

12 "Papers of the Tuttle Family, 1895–1975 (Inclusive), 1900–1953 (Bulk)," Hollis for

Archival Discovery, Harvard Library, https://hollisarchives.lib.harvard.edu/reposito
ries/8/resources/4962, accessed March 15, 2008.

13 David Schiff, *The Music of Elliott Carter* (Ithaca, NY: Cornell University Press,
1998), 155.

14 "Boston Symphony Orchestra Concert Program, Subscription Series, Season 64
(1944–1945), Week 22," Boston Symphony Orchestra Archives, https://cdm15982
.contentdm.oclc.org/digital/collection/PROG/id/228960, accessed January 10, 2018.
In an unusual pairing, the program also featured Shostakovich's Symphony No. 8.

15 "Performance History Search: Randall Thompson," Boston Symphony Orchestra,
https://archives.bso.org/Search.aspx?searchType=Performance&Composer=Ran
dall+Thompson, accessed January 10, 2018.

16 Snoddy also served in Korea and commanded the Seventh Marines in Vietnam.
Originally staunchly anti-Japanese, his attitudes started to shift as he served alongside
Japanese officers and staff during the Korean conflict. He later led Reunion of Honor
missions to reunite American and Japanese veterans of the Battle of Iwo Jima, starting
in 1985.

17 Beaman was an attorney for General Electric for thirty years; Hamm was a
musicologist who is credited with some of the first serious study of American popular
music.

18 "Capacity Yuletide Crowd Hears Glee Club and Madrigal Group," *College Topics*,
January 5, 1945, 1.

19 "Arthur Hyde Buell Jr. Marries Miss Sweet," *New York Sun*, February 22, 1946, 13.
Chamblin turned to teaching after returning from the war and, after thirty-three
years as a French and Spanish teacher in Delaware and New Jersey, took on an assign-
ment with the Peace Corps in Liberia.

20 Robert R. Fair, interview by Gordon Holloway, February 17, 2009, transcript,
Virginia Military Institute, Military Oral History Project, John A. Adams '71 Center
for Military History and Strategic Analysis, http://digitalcollections.vmi.edu/digi
tal/collection/p15821coll13/id/178, accessed November 12, 2017.

21 "Virginia Music Fete Proves Successful," *New York Times*, June 18, 1947.

22 Harvard Glee Club, Radcliffe Choral Society, Boston Symphony Orchestra Brass
Choir, E. Power Biggs, "Processional and Ceremonial Music for Voices, Organ and
Brass," Discogs.com, RCA Red Seal, October 1943.

23 Virginia Polytechnic Institute Glee Club, "Glee Club," discogs.com, Columbia,
1948.

24 Date approximate. The only photos of the recording sessions in the University
of Virginia Library's collections are dated 1948 along with a set of other Glee Club
photographs of varying years, but MacInnis's involvement pins the date to sometime
between 1950, when he joined the faculty, and 1951, when the album was released.

25 "Virginia U. Band and Glee Club Put Songs 'On the Record,'" *Washington Post*,
April 22, 1951, L7.

26 As of 2021, Chase was one of the oldest living active Virginia Glee Club alumni,
having served on the board of the Virginia Glee Club Alumni and Friends Association from its founding in 2006 until 2015.

17 THE 1950S AND EARLY 1960S: MACINNIS AND DAVIS

Murdock Donald MacInnis (1923–2003) was just twenty-nine years old when he became director of the Virginia Glee Club in 1952, the youngest director since Kirk Payne in 1918. Like Stephen Tuttle, he came from outside the University, having completed his undergraduate degree and a master's in music at Princeton University. While at Princeton, he was the student director of the university band, the manager of the glee club, the musical director of one of the theaters, and an organizer of the Tigertones. During the war he had served in Germany with the Thirteenth Armored Division as assistant to the division chaplain.[1] He studied composition and theory with Milton Babbitt, Edward Cone, Joseph Kerman, Bohuslav Martinů, Roger Sessions, and Randall Thompson and conducting with Leonard Bernstein at Tanglewood.[2]

MacInnis was elected an instructor in the faculty of music at the University in 1950, replacing James E. Berdahl (who joined the faculty at the same time as Tuttle but left in 1950, eventually becoming director of bands at the University of California at Berkeley).[3] In 1952, MacInnis was promoted to assistant professor, formalizing his assumption of Tuttle's duties upon the latter's departure.[4]

MacInnis assumed the directorship of the Glee Club after the great postwar tide of student enrollment had ebbed. The 1952–1953 club, under the leadership of president Charles C. Tarkenton and business manager James Clifton Barlow, had only forty-five members, half the size of the 1950 group. The repertoire hewed close to Tuttle's standards at first, with performances of

The Testament of Freedom alongside works by Bach, Vaughan Williams, Haydn, and Handel in the fall, and Mozart, Thomas Weelkes, and John Dowland ("Come Again, Sweet Love," in an arrangement by Archibald Davi-son) in the spring.

The concert season schedule was expanded under MacInnis. During Tuttle's tenure, a typical season might include the Christmas concert, a spring concert, one or two women's college concerts, and a short tour. MacInnis expanded the concert list in his first season, adding a joint concert in the early fall that inevitably paired the Virginia group with a men's glee club from a football opponent. (The first concert in the series was held November 21, 1952, with Washington and Lee's glee club as the guest group; Virginia defeated Washington and Lee the following day 21–14 in a home game. Unfortunately the following seasons were not so lucky, as the Virginia squad was defeated by University of North Carolina, 7-33, the night after the 1953 fall concert, and 14–26 in 1954 and 1955.[5])

It was sometime in 1953 that the next significant development of MacInnis's tenure occurred: the appearance of the Glee Club Octet. Small-group performance had been a mainstay of the Harry Rogers Pratt days but had fallen off in Tuttle's years of directorship. However, MacInnis had been a founding member of Princeton's Tigertones, and the times apparently demanded a resurgence of smaller men's singing groups. Harvard's Krokodiloes and the Tigertones had debuted in 1946, and Cayuga's Waiters appeared as the Cornell Glee Club subset in 1949. Official history of the group records that MacInnis initiated it by "choosing eight Club singers to perform his 5-part a cappella rendition of *Perfidia*," but at least one founding member, Frederick "Fritz" Berry, recalls members of the group spontaneously coalescing into four-part harmony while in an elevator.[6]

Starting in the 1953–1954 season, the octet, soon renamed the Virginia Gentlemen, became a feature of Glee Club performances on Grounds and off, including an alumni dinner in Washington, DC, in 1954.[7] Concert programs do not record the repertoire of the early Virginia Gentlemen, but their records indicate that the first work ever sung in concert by the group was MacInnis's arrangement of *Perfidia*, originally composed by Alberto Domínguez with English lyrics by Milton Leeds. Interestingly, *Perfidia* was also the founding song of the Princeton Nassoons, who premiered a five-part arrangement in a concert in fall 1941 after Princeton Glee Club director J. Merrill Knapp explicitly forbade its performance. (Apparently the last-minute change was made when the Nassoons' performance of more conventional material bombed during a joint Princeton-Yale concert.[8]) It seems MacInnis heard the work while at Princeton and brought it to Virginia.

For their first few performances, the group was credited as the "Glee Club Octet," but by the time of the Glee Club's spring performance with the Madison College Glee Club in Old Cabell Hall in 1954, they were credited as the "Virginia Gentlemen." Still performing, they maintained the format of an elite group drawn from within the Glee Club for many years.

UNIVERSITY OF VIRGINIA
DEPARTMENT OF MUSIC

JOINT CONCERT

by the

MADISON COLLEGE GLEE CLUB

and the

UNIVERSITY OF VIRGINIA GLEE CLUB

Tuesday Evening, May 4, 1954

Cabell Hall — Eight o'clock

PROGRAM

I.

Salutation..............................Samuel Richard Gaines
Pueri Hebraeorum......................Randall Thompson
Omnipotence................................Franz Schubert
Soloist: Jo Ellen Worth, Soprano
Easter Alleluia............................T. Tertius Noble
Fantasy on a Russian Folk Song........Samuel Richard Gaines
Accompanist: Doris Rutherford
Violinist: Mildred Gunn

MADISON COLLEGE GLEE CLUB

II.

Crucifixus, from the B minor Mass.................J. S. Bach

COMBINED GLEE CLUBS

INTERMISSION

III.

The God who gave us life (from the Testament of Freedom)
....Randall Thompson
Ave Maria (a four-part canon)...............W. A. Mozart
De Animals a-Comin'.........................Negro Spiritual
arr. Marshall Bartholomew
Mobile Bay.....................................Sea chantey
arr. M. B.
Careless Love...........................American folk song

UNIVERSITY OF VIRGINIA GLEE CLUB

Selections by the "Virginia Gentlemen" Octet

IV.

Let There Be Song................................Klemm
Pan.............................David Stanley Smith
Soloist: Jo Ellen Worth, Soprano
Carnival..Fourdrain
Soloist: Julia Freeman, Soprano
Aria: Habanera, from "Carmen"...............Georges Bizet
Caroline Blair, Contralto
Mildred Brown, Accompanist
Think On Me...............................Alicia Ann Scott
arr. Marshall Bartholomew
Joy..Winter Watts
Joyce Gwaltney, Soprano
Malaguena.....................................Lecuona
arr. Clay Warnick

MADISON COLLEGE GLEE CLUB

Officers of the Madison College Glee Club
Edna T. Schaeffer, Director
Doris Rutherford.................President and Accompanist
Sarah Thompson..........................Vice-President
Joyce Gwaltney................................Secretary
Rita Ritchie.................................Librarian
Julia Freeman..........................Business Manager

Officers of the University of Virginia Glee Club
Donald MacInnis, Director
T. Walley Williams, III, '54................President
William Hazen, '54...........................Manager
Mark H. Jander, '54.........................Librarian
George R. Silvernell, Law School.........Accompanist
Kermit Lowry, '56   )
Frederick Emerson, '55)...........Section Leaders
Robert Nuckles, '56   )
Harold Cloutier, '55)

ANNOUNCEMENT

Friday, May 14 — Annual Concert-on-the-Lawn. (Traditional light music sung from the steps of the Rotunda)..................7 o'clock

FIGURE 9. May 5, 1954, Virginia Glee Club concert program, featuring the first named appearance of the Virginia Gentlemen (Glee Club archives).

The Glee Club's concerts at women's colleges continued during this time. They had been a regular feature of Glee Club seasons since at least the 1933–1934 season, when Harry Rogers Pratt's groups began planning several trips a year to neighboring colleges, and dated back as far as a February 25, 1911, concert at Sweet Briar.[9] MacInnis took the tradition to another level, collaborating with Madison College (twice), Hollins College (twice), Goucher, Sweet Briar (three times), Mary Washington (twice), and Longwood College during the five seasons from 1952 to 1957. Some of the collaborations, unusually, took place over Christmas, with Mary Washington appearing in the 1955 Christmas concerts.

The 1955–1956 season in general hit several high points. Sometime during or prior to the season, MacInnis and the Glee Club recorded a promotional record, a 7-inch acetate containing repertoire from the previous two seasons. The recording included Bach, an arrangement of "Careless Love," and Tom Lehrer's "The Hunting Song." The record apparently helped the Glee Club secure a spot on WTVR's broadcast schedule in April 1956.[10]

Also during 1955–1956, on February 20 and 21, 1956, the Glee Club joined with the Roanoke Symphony Orchestra and choruses from Hollins, Lynchburg College, Radford, Randolph-Macon, University of Richmond, Roanoke College, Sweet Briar, Virginia Tech, and Washington and Lee, in a concert commemorating the two hundredth anniversary of Wolfgang Amadeus Mozart's birth that featured the Mozart *Requiem*. The club also performed a Founder's Day concert, the first since 1943, in collaboration with the Hollins Chapel Choir.

The following season saw the arrival of assistant conductor David Davis. MacInnis had been tapped as acting head of the McIntire Department of Music in 1955, which may explain the need for an assistant.[11] Davis had completed his undergraduate degree in music theory and composition at Peabody College of Vanderbilt University and his master's in music history and composition at Harvard. The club in 1956–1957 numbered sixty-five singers, up from forty-five in MacInnis's first season in 1952–1953. Otherwise the season was unremarkable for the 1950s, except that it marked the end of the recent tradition of fall football concerts in favor of a show that featured the Glee Club and the Virginia Gentlemen. As of the previous season, the record of the University of Virginia versus their fall concert weekend opponents was one win, three losses, and one win by forfeit (North Carolina, fielding an ineligible player in the 1955–1956 season, forfeited all their games that season, including a 7–21 defeat of Virginia). The tradition would return in the 1960s and 1970s, but the record would not improve. These were not good times for Virginia football.

The following season MacInnis withdrew entirely from conducting as his administrative and other duties became more consuming, leaving David Davis as the sole conductor in charge. During the 1957–1958 year, the schedule included performances with the Roanoke Symphony Orchestra, alumni concerts in Norfolk, and a collaboration with the newly formed University Singers during the annual Christmas concert. The season also included television appearances, a return to performances at the Greenbrier, and even a performance with the National Symphony Orchestra of *The Testament of Freedom* to be used as the soundtrack for a television special on the life of Thomas Jefferson.[12]

The University Singers debuted during the 1957–1958 academic year under the direction of MacInnis, who apparently did not wish to direct both of the University's choruses at the same time. The University Singers was a mixed chorus from the start, unlike the still all-male Glee Club, and had as its explicit purpose "to give all women with any University connection an opportunity to sing in some choral organization." The initial membership consisted of a mix of women students, faculty wives, male graduate students, and a "few members of the Glee Club."[13]

The other happening of note was a look forward, as the Glee Club took the step of becoming the "exclusive sales agents of the *Virginia Spectator* magazine," planning to use its returns to help finance a European tour, according to Glee Club president Palmer Rutherford. The action to seek revenues was more farsighted than the group realized; it would be years before a tour could actually take place.[14]

But the foundation of the University Singers and the desire to tour internationally were the first notes of significant change in the Glee Club's existence since the postwar boom. The Glee Club was now on its third conductor in six years, but unlike the periods of high turnover that preceded Fickénscher, membership and the program remained relatively stable. A few factors contributed to this increased stability, including the shift away from expensive musical comedy productions toward a predictable schedule of concerts at fall, Christmas, spring, and women's college visits; the lack of a major world war (or, indeed, significant conflict, though more than a few Glee Club men in the early 1950s were veterans of Korea); and perhaps most of all the continued support of the Glee Club as a curricular option conducted by a faculty member. Despite the occasional change in the faculty filling the role, there was now enough institutional memory and stability to continue to support the group's activities.

The stability seems, from the evidence, to have led to a certain settling in the Glee Club's affairs. The seasons from 1957 to 1961 seem to have been largely marked by repetition. The most exciting thing appears to have been the 1961 tour to Emory University in Georgia, during which there was a report that the Glee Club participated in a panty raid while on campus.[15] Such raids, with a goal of entering the women's dormitories and making off with a "prize" of women's underwear—sometimes bought specifically for the occasion— were commonplace in postwar universities, stemming from rules that strictly separated the genders at school colliding with the same spirit of student rebellion that led to the University of Virginia calathumps of a century earlier. The activity reached an early peak in 1952 and continued off and on until a series of "riots" at Ivy League schools in the spring of 1963 occasioned more moral panic than the customary response of "boys will be boys."[16] These weren't the musical comedy years, but spirits were as high as the level of musicianship was apparently low.

If the Glee Club was stable, suddenly the University may have seemed less so. Like much of the rest of Virginia and the American South, by the late 1950s the issues of race, civil rights, and equal opportunity for education were thrust onto the main stage. The University was first integrated in 1950, when Gregory Swanson, a graduate of Howard Law School, applied to take graduate courses at the University of Virginia, was denied admission, sued, and won, becoming the first black student at the University—only to drop out in the summer of 1951.[17] The University's president, Colgate Darden, said he "was not well prepared for the work." In the early 1950s two other African Americans followed in Swanson's footsteps, and Walter N. Ridley became the first black student not only to gain a degree at the University but also the first black student to receive a doctorate from any southern university.

It took the undergraduate schools a few more years, but in September 1955, following on the heels of the 1954 *Brown v. Board of Education of Topeka* decision, three black students matriculated in the engineering school. Theodore Thomas and George Harris dropped out by the following spring, but Robert Bland continued on and was the first African American undergraduate to graduate from the University in 1959, nine full years after the struggle for integration started.

Those nine years were full of racial challenges. By 1957, when William Faulkner began his first term as writer in residence at the University, there were African American students enrolled, but the editorial board of the *Cavalier Daily* could still write paragraphs like this one:

We feel that the success or failure of race relations at the
University now rests largely in the hands of Negro students

enrolled. Desegregation has gone over smoothly here because it has not been rushed by the colored race and because it has not caused social mixing between white and Negro. Even when the two have attended dances together in Memorial Gymnasium, there has been not the slightest hint of trouble or violence.[18]

The *Virginia Spectator*'s Jim Crow issue, published in May 1958, reprinted Faulkner's "Letter to the North," arguing for a more slowly paced desegregation, alongside newly written articles entitled "Segregation or Death" and "Segregation Means Degeneration." Most dramatically, in 1956, Senator Harry Flood Byrd's massive resistance campaign declared its opposition to the *Brown v. Board of Education* Supreme Court decision and others addressing racial integration, passing laws designed to institutionalize opposition to integration. One law forbade integrated schools from receiving state funds and authorized the governor to order any such school to close. Another created tuition grants that channeled funds from closed schools to individual students so they could attend private, segregated schools of their choice, the so-called segregation academies.[19]

The Glee Club moved with the speed of the rest of the University in integrating—that is, slowly. The first known black student to join the group was Edwin S. Williams of Smithfield, a member of the Young Democrats who joined in 1961 as a first year, some three years after Leroy Willis transferred from the engineering school and integrated the College of Arts and Sciences for the first time and eleven years after the first black students matriculated. In 1960–1961 there were only twenty-five black students enrolled at the whole University. Williams would go on to play an even more dramatic role in the Glee Club's history several years later.

The same season also saw the Glee Club resuming symphonic performances with a pair of concerts with the National Gallery Orchestra, their first symphonic collaboration since the performances with the Roanoke Symphony in 1957 and only the second since the second Virginia Music Festival in 1948. The club performed *The Testament of Freedom* in the East Garden of the National Gallery of Art on May 6, 1962, followed by a second *Testament* performance commemorating the two hundredth anniversary of the City of Charlottesville at Memorial Gymnasium the following day.

Much of the invisible activity of the Glee Club continued, rarely recorded in official concert programs. Though few documents survive of the Glee Club's

Concerts on the Lawn, enough evidence remains to suggest that they continued as a regular feature of Glee Club seasons. In particular, the 1962 *Corks and Curls* contains a photo of David Davis with the 1961–1962 president Michael Stillman that shows a Concert on the Lawn flier on the bulletin board behind them.[20]

There are several significant club alumni from the MacInnis and Davis years. John Carter Clary (1941–2009) was a Glee Club member in 1959–1960 and went on to serve in the US Navy in the Vietnam War, building a career as a prosecutor in Alabama and New Mexico and a law professor at Wake Forest, the International School of Business in Tokyo, and other universities and schools. William S. Cudlipp (1940–2016) was the accompanist of the Glee Club from 1959 to 1962 and was a professor on the Spanish faculty at University of Richmond and the University of Wisconsin. Lloyd Lawrence Bird (1938–1992), who sang with the Glee Club from 1956 to 1959, sang with the National Opera of Belgium and taught at the conservatory at Liège.[21] Kermit Lowry Jr. (1935–2006) was a Glee Club member from 1952 to 1956 and helped to establish the medical school at East Tennessee State University.[22] Vito Perriello (1941–2009), a member from 1958 to 1960, founded Pediatric Associates in Charlottesville. William Clarence Poole (1939–2016) was CEO of Applied Micro Controls. Paul Tipton (1939–2008) was president of Spring Hill College and of Jacksonville University and served as president of the Association of Jesuit Colleges and Universities, where he brought to light the murder of six Catholic priests, their housekeeper, and her daughter by the Salvadoran army.[23] Michael Stillman, who would later collaborate with David Davis on the Glee Club repertoire staple *Summer Songs*, became a published poet, leaving his doctoral studies at Stanford to pursue many projects in literature and music in Silicon Valley; his poem "In Memoriam John Coltrane" appears in many anthologies.[24]

But the Davis era was about to draw to a close. The 1962–1963 season saw MacInnis taking over the Glee Club again as Davis took a brief hiatus. Little is recorded about this season, which would prove to be MacInnis's last as Glee Club director. Membership fell during this season to thirty-six (as recorded in the Christmas concert program). The known collaborations included the University Singers and the Mary Baldwin College Choir. The following season, Davis returned for what would prove to be his last season. Membership rebounded to fifty-four, but the programming remained consistent, including a collaboration with the Westhampton College Glee Club under the direction of James Erb.[25]

Following the 1963–1964 season, both MacInnis and Davis moved on to other priorities. Davis became head of the McIntire Department of Music from 1964 to 1966, and then resigned his post at the University and relocated to California to compose film soundtracks.[26] MacInnis remained at the University as a professor, now focusing on twentieth-century music. The main project for his course was a multimedia performance that could include music, film, performance art, or nearly any other work. One of MacInnis's students recounts,

> Multi-media night in Old Cabell Hall [was] an advertised event that drew a large and disparate audience. Professor MacInnis had a rather laissez-faire approach to these projects—he didn't inquire as to what you were doing and there were no previews....
>
> One group set up strobe lights around the auditorium, climbed into the auditorium ceiling (which for some reason has windows at the apex), turned on the strobes and dropped wet spaghetti down on the unsuspecting audience. It was a great effect which drew much applause—from everyone but the Cabell Hall maintenance crew, which had to spend days cleaning the now-dry pasta off the auditorium carpet.
>
> Another group's project featured an old 8-millimeter film set to some mondo-bizarro music. The film involved a woman and a German Shepard, and I need say no more.[27]

MacInnis's University career survived the subsequent uproar and he remained a professor until his retirement in 1994.[28]

---

1 "Murdock Donald MacInnis, '45 * 50," *Princeton Alumni Weekly,* https://paw.princ eton.edu/memorial/murdock-donald-macinnis-%E2%80%9945-50, accessed April 19, 2018.
2 "Donald MacInnis," Edward B. Marks Music Company, http://www.ebmarks .com/composers/donald-macinnis/, accessed July 12, 2018.
3 "Minutes of the Board of Visitors of the University of Virginia," July 14, 1950; "Obituary—James E. Berdahl," *San Francisco Chronicle,* March 19, 1996, https://www .sfgate.com/news/article/OBITUARY-James-E-Berdahl-2989963.php.
4 "Minutes of the Board of Visitors of the University of Virginia," October 10, 1952.

5   "All Time Results," Virginia Sports, https://web.archive.org/web/2018062614232
6/http://www.virginiasports.com/sports/m-footbl/spec-rel/all-time-results.html,
accessed June 11, 2018.
6   "History," *Virginia Gentlemen,* accessed April 20, 2018.
7   Program available at "Alumni Concert in Washington (1954)," Virginia Glee Club
Wiki, https://virginiagleeclub.fandom.com/wiki/Alumni_Concert_in_Washing
ton_(1954).
8   David Mehnert, "Nassoon or Nasshound?," *Princeton Alumni Weekly* 92, no. 15 (May
6, 1992): 23.
9   "College Topics," *Sweet Briar Magazine* 2, no. 2 (February 1911): 155.
10   According to a note on the reverse side of a photograph of the Glee Club being
directed by Thompson, in the University of Virginia Visual History Collection,
https://search.lib.virginia.edu/sources/images/items/uva-lib:2162044.
11   *The University of Virginia Record,* vol. 41 (1955).
12   Ballowe, "A History," 11.
13   "Glee Club Gives Yuletide Concert Tuesday Evening," *Cavalier Daily,* December
14, 1957, 1.
14   "Glee Club to Promote Spectator Sales Today," *Cavalier Daily,* October 12, 1957, 4.
15   The rumors may have been overblown. Although Ballowe cites the student newspaper at Emory—the *Emory Wheel,* with a page 1 article about the raids—a review of
the actual paper on the dates he cites reveals no mention of any such hijinks or of the
University of Virginia.
16   Troy Patterson, "The Guerrilla Skirmishes of the Sexual Revolution," *Slate,* May
9, 2013.
17   Atima Omara-Alwala, "An Epoch of Change: A Timeline of the University
1955–1975," Trailblazing against Tradition: The Public History of Desegregation at
the University of Virginia, 2003, http://xroads.virginia.edu/~ug03/omara-alwala/
Harrison/Timeline.html, accessed July 2, 2018.
18   "Desegregation at the University," *Cavalier Daily,* May 22, 1957: 2.
19   Jessica Hanthorn and Kimberly Lenz, "Overcoming Exclusion," *Daily Press,* May
16, 2004.
20   *Corks and Curls* 75 (1962): 159.
21   "Lloyd L. Bird," *Desert News,* November 22, 1992.
22   House Joint Resolution 988, Tennessee State Legislature, April 5, 2006, https://
www.capitol.tn.gov/Bills/104/Bill/HJR0988.pdf.
23   Patricia Sullivan, "Paul Tipton; Exposed Jesuit Deaths in El Salvador," *Washington
Post,* May 31, 2008.
24   Dana Gioia, Chryss Yost, and Jack Hicks, eds., *California Poetry: From the Gold
Rush to the Present* (Berkeley, CA: Heyday Books, 2003), 228.
25   *Westhampton College Glee Club* (sound recording), 1964.
26   Board of Visitors Minutes, June 5, 1964, and April 2, 1966.
27   "Jim Heilman Recounts Censorship in Old Cabell Hall in the Early 1970s," Letters to the Editor, George Edward Loper, December 2003, http://george.loper.org/
trends/2003/Dec/923.html.
28   "In Memoriam," *Inside UVA,* May 9–15, 2003.

18

1964 TO 1972: THE LOACH YEARS BEGIN

I t would be poetic to report that the Davis years saw an artistic blossoming of the Glee Club in response to the nourishment of relative organizational stability and consistency. It would also be false. By all accounts the Glee Club of the late 1950s and early 1960s was busy but not at any sort of artistic peak, a state which led 1961–1962 Glee Club president Michael Stillman to remark in November 1961: "For the last three years and longer we have held our bachotic celebrations as often as possible without fully validating the lingering tremor that we really don't intend to sing at all."[1]

The club's complacency was soon to end with the arrival of its next conductor, the fifth faculty member (sixth counting Randall Thompson) to lead the group and the man who would set the record for the longest tenure of any director of the group: Donald Loach.

Born in Denver, Colorado, in 1927, Loach began his musical studies early, at age fourteen becoming a conducting student of Antonia Brico.[2] He attended the University of Denver as an undergraduate and went on to study music theory and organ at Yale University, where he studied under Paul Hindemith, managed Hindemith's Collegium Musicum, and was an assistant in instruction.

Loach received an appointment on April 18, 1964, as acting assistant professor of music for a one-year term to begin September 1, 1964.[3] Among his first tasks (which also included courses in music theory, music history, and the development of the graduate program): the direction of the Glee Club.

In some respects this first season was much like the ones that preceded it: a Christmas concert and a spring concert featuring the Westhampton College Glee Club under the direction of James Erb, performed at Richmond and at the University of Virginia. But the repertoire was deeper: Bruckner's *Mass in E minor* and the music of Heinrich Schütz. Even the Christmas concert eschewed more familiar elements for a set of "Ave Marias" (by Adam Gumpelzhaimer, Tomás Luis deVictoria, Mozart, Stravinsky, and Josquin des Prez), carol settings (medieval and by William Byrd), and madrigal settings by Loach's New Haven colleague David Kraehenbuehl (who had dedicated a wedding anthem to the Loaches just eight years previously).

As significant, if not more so, was the accelerating pace of racial change at the University, which Loach was to play a significant role in bringing to the Glee Club. University president Edgar F. Shannon, who had taken over from Colgate Darden in 1959, turned his attention early in his presidency to the challenge of race relations at the University. Shannon asked his public relations adviser Paul Saunier to work to improve black student admission. Saunier realized that "if they were going to try to recruit black students, they would have to do something to improve life for black students." Saunier worked with University professors, including Paul Gaston and William Elwood, and community leaders, including Billy Williams, owner of Anderson Brothers Bookstore, to overcome the systemic challenges facing black students.

One of the first challenges that Saunier took on was desegregating businesses on the Corner. Working with Williams, Saunier went from business to business, convincing them to change their ways. Saunier recalls, "The basic thing I used was: you may turn down a black [student] in your restaurant thinking he's a local [townsperson], but with all the international students we've got, he could be a prince. It would be all over the *Washington Post* and the *New York Times*." The tactic was effective, with all Corner restaurants except the White Spot becoming integrated a full two years ahead of the mandate of the Civil Rights Act of 1964.[4]

Against this background, Loach's Glee Club ran headlong into the ongoing challenges over public accommodation of black students in December 1964. The Glee Club was on the bus, returning from giving a Christmas concert at the National Gallery of Art, when they stopped at a truck stop on Route 29. To Loach's surprise, the club was refused service due to the presence of Edwin S. Williams. Now a fourth-year student, Williams had been in the Glee Club for four years and was the baritone section leader. Loach recalls, "At the truck stop the guys went in and most had eaten when we discovered that the servers at the counter wouldn't let Williams order. I'd just come from California and I couldn't abide this nonsense. We ordered his dinner and watched him eat it."[5] Loach turned to Shannon after the tour, and Shannon turned to Saunier. As a result of Saunier's investigation, the truck stops "all up and down Route 29 were integrated."[6]

The following season was less dramatic, but still featured the Glee Club's first performance at Washington National Cathedral, a collaboration with the Madison College Choir, and a tradition that would continue every two or three years into the future. The year 1966–1967 Loach was on sabbatical, as he continued research on his dissertation at the University of California, Berkeley. He would complete his PhD in musicology in 1969 with a dissertation entitled "Aegidius Tschudi's Songbook."[7]

In Loach's absence, Frederic H. Ford directed the Glee Club. Ford, a graduate of Harvard University, had directed the Krokodiloes in 1959–1960 and had roomed with David M. Park, a fellow Harvard Glee Club member, whose son John would join the Virginia Glee Club twenty-four years later. During this season, Ford left a lasting contribution on the Glee Club's repertoire with an arrangement of the "Virginia Yell Song" accompanied by piano four hands.

Loach returned in 1967–1968 and began expanding the club's concert season. He reinstituted the Openings concert (November 10, 1967, with the University of North Carolina Glee Club; Virginia won the game against North Carolina 40–17 the following day). The Christmas concert was more broadly ambitious, including a full performance of the anonymous eighteenth-century cantata *Uns ist ein Kind geboren*. And Loach made elaborate plans for the spring concert, including a performance of Handel's *Dettingen Te Deum* with the Sweet Briar Glee Club and an orchestra. The spring concert was announced in December as being scheduled for April 9, 1968, but a performance was added at Sweet Briar on April 5.

So it was that Loach and his Glee Club found themselves preparing for the concert when the rehearsal was interrupted to announce that the Reverend Martin Luther King Jr. had been assassinated in Memphis, Tennessee. David B. Witt recalls, "To be in the relative shelter of UVA—at the time almost totally white and male—made the event seem unreal to me."[8] David Temple, who was only the second black member of the Glee Club, remembers the room falling into silence: it "had an extraordinary and profound impact on those of us who were watching the world evolve before us and seemingly and predictably dissolve around us."[9] Witt concurs: "I believe that UVA was a different place afterward—a place where uncertainty and protest were no longer abstractions, but part of our consciousness."

Temple was noteworthy for much more than his Glee Club membership. In his time at the University of Virginia, Temple became the first African American to desegregate the interfraternity council system, helping to recolonize Pi Lambda Phi.[10] The late 1960s were a time of significant social change at the University. Joel B. Gardner notes in his history of the period that race issues came into sharp relief in early 1968, beginning with an NAACP-led protest against discrimination in recruiting black athletes and the subsequent establishment of the University's first formal nondiscrimination policies. That fall, students led a boycott of two Corner barbershops who refused service to black patrons, with the full support of the student council, which issued a resolution encouraging the boycott, and the administration. The University may have existed in a bubble, to use Gardner's metaphor, but the walls of the bubble were thinning.[11]

David Temple was one of a number of notable alumni who sang with the club in Loach's early years. Jerry Lee Coffey (1942–2018) sang with the Glee Club from 1960 to 1966 and worked for the Office of Management and Budget under three US presidents. Douglas Dixon (1955–1990) was president of the Glee Club in 1966–1967; he became a medical examiner working with the Army Medical Corps (during which time he investigated the runway crash in Tenerife and the mass suicide at Jonestown in Guyana) and in the DC Medical Examiner's Office, where he led the investigation into the 1982 Air Florida plane crash. He concluded his career as associate chief medical examiner for the Commonwealth of Massachusetts, and he died of AIDS in 1990.[12] James F. Jones sang in the Glee Club from 1965 to 1968, serving as the assistant director, and went on to study at the Sorbonne, receiving the Chevalier, Ordre des Palmes académiques. He served as president of Trinity College in Hartford, Connecticut, from 2004 to 2014 and was interim president of Sweet Briar College until he resigned amid controversy regarding the attempted closure of the school in 2015.[13]

Another notable piece of Glee Club history premiered shortly after the memorable spring concerts of 1968. Donald Loach had connected with Arthur Kyle Davis Jr., who had served as the Glee Club's secretary in 1916–1917 and then, following his army service in World War I, attended Oxford on a Rhodes scholarship. Davis, a native Virginian (his parents had founded the Southern Female College in Petersburg, Virginia), spoke for the rest of his life with a strong Oxonian accent. Together they conceived of the idea of writing a song about the University to a tune by Handel from *The Beggar's Opera*, with a text contributed by Davis (who naturally rhymed "thunder" and "Rotunda"). The song premiered before the Jefferson Society in honor of the University's Sesquicentennial in April 1968.[14]

The first phase of Donald Loach's directorship of the Glee Club can be said to have culminated with the 1969–1970 season. The fall concert saw the premiere of the David Davis/Michael Stillman collaboration *Summer Songs*. Ostensibly a light work, it entered the Glee Club's repertoire, appearing in concert in eight seasons and on two Glee Club recordings. Then on February 7, 1970, the Board of Visitors promoted Loach from acting assistant professor to full assistant professor.[15] Loach could now make longer-term plans for the group, and he began to do so almost immediately. One of the first signs of the transition to longer-term building of the group was the adoption of a logotype for the group, in the form of a conductor with Y-shaped outstretched arms directing a chorus of circular dots. The logo, which appears for the first time on the program for the spring 1970 concert, became a regular feature of Glee Club posters and programs for the next fifteen years.

FIGURE 10. Members of the Virginia Gentlemen perform at the Concert on the Lawn, spring 1966. Left to right: Elbert Gary Cook, Jerry Lee Coffey, Peter Zwanzig, Steve Middlebrook. Photo courtesy Peter Zwanzig.

Hollins College Chapel Choir
JAMES LELAND, *Conductor*

University of Virginia Glee Club
DONALD LOACH, *Conductor*

University of Virginia Orchestra
JOEL LAZAR, *Conductor*

celebrate the bicentennial of

LUDWIG VAN BEETHOVEN

Assisted by

CHARLENE PETERSON, *soprano*   JOHN ROBERTS, *tenor*
SARA FISHBACK, *contralto*   OSCAR McCULLOUGH, *baritone*

Cabell Hall Auditorium   Hollins College Chapel
University of Virginia   Hollins College
March 13, 1970   March 15, 1970
8:30 P.M.   7:30 P.M.

FIGURE II. First page of the spring 1970 concert program featuring the Glee Club
Y logo.

These years also saw the expansion of a tradition started by Harry Rogers Pratt and continued under David Davis, the Concert on the Lawn. Loach recalls:

> In the early 1960s David Davis instituted a Concert on the Lawn in late spring. When I came on board I continued the tradition from 1965–1989. These concerts were sung primarily from the Rotunda Steps although I did hold them for a few years on the steps of Old Cabell. Davis's concerts were intended for a student audience and were held, I think, on a Friday afternoon. I refocused them to be family oriented on Saturday afternoons and included fun songs for everyone to sing.[16]

The 1970–1971 season was notable mostly for the club's increasing musical ambition. The fall concert featured the Virginia Military Institute Cadet Glee Club and so might have been a traditional football concert, but it opened with brass fanfares by Gabrieli and Handel and featured Poulenc's *Lauds of Saint Anthony of Padua* and, unusually, two musical parodies: the *Requiem Populorum* (based on "Requiem for the Masses" by the Association, a pop band, with new text by Howard Hanson and "reconception" by Loach and Glee Club member Thomas Diklich) and *Songs Mein Grossmama Sang* by Lloyd Pfautsch. The spring concert featured a joint performance with the Hollins College Choir of Arthur Honegger's *King David*, an oratorio for chorus and orchestra in twenty-seven movements. This was the first time that the Glee Club mounted a concert dedicated to a single large work.

But 1970 was a milestone in other ways. This was the year that, after hedging and half measures, the University finally admitted women as undergraduates. This was unprecedented; women had been permitted to enroll as nursing and education students, and eventually as graduate students, but undergraduate education had remained a closed door until Virginia Scott sued for the right to enroll in 1969. John Lowe brought the suit, seeking to compel the University to accelerate its plan to ease into coeducation over ten years, with a 35 percent female enrollment cap. After the judge learned that the University had withheld from evidence the minority report of the coeducation committee that created the ten-year plan, he called the parties to chambers and strongly suggested that the University avoid serious reputational damage by voluntarily going coeducational, and the University complied.[17] The arrival of coeducation would not significantly affect the Glee Club, which opted to remain single-sex; some of its peers at coeducational schools did the same, while others including Yale and Princeton would later become mixed-voice choirs.

In the seven years of the Loach era, the group had increased significantly in musical sophistication but still remained a relatively local phenomenon. That was about to change.

1 Ballowe. "A History," 12–13.

2 Brico was the first American to graduate from the Berlin State Academy of Music's master class in conducting (in 1929), the first woman to conduct the New York Philharmonic (in 1938), and the founder of the Denver Philharmonic. Her other students of conducting and piano included James Erb and Judy Collins.

3 University of Virginia Board of Visitors minutes, April 18, 1964.

4 Charlie Tyson, "Now 95, Saunier Reflects on Efforts to Expand U.VA.'s Black Enrollment," *UVA Today*, July 7, 2014.

5 Donald Loach, "Glee Club History Notes" (email), May 12, 2021.

6 Tim Jarrett, "Integrating the Virginia Glee Club in 1961" (blog post), Jarrett House North, April 27, 2016.

7 "Earlier Ph.D. Dissertations," Berkeley Music, https://music.berkeley.edu/grad uate-studies/recent-ph-d-dissertations/earlier-ph-d-dissertations/, accessed July 13, 2018.

8 Sarah Lindenfeld Hall, "Where Were You When . . . ?" *Virginia Magazine*, Summer 2020, https://uvamagazine.org/articles/where_were_you_when.

9 Atima Omara-Alwala, "David Temple," Trailblazing against Tradition, http:// xroads.virginia.edu/~ug03/omara-alwala/Harrison/DavidT.html, accessed July 15, 2018. Temple also later served as the Virginia deputy secretary of education and as an adviser to the Welfare to Work initiative in the Department of Commerce during the Clinton administration.

10 *Recolonizing* is a term used by fraternities to describe establishing a new chapter at a university where one previously existed; see "Glossary of Greek Terms," Oregon State University, Office of the Dean of Students, https://studentlife.oregonstate.edu/ cfsl/glossary-greek-terminology.

11 Joel B. Gardner, *From Rebel Yell to Revolution: My Four Years at UVA 1966–1970* (Richmond, VA: Brandylane Publishers, 2018), 112, 129ff.

12 Richard Pearson, "Douglas Dixon Dies, Was Top DC Coroner," *Washington Post*, October 9, 1990, B7.

13 Kathleen Megan, "Trinity College President James Jones Will Retire Early, " *Hartford Courant,* May 6, 2013, https://www.courant.com/education/hc-xpm-2013-05 -06-hc-jimmy-jones-trinity-0507-20130506-story.html; Susan Svrluga, "Agreement Reached to Keep Sweet Briar Open; Needs Court Approval," *Washington Post,* June 20, 2015, https://www.washingtonpost.com/local/education/agreement-reached- to-keep-sweet-briar-open-needs-court-approval/2015/06/20/6c9c43e4-179e-11e5- 9ddc-e3353542100c_story.html.

14 Patti Kyle, "Singers Invade Europe at Spring Break," *Cavalier Daily*, February 29, 1972.

15 University of Virginia Board of Visitors minutes, February 7, 1970.

16 Donald Loach, "Concerts on the Lawn" (email), March 27, 2016.

17 Jane Kelly, "Going Co-Ed," *UVA Today*, September 28, 2017. The trial included a question from the opposing council, state senator James Harry Michael: "Isn't it true, you have all these men's bathrooms on the Grounds of the University? You don't have any women's bathrooms. How do you work that out?" The plaintiff's witness, Kate Millett, then dean of Barnard College, replied, "Oh, shucks, Senator, all you do is plant geraniums in the urinals and you've got a women's bathroom."

19 CLUB ABROAD

The 1971–1972 season marked a number of milestones. The group, having dug deeper into its history, marked 1971 as the one hundredth anniversary of the Glee Club. James Ballowe, who published the only previous history of the Virginia Glee Club in 1977, notes that "by way of celebration, the Club made plans for a spring European tour." This was unprecedented for the Virginia Glee Club, but not for collegiate glee clubs in general; by this time, the glee clubs of Yale and Cornell, among others, had already done numerous international tours. But this was a major step forward for what the *Atlanta Chronicle* had called nearly eighty years previously "The Virginia Boys."

The tour capped a major resurgence in the group and its reputation, in much the same way the 1893 tour and the 1936 New York performances had done. Among other points, the tour signaled that the group was ready and able to handle not only the international exposure but also the considerable logistics. And the club rose to the challenge. The plans for a European tour were to have several lasting effects on the Glee Club, including its long-overdue return to making records.

In the twenty years since Stephen Tuttle had left the Glee Club for the greener pastures of Harvard University, the group had carried forward many of the traditions that he had left them with, including frequent guest choir collaborations, the Christmas concert, and an abiding affinity for Renaissance music. But one of Tuttle's innovations had not been repeated: *Songs of the University of Virginia* remained the club's only generally available recording, having been reissued twice (once on a 10-inch 33-1/3 rpm record with a facsimile of the original blue and orange cover, once on a 12-inch LP with a generic cover with no art). The club had not made a studio recording during the MacInnis or Davis years, nor during the first few years of Donald Loach's tenure.

The long drought was about to end. The Glee Club released *A Shadow's on the Sundial* in the 1971–1972 season. It featured repertoire that reflected the history of the Glee Club, including the Chesnokov *Spaséniye sodélal,* here titled "Salvation Belongeth to Our God"; the first and fourth movements of *The Testament of Freedom;* and a set of University songs: "Vir-ir-gin-i-a," "Virginia Yell Song," "The Good Old Song," "Virginia, Hail, All Hail," and inevitably "From Rugby Road to Vinegar Hill/Fill Up Your Silver Goblet/Glory, Glory to Virginia." It also featured the repertoire that was becoming the cornerstone of Loach's Glee Club: a set of expertly performed madrigals by Weelkes ("Hark, all ye lovely saints," which would open concerts for years to come), Lassus, Monteverdi, and Morley; Poulenc's *Lauds of St. Anthony of Padua;* Dieterich Buxtehude's *Cantate Domino*; and David Davis's *Summer Songs.*

Much had changed in the twenty years between the two recordings. Not least of the changes involved the quality of the recording technology itself; *A Shadow's on the Sundial* sounds much crisper and more immediate than its predecessor. More importantly, the quality of the Glee Club itself had risen immeasurably. Much of the performance on *Songs of the University of Virginia* features homophonic or two-part singing, inevitably slightly out of pitch and performed with little or no dynamic variation or shouted over the sound of the University Band. The performances on *A Shadow's on the Sundial* are nuanced, impeccably pitched, with a broad variety of tonal colors and dynamics. The performance is, in a word, stunning.

It was this sound that the Glee Club would take on tour to Europe in 1972 for the first time in its history. Sales of *Shadow* helped to finance the trip, as did the first recorded donation to the Glee Club from the University's secretive Seven Society.[1] More significant were the other measures the group took to ensure that its members could travel abroad.

The economics of mounting an international tour must have been daunting for the students to contemplate, but the organization rose to the challenge. It was during this season that the first Glee Club newsletter was published, in the fall of 1971, constituting the Glee Club's most formal outreach to its alumni to date. The fundraising proceeds would eventually lead to the establishment of a small endowment account at the University of Virginia Alumni

Hall, intended to help offset expenses for club members who could not afford to travel. The club also performed a concert on March 24 to benefit the tour fund, with Randall Thompson's *Tarantella* and works by Orff, Britten, and Schütz joining Poulenc and *Summer Songs*.

FIGURE 12. Letter from the Seven Society to the Glee Club, marking a donation for the 1972 international tour.

Still, these measures defrayed only about 20 to 25 percent of the cost of the tour; the remainder was raised by the members themselves.

The trip itself was ambitious for a first outing. Scheduled during spring break in 1972, the tour visited Sacrofano (outside Rome), Florence, Venice,

Padua, Munich, Salzburg, Innsbruck, Lucerne, and Weggis (Switzerland), all with accompaniment by the University of Virginia Music Department's harpsichord. Loach notes, "It needed to be 'packaged up' for the trip. I remember Jim Richardson, who would be playing it, working very hard getting it ready."[2] Of the tour, John Wood recalls:

> Munich with lots of beer drinking at the Hofbrau Haus, Lucerne, Switzerland where we sang a tune entitled "From Lucerne to Weggis on," and I think we also went to Rome and Venice. The one memory that stands out was singing Poulenc's Lauds of St. Anthony of Padua in Padua! We were also in Salzburg. A friend of Charley Mayhew's was serving as a governess at a schloss where the gazebo was used in filming Sound of Music. I couldn't resist serenading her with "You are 16 going on 17."[3]

The tour began in Sacrofano, 30 km northwest of Rome. In a *Cavalier Daily* article from May 12, 1972, business manager Richard Hanger recalled the event:

> "It was by far, I think, the most interesting concert." Fittingly enough, Good Friday provided the occasion, and the Glee Club culminated a traditional procession through the streets of the city with a performance at a church dating from the fifteenth century. With torches waving and children singing a medieval chant, the entire affair was spectacular, if anachronistic. "The people followed this procession with three crosses and a wooden statue of Jesus, and you really had the feeling that this was something right out of the middle ages," continued Mr. Hanger. "After the concert, the mayor invited us to a reception at the town hall." The mayor's idea of a reception involved a generous distribution of wine—"some of the best on the whole tour."[4]

The tour featured only five planned concerts, one of which, the Munich performance, had to be canceled due to a conflict with a concert by the Munich Symphony. However, Hanger noted, "wherever we went, we'd often sing. Let's say we went to Mozart's birthplace, we'd sing a Mozart piece. In Venice, we went in Saint Mark's cathedral, where we did several songs which were especially written for the church there." As another member phrased the situation, "We did more impromptu concerts than we did scheduled."[5]

FIGURE 13. Glee Club members in Salzburg. Photo courtesy John W. O'Neill.

Following the tour, the Glee Club returned from Rome in triumph, albeit without the harpsichord, which, mistakenly left behind, arrived in Charlottesville seven months later.[6] The club performed a Concert on the Lawn on May 13. Hanger noted the most significant effect of the tour: "What it did for the Club, you couldn't measure. When you see someone just twice a week you sort of just know them by face. By the time we got back, everyone knew everyone that went very well. It did a lot to bring the Club together. You can't sing well unless you really feel part of the group."[7]

For any other conductor, the 1972 tour might have proven the high-water mark of his ambitions. For Loach, it was just the beginning. The following season saw no international tour, but it did mark the Glee Club's first joint tour with a women's college choir: they toured the South with the Mount Holyoke Glee Club, with stops in Chapel Hill, Charleston, Williamsburg, and Washington, DC (appearing at Washington National Cathedral), and performances of Bach's "Komm, Jesu, komm," Schütz's "Herr, unser Herrscher," and Stravinsky's *Mass for Mixed Chorus and Double Woodwind Quintet*. The membership of the club, reflecting the highs of the previous season, stood somewhere north of seventy.

The next season, by contrast to 1972–1973, saw multiple changes to both the club and the University. Loach took a sabbatical semester in the spring of 1974 to study the motets of Josquin des Prez in Italy; his substitute for the semester was James Dearing. Dearing had become part of the McIntire School faculty in the fall of 1973 and was conducting the University Singers. He also started the Virginia Women's Chorus that spring.[8]

The Women's Chorus was a response to the success of coeducation. While coeducational undergraduate enrollment had been capped at 450 in 1970 under the University's revised plan, it grew to 550 in 1971 and the cap was removed in 1972. By 1974 the undergraduate class was nearly half women, and they sought opportunities to participate in University life. Women had been welcomed in the University Singers from the beginning of coeducation, but the Virginia Women's Chorus offered an opportunity for female singers to explore single-sex repertoire in the same way the Glee Club did for men. Dearing led the chorus in its inaugural seasons before leaving the University to become director of choral studies at Indiana University of Pennsylvania, a post he held for thirty years until his death in 2010.

The 1973–1974 season was largely unremarkable. During Loach's sabbatical in the spring of 1974, Dearing led the Glee Club on tour to Pennsylvania and New York City with the Carlow College Choir from Pittsburgh; otherwise the schedule was much more sedate than the prior years. But one tradition quietly began that year, as Croxton Gordon took up residence in 5 West Lawn.

The original Jeffersonian Lawn rooms had, over the years, become a less than desirable accommodation; the Reverend Beverley D. Tucker Jr. noted in a letter in the 1930s, "I can remember when Dawson's Row was the promised land of social prestige and rooms on the Lawn and Ranges were rated rather low in the scale."[9] The rooms became more popular beginning in 1949, when eligibility for Lawn residency, formerly restricted to Virginians, was opened to all student leaders regardless of geographic origin; the addition of hot water to the West Lawn rooms probably also helped.

The Glee Club, unlike other old organizations on Grounds, such as the Jefferson Society, Kappa Sigma, Trigon Engineering Society, and the Honor Committee, did not have a dedicated room. Over the years more than a few Glee Club students resided on the Lawn or Ranges, but beginning in 1973, they increasingly gravitated to 5 West Lawn. Beginning with Gordon, the room was occupied by Glee Club members for sixteen of the following twenty-two years, including a seven-year streak between 1987 and 1994.

The University continued to change and evolve as well during this season, with the decade-old "new" Alderman Road dormitories overflowing with students and with Terry Holland arriving as head coach of the men's basketball team. This was nothing compared to the changes to the Glee Club that were to come when Loach returned in 1974–1975.

The Glee Club was enjoying renewed visibility at the University. The fall of 1974 saw the inauguration of Frank Hereford as University president following Edgar Shannon's retirement from the post, and the Glee Club performed excerpts from an old staple of their repertoire, *The Testament of Freedom,* during his inaugural ceremony. The group would dig deep into a different corner of their repertoire, thanks to Loach's studies during his sabbatical. Loach had programmed Renaissance music since the beginning of his tenure as the Glee Club's director in 1964, but it became a keystone of the club's performances in this season. The fall Openings concert in 1974 featured the Hans Leo Hassler *Cantate Domino* and the Palestrina *Lamentations,* as well as works by Mozart, Vaughan Williams, Elliott Carter, and Schubert. Loach would steadily increase the Renaissance programming, adding works by Tomás Luis de Victoria, Josquin des Pres, and Dieterich Buxtehude to the Christmas concert repertoire and the Gabrieli *Surrexit Christus* to the spring concert program. Even the normally lighthearted Concert on the Lawn (performed in McIntire Amphitheatre due to Rotunda renovations) saw a redoubled attention to repertoire, with the group performing a premiere of a work by University professor Walter Ross and works by Carter, Hindemith, Kodály, Schubert, and Brahms, as well as the chorus and finale from Wagner's *Die Meistersinger.*

Loach's return apparently reversed a short-lived downward trend in the group's esprit de corps. Incoming Glee Club president Laird Boles wrote in a July 1974 letter to the membership, "I would be less than honest if I said I wasn't seriously disturbed by the general decline in attitude and moral [*sic*] of the Club during the past year. I'm sure we can turn things around this year. In light of the time, money, and effort that will be going into our performance as a club, the investment cannot possibly be worth our while unless we're all pulling together."

But turn around the club did, and the 1974–1975 season saw the Glee Club successfully return to international touring, signifying the intention that the 1972 tour would not be a onetime event. The 1974–1975 European tour (undertaken over winter break; the group flew into Luxembourg two days after Christmas and returned home from the same location almost two weeks later) went further afield than the trip three years earlier; rather than stops in Italy, France, and Germany, the tour had thirty-seven Glee Club members performing in Zagreb and Belgrade (in Yugoslavia at the time, now the respective capitals of Croatia and Serbia), Budapest, Vienna, Prague, Luxembourg, Trieste, and Heidelberg.[10] The music included Buxtehude's *Laude Sion*, Antoine Brumel's "Mater Patris," Josquin's *Missa Mater Patris*, Carter's *Emblems*, and Thompson's *Tarantella*, alongside the more familiar David Davis *Summer Songs*, Davis's second joint composition with Michael Stillman, *Broken Glass*, and a set of American songs.

December 27, Friday	Arrive Luxembourg –	
12.00	Arrive Luxembourg, transfer to railway station	
Afternoon	Free	
6.00	Dinner at Hotel Alfa	
9.21	Depart on train to Trieste	
December 28, Saturday	– Trieste	
8.20	Arrive Milan - breakfast	
9.10	Depart Milan	
12.35	Arrive Mestre	
1.06	Depart Mestre	
3.10	Arrive Trieste, transfer to hotel	
6.00	Dinner at your hotel	
Evening	Free	
December 29, Sunday	Trieste - Zagreb	264 km
9.00	Orientation tour of Trieste	
10.00	Depart for Zagreb	
Lunch	En route, individual arrangements	
4.00	Arrive Zagreb	
4.30	Rehearsal	
6.00	Dinner at your hotel	
8.00	Concert at Povijesni Musej	
December 30, Monday	Zagreb - Belgrad	400 km
8.00	City tour	
9.30	Depart Zagreb	
Lunch	En route, own arrangements	
4.30	Arrive Belgrad	
5.00	Rehearsal	
6.00	Dinner at your hotel	
8.00	Concert as guests of Branko Krsmanovic Choir	
December 31, Tuesday	Belgrad - Budapest	335 km
9.00	Depart Belgrad	
Lunch	En route, individual arrangements	
4.30	Arrive Budapest	
6.00	Dinner at your hotel	
Evening	Free to celebrate New Year's Eve	
January 1, Wednesday	Budapest HAPPY NEW YEAR!	
Morning	Sleep-in	
Lunch	Individual arrangements	
Afternoon	Free time	
6.00	Dinner at your hotel	
Evening	Free time	
January 2, Thursday	Budapest	
9.00	City tour	
Lunch	Individual arrangements	
4.00	Rehearsal	
6.00	Dinner at your hotel	
8.00	Concert	

FIGURE 14. Itinerary, Eastern European Tour of 1974–1975.

The repertoire was more ambitious, and the documentation was also more thorough. Many photographs of the concert performances survive in the University's Special Collections and in members' scrapbooks, particularly from the Vienna performance. Members also recalled numerous details from the trip. One recalled that some of the students, including Bill Piper, were stranded "on the wrong car when the overnight train from Amsterdam (Luxembourg City) to Trieste split into two parts somewhere in Switzerland." (Piper and his fellow ROTC students successfully found their way to Trieste on their own.) Others spoke fondly of Loach's guidance: after "drinking Italian white wine like water," he urged a mandatory "two aspirin and two tall glasses of water" for the members before bed. Loach himself recalled the members spending New Year's Eve in a lounge in Budapest listening to Bulgarian folk music and hearing a cimbalom, as well as a joint concert with a local men's group in Bucharest.[11]

FIGURE 15. Virginia Glee Club in performance in the Schottenkirche, Vienna, January 4, 1975. Photo courtesy John Madden.

The performance locations in Eastern Europe were enough to merit additional precautions and preparations. The office of Secretary of State Henry Kissinger sent an advance cable about the performances to the embassies in Belgrade, Bonn, Budapest, Munich, Sofia, and Vienna, noting "PANEL EVALU-

ATION OF EXCELLENT OBTAINED ON UNIVERSITY OF VIRGINIA GLEE CLUB WHICH PLANNING TOUR DECEMBER 27, 1974–JANUARY 12, 1975. KISSINGER."[12] And for this tour, the group enlisted local help. As the group traveled into Eastern Europe, the tour agency's guide, Katalin Brosman, helped them navigate through the complex geopolitical and cultural landscape, despite being, in Douglass List's words, "one twentysomething female on a bus with forty-some college guys." [13] Though the performances were received warmly—members spoke of the "local delight at our performances of [Hungarian] folk songs arranged by Kodály"—off the stage the reception might have been less warm. Members spoke of "the feeling of being watched all the time" and of their feeling of helplessness as they passed through the armed border between Austria and Hungary, where they were detained for eight hours while the Hungarian police searched the bus for contraband. In one instance, during the group's visit to the Hungarian-born tour guide's hometown of Tata, the guide anxiously feared a dispute with the Hungarian authorities over her Austrian passport. But the excursions, including a New Year's Eve visit to a Budapest disco with Katalin, made up for it.

The members eventually made it home, despite a last-minute hassle with the return flight. The club had booked Icelandic Air, which did not officially offer direct flights from the United States to Luxembourg (but which nevertheless offered cheap flights with a brief stop in Reykjavík). The return flight was late, and the airline substituted a smaller plane. Some members had to stay behind and were given the choice of catching the bus to Frankfurt to get on a flight or taking Air Bahama to Nassau and then on to New York via Miami. Opting for Nassau, those members lucked out when their flight to Miami arrived late and they had to be put up in a hotel overnight, enjoying a day on the beach before returning.

After the tour, the rest of the season might reasonably be expected to be an anticlimax. However, there were two more highlights to come. First, the spring concert featured a collaboration with the University Wind Ensemble and music ranging from Gabrieli to Bartók and Schubert. Second was the first collaboration with the Harvard Glee Club. As we have seen, the Virginia Glee Club was founded in awareness of the glee clubs of Harvard and Yale, and though the clubs exchanged (at a distance) repertoire, leadership, and performance ideas (the Virginia Gentlemen were still performing alongside the Glee Club at this time), they had yet to meet in person.

This changed when the Harvard Glee Club, under the baton of F. John

Adams, traveled to Charlottesville for a performance as part of a tour that also took them to Williamsburg and Washington, DC.[14] Logistically and musically the performance was a revelation. Douglass List recalls "the extraordinary performance" and the "spectacle of the piano four hands accompaniment to the football song they performed," as well as "the determination in [Virginia Glee Club accompanist] Jim Richardson's face to find an opportunity to respond"; he got his chance with a performance of Carter's *Defense of Corinth,* featuring its own piano four hands accompaniment. There were also less positive surprises: the officers of the Glee Club were apparently unaware that Harvard commanded an honorarium for their performances, and they transitioned from initial outrage through determination to pay the fee. The men of Virginia would get their opportunity to respond to Harvard's performance, but it would take another three seasons. First, there was a bicentennial to celebrate.

The 1975–1976 season saw the Virginia Glee Club stretching out domestically, incorporating symphonic performances alongside the customary collaborations with women's choruses (Mount Holyoke and Radcliffe) and a domestic tour to New England with stops at Mount Holyoke, the University of New Hampshire, and Harvard.

The season started in the light mode, with a joint kickoff concert with the Virginia Tech Glee Club. About two weeks later, the Glee Club shifted into a more serious mode with its first appearance at the Kennedy Center. Appearing as part of the Bicentennial Parade of American Music, the Glee Club's appearance for a Sunday evening concert included performances of parts of Thompson's *The Testament of Freedom* and Davis and Stillman's *Broken Glass.* A week after that, the Glee Club revisited one of its most enduring partnerships: its collaborations with the Mount Holyoke Glee Club.

The Glee Club had begun collaborations with Mount Holyoke in 1972 with a joint tour; the collaboration has continued into the twenty-first century with almost twenty joint performances and tours. The early years of the collaboration were given life by the working partnership of Loach and Catharine Melhorn, conductor of the Mount Holyoke Glee Club from 1970 to 1996.[15] The Mount Holyoke Glee Club remains the only women's chorus to tour with the Virginia Glee Club. Ambitions for the 1975 fall concert collaboration with Mount Holyoke were high: the performance featured the Vaughan Williams's *Mass in G Minor,* Schoenberg's *Friede auf Erden,* Schubert's "Standchen" and "Sehnsucht," and Brahms's "Fest - Und Gedenksprüche."

After the Christmas concert—and it seems a disservice to call the 1975

Glee Club Christmas concert "merely" a Christmas concert, with its program of three "O magnum mysterium" settings combined with Buxtehude's "In dulce jubilo" and works by Britten and Franck—the Glee Club returned to symphonic performances and bicentennial celebrations. On January 12 and 13, they performed *The Testament of Freedom* with the Norfolk (Virginia) Symphony Orchestra, among works by Howard Hanson, Ferde Grofé (the redoubtable *Grand Canyon Suite*), and Alan Hovhaness.

The spring tour programs were far from a walk in the park after the symphonic performances. The tour included collaborations with two women's choruses with entirely different repertoire. The Mount Holyoke performances featured a repeat of the fall performance, including the Vaughan Williams Mass, *Friede auf Erden,* works by Brahms, and the two Schubert songs. The club's performance with the Radcliffe Choral Society four days later included the *Deutsches Magnificat* by Heinrich Schütz, Verdi's "Pater Noster," and Brahms's *Selections from the 51st Psalm* as joint works, alongside the Virginia Glee Club's performance of Poulenc, *Quatre Petits Prières De Saint Francois D'Assise,* and Carl Orff's *Sunt Lacrimae Rerum.* This latter program was repeated a few weeks later when the Glee Club returned to Grounds, with Radcliffe joining as guests.

This being *the* bicentennial year, a Founder's Day concert on Thomas Jefferson's birthday was inevitably part of the celebration. The Glee Club responded with a triple-threat performance: of course there was *Testament,* with the University of Virginia Symphonic Band. But the program also included Carter's *Emblems* and a lesser-known *Fantasy on American Folk Ballads* by Richard Donovan.

Last but not least was the Concert on the Lawn, which in 1976 could actually be held on the Rotunda steps. For the last few years, Mr. Jefferson's centerpiece had been undergoing extensive renovations to remove Stanford White's modified interior and return the building to something closer to Jefferson's original design. The renovations drew international visitors, including (in late July) Queen Elizabeth II, whose visit occasioned a frantic round of strategizing when University history and protocol officer Alexander "Sandy" Gilliam paced her route and realized that the newly renovated Rotunda oculus would send a blinding shaft of light directly into the queen's eyes when she arrived for her address. Psychology professor Raymond Bice solved the problem; with typical ingenuity, he accessed the Rotunda roof through a trap door and glued white butcher paper over the oculus to diffuse the sunlight, using water-soluble glue so that it would eventually wash away.[16]

FIGURE 16. Glee Club performance at the Rotunda, April 24, 1976, Donald Loach conducting.

The Glee Club faced no such hurdles in its performance. Joined by the Virginia Gentlemen, the club performed lighter highlights from a season rich with musical choices: a set of Elizabethan madrigals (including what was rapidly becoming a Loach signature, Thomas Weelkes's "Hark! all ye lovely Saints"), Fenno Heath's "Death, be not proud," the Kodály "Tavern Song," Davis's *Broken Glass,* and Schubert's "Sehnsucht." The crowd, judging from contemporary photographs, was large and appreciative. It also included women; the transition from the single-sex undergraduate experience had come rapidly after the advent of coeducation in 1970.

The evolution of the Concert on the Lawn is a good summation of this period of the Glee Club's activities. The first Concerts on the Lawn were literally boozers, accompanied by kegs and juleps; the modern version was a light classical concert, albeit one outdoors. But the Glee Club had not lost its sense of humor, as a photo of the men carrying a grand piano up the Lawn from Old Cabell Hall to the Rotunda shows. Nonetheless, by the mid-1970s it took its performances very seriously. That seriousness of purpose, with an underpinning of fun, was Loach's developing style. It was to pay dividends for the Glee Club in the latter half of the 1970s and beyond.

FIGURE 17. Glee Club men moving a grand piano from Old Cabell Hall to the Rotunda for the Concert on the Lawn in the mid-1970s.

1 The donation seems to have been solicited by the Glee Club's president, John Wood, but it was given good-naturedly: above the signature of the seven astronomical symbols, the Sevens wrote, "With all good wishes for a most successful tour."

2 Donald Loach, interview with the author, May 22, 2021.

3 John Wood, email to the author, August 20, 2014.

4 David Foster, "Around the Western World in Eighteen Days: A Glee Club Diary," *Cavalier Daily*, May 12, 1972.

5 Ibid.

6 Donald Loach, email to the author, May 21, 2021.

7 Foster, "Around the Western World in Eighteen Days."

8 Dearing (October 20, 1943–November 26, 2010) was a native of Lynchburg. He completed his undergraduate education at UCLA and his graduate work at the University of Wisconsin; he had been a featured soloist in the Roger Wagner Chorale before serving in the United States Army in Heidelberg, Germany.

9 Beverley D. Tucker, quoted in Dabney, *Mr. Jefferson's University*, 121.

10 The full membership was closer to sixty; apparently financial and artistic considerations held back the other members.

11 Donald Loach, email to the author, May 21, 2021.

12 Cable from the State Department, 1974-129715, April 10, 1974, https://archive
.org/details/State-Dept-cable-1974-129715/mode/2up?q=%22university+of+virgin
ia+glee+club%22.

13 Memories of the tour were provided by Douglass List, John Flack, and others on
the Virginia Glee Club Wiki.

14 "1975 Tour," *Harvard Glee Club Foundation,* accessed November 27, 2018.

15 "April 29 Concert to Honor Catharine Melhorn," Mount Holyoke College, April
10, 2006, https://www.mtholyoke.edu/offices/comm/news/melhorn.shtml.

16 "1976: A Royal Visit," *Virginia Magazine,* Spring 2012, https://uvamagazine.org/
articles/a_royal_visit.

20 "WHO'S YOUR RECORD CONTRACT WITH?"

I n many respects, the 1976–1977 season opened as others had. The fall con-cert, billed as Chorkonzert due to its focus on German repertoire, was a col-laboration with a women's chorus, this time the Chatham College Choir. Only one work, the Lassus "De Profundis," was not by a German composer, and the rest ran the gamut from the early Renaissance with works by the ob-scure organist and composer Paul Peuerl as well as by Heinrich Schütz, to the later classical and romantic works of Robert Schumann and the Brahms *Lieb-eslieder Waltzer*, into the twentieth-century with Hindemith.

But it is the end of the program, in the season concert schedule, that the group's ambitions are signaled. In addition to the Christmas concert and the *Messiah* Sing-In, the season promised an appearance in Roanoke, a collabo-ration with the Lehigh University Women's Chorus at both the University of Virginia and Lehigh, and "three concerts with the Glee Clubs of Amherst and Harvard University, honoring the memory of G. Wallace Woodworth, at Har-vard." Were this not enough, a note at the bottom suggested that a tour of northern France was "under consideration."

The late 1970s saw some of the most varied artistic partnerships in Glee Club's history, as evidenced by the collaborations with Chatham, for only the second of three times in Glee Club history, and Lehigh, for the second and last time. Donald Loach and his officers, which this season included club president Douglass List, were reaching more broadly and ambitiously for musical collaborations and performance venues. If the Christmas concert for

1976 followed a familiar formula, it was still ambitious, with a raft of "Salve Regina" settings by Orlando di Lasso, Francis Poulenc, Claudio Monteverdi, and Franz Schubert alongside the familiar "Twelve Days of Christmas."

But the Glee Club was just getting started, as it began perhaps the single most jam-packed semester it had yet performed. On March 27, 1977, the Glee Club collaborated with Lehigh University Women's Chorus in a performance of Honneger's *King David* in Old Cabell Hall. Then a month later, on April 25, the club held a concert of sacred music in the University Chapel. The repertoire included motets by Jacob Handl, Adrian Willaert, Josquin and Costanzo Festa, the Schubert "Salve Regina," and a full performance of the Tallis *Lamentations of Jeremiah*.

The *Lamentations* performance is noteworthy as it took advantage of a newly established countertenor section. Loach had created the unique section in part to take advantage of the arrival at the University of David Quittmeyer from Williamsburg. Quittmeyer had been trained as a boy soprano in the choir of Bruton Parish, whose music director worked with him to maintain his alto register when his voice changed in adolescence. He came to the University "ready to use that voice," Loach recalls, calling him, "a gift. . . . [I] could use David to develop a section within the Glee Club capable of singing alto parts; thus, the Club now had five sections when needed: ATTBB." This made possible the performance of many English madrigals as well as much Renaissance sacred music composed for male voices at a time when women and girls were not permitted membership in Roman Catholic and English choirs.[1]

And then, beginning four days later: the Harvard Festival of Men's Choruses. However it came together, the concerts, sponsored by Harvard in memory of the deceased Harvard Glee Club conductor and hosted by the Harvard Glee Club under F. John Adams, brought together the famed group with the Amherst Glee Club and Loach's Virginia Glee Club. We have very little direct documentary evidence of many of the Glee Club's performances during this time, but thanks to the Harvard Glee Club archives, we can hear their performances this weekend from one of the three concerts. Over the weekend, the Glee Club performances included Jacob Handl's "Confirma hoc" and "Ascendi Deus," Willaert's "O Domine Jesu Christe," Josquin's "De profundis clamavi," and the Tallis *Lamentations of Jeremiah*, reprising most of the repertoire from the April 25 Musica Sacra concert.

The final concert featured all the groups performing Schubert. The program opened with Amherst performing "Nachtgesangim Walde," "Die Nacht," and "Widerspruch"; Virginia performed "Salve Regina," "Nachthelle," and "Geist der Liebe"; and Harvard performed "Grab und Mond" and "Gesang der Geister über den Wassern." The combined glee clubs then performed a set of works by composers including Jacob Handl, Schubert, and Giovanni Gabrieli, as well as a performance of Biebl's "Ave Maria." This was the first time the men of the Virginia Glee Club heard the work, which had only been introduced into the United States by the Cornell Glee Club in 1970.[2]

All three Virginia performances are light-years ahead of the 1950s and 1960s performances but also show a substantial advance over the recorded performances on *A Shadow's on the Sundial*. The pinnacle, though, is probably "Nachthelle." The performance features sensitive piano accompaniment by James Richardson, by then in his final season of seven as Glee Club member, assistant conductor, and accompanist, and a transcendent solo by Louis Burkot (later an operatic performer and director of the Dartmouth Glee Club from 1981 to 2018). Loach has called it among the most spectacular performances the Virginia Glee Club ever gave.[3]

The three-day weekend ended on May 1, 1977. The tour followed with a Concert on the Lawn. Then after Finals came the 1977 Finals concert. Conceived as a fundraiser for the next international tour by president Douglass List, the May 21 concert featured works from the season and also celebrated the group's graduating members.

And then, four days later, a handpicked subset of twenty-five Glee Club members left for France. The third international tour in five years, this one saw the Glee Club performing in the cathedrals at Reims, Notre-Dame in Paris, Chartres, and Arras, with additional stops in Amiens, Rouen, and Versailles. This trip's repertoire included the Tallis *Lamentations of Jeremiah;* settings of the "Salve Regina" by Lassus, Schubert, and Poulenc; Poulenc's "Quatre Petits Prières de Saint Francois d'Assise," and a series of love songs written by John Crawford which set the poetry of Joachim du Bellay.

The tour, though occasionally a challenge—List recalls "the frustration of the incredible level of tourist background noise during our performance at Notre-Dame"—also had its rewards, including a champagne tasting in the Moët cellars in Reims.[4] Club member Barry Germany wrote, "Eight singers, seeking the highest in haute cuisine, dined one evening in splendor at the Plaza Athénée in Paris. They experienced the delights of civilization and the sumptuousness of the French cuisine and returned to the hotel sated, cultivated, and quite dreadfully poor"; he also recalled spotting Andy Warhol at the Hôtel de Crillon.[5] Loach noted, "The most memorable event of the tour was our visit to the cathedral at Chartres and our singing there. It was late afternoon. We stood at the east end of the nave facing the gorgeous stained glass windows in the west, blinded by their brilliance in the afternoon sun, astonished by such beauty."

While the Glee Club had previously performed the Biebl at Harvard with the other groups, the tour also saw its first solo, impromptu performance of the "Ave Maria" in the ruins of the Abbey of St. Jean des Vignes in Soissons. Loach recalls:

> It was in Rouen that we sang through for the first time Biebl's *Ave Maria*. We had walked a short distance from the Cathedral to a small, empty church where we stood in a circle in the nave, and let it happen. We did not include it in our repertory for the tour after that but saved it (I think) for the Christmas program the following December. I did not give it a permanent slot in every concert, but kept it in reserve for special programs over the next several years.[6]

FIGURE 18. Virginia Glee Club performing at Reims, May 29, 1977. Photo courtesy Dr. Anthony Gal.

If the events of 1976–1977 seem hard to top, they were; the 1977–1978 season was relatively more sedate—but only by comparison. The season opener was a joint concert with the University of North Carolina Glee Club, with both clubs performing music of Schubert and Bruckner in alternating sets, culminating with a joint performance of the chorus "O welche Lust" from Beethoven's *Fidelio*. While the hapless Virginia football team lost the following day's football game, 14–35, the score of the Schubert and Bruckner contest sadly went unrecorded.

Christmas went on as it was now regularly doing under Loach, with a program both highbrow (Josquin's *Missa L'Homme Armé Sexti Toni*, Lloyd Pfautsch's "A Day for Dancing") and jovial. Indeed, by now certain aspects of the club's Christmas programming had hardened into tradition. Loach would open with an antiphon or a conductus and, beginning sometime between 1968 and 1971, would lead the audience in a sing-along of "The Twelve Days of Christmas." Somewhere along the way the observation had been made that Old Cabell Hall auditorium could be neatly divided into enough parts that each section of the audience could call out one of the twelve days' gifts at the appropriate part of the song. Over time, the audience came to know what was coming, and indeed to plan their participation. The "three French hens" were especially persistent in returning to their location at stage left year after year and in steadily escalating the tenor of their participation. And their participation was noted and encouraged from the stage. Loach recalls, "French organist Yvaine Duisit accompanied 'Twelve Days of Christmas.' When we got to 'Three French Hens,' she would play the first phrase of 'La Marseillaise.'"[7]

Spring saw a joint performance with the Virginia Women's Chorus, for the first time since the latter group's premiere concert in 1974; a tour of southern US destinations in Georgia, Alabama, Tennessee, and Louisiana; a spring concert of Renaissance music; and the requisite Lawn and Finals concerts.

And, in April, a few days following the spring concert, there was a return to Harvard for the second Festival of Men's Choruses. As before, the performances each night featured sets from the invited groups, this year including Union College Men's Glee Club and the St. Paul Men's Schola of St. Paul's Church in Harvard Square instead of Amherst. The theme for the year was "composers attached to the Renaissance court of the French King Louis XII."[8] The Virginia Glee Club performed Josquin, *Missa L'Homme Armé*, thriftily reprising the work from earlier concerts, on Saturday, April 15, and the following day performed a set of sacred and secular motets by Josquin and Jean Mouton.

Loach recalls, "At one of the concerts in St. Paul's Church, as we were singing the concluding 'Angus Dei' of Josquin's Mass, we were threatened by a blast of sirens from the street. At the next cadence, I interrupted Josquin until the sirens passed, then we simply picked up where we'd left off and completed the remaining measures of the Mass. The Harvard men in the audience went wild over our recovery."[9]

At the Saturday concert, a *Cavalier Daily* correspondent—who happened to be a member of the Glee Club— captured an exchange between Loach and Yale musicologist Craig Wright:

> A somewhat disheveled gentleman breaks through the crowd and approaches Director Donald Loach.
>
> "My name is Craig Wright," he begins. "I'm a musicologist at Yale and I . . ."
>
> "Oh, you don't have to introduce yourself to me," interrupts Loach. "I've read your book on Renaissance music and I was ecstatic that you could come up from New Haven to give this year's special guest lecture."
>
> "Well, thank you. I just wanted to tell you that I was tremendously impressed with the sound of your group. I'm anxious to hear some of your other efforts. What record label are you on?"[10]

That Wright, who later served as the chair of the Yale Department of Music and who spent his early career focused on the study of early music from original manuscripts, would single out the Glee Club for praise serves as perhaps the best independent testimony for the sound of the group that Loach achieved during this time.[11]

The article also captures some of the Glee Club's emerging musical distinction. Sounding a note that would recur later, the article points out the limited selection of music for male chorus, quoting Loach as saying, "We found ourselves having to repeat the same pieces every four years or so." But it also notes Loach's unique solution: the cultivation of a countertenor section so that the group could perform a broader selection of Renaissance music; he said, "No other glee club, to my knowledge, has a countertenor section so they can't really do the same pieces we do."

But the article also captures some of the strains that the group was feeling at this time. The writer imagines Loach's response to Wright, "Loach, taken aback, wonders how he can explain to this famous scholar that his group can't afford the studio time necessary to produce a record—that the only way the singers have been able to come to Harvard was by dipping into their own pockets to cover expenses." The article notes that, unlike the "heavily endowed" Harvard Glee Club, the Virginia group made its members pay their own way for foreign and some domestic tours, with costs for the French tour cited at around $1,200 per person. Its operating budget was paid with ticket sales and other fundraising efforts; only about 2 percent of its operating budget was money from the University, via student activity fee allocations.

The University had begun to charge student activity fees years before, collecting a flat sum from each student and allocating the proceeds among student groups through a special committee of the student council. The process, which required review of a proposed budget submitted by each student group, was unpredictable. Even in the best case, an inexperienced business manager might easily make an error or submit a budget that did not describe the benefit to the overall student body and thus get a reduced rate. Often, it was worse; new student body reps unfamiliar with the Glee Club might come in with an agenda to fund newer groups at the expense of well-established ones, or might change the allocation policy so that previously eligible budget items were now ineligible. While the process provided seed money for smaller groups, even when it worked, it did not come near to providing sufficient operating capital for a fifty-person men's choir, especially not one with touring ambitions as high as the Glee Club's.

So the club leaned on its alumni for supplemental donations. Beginning in 1971, the group had started to publish the "Virginia Glee Club Bulletin," a two- to four-page glossy newsletter featuring highlights, photographs, and narratives from members about the year's planned and concluded activities. But the hoped-for outcome of the bulletin was signaled by a discreet box, usually somewhere on the back cover, requesting donations to the Glee Club Tour Fund. This fund had begun in recognition of the obstacles that the trip cost would pose to student participation in international tours; money from the fund was meant to defray tour costs to allow more students to participate. Though the funds raised were comparatively modest, amounting at most to a few thousand dollars, the existence of the fund would prove pivotal a few years later.

The Glee Club entered its 1978–1979 season with challenges but also with mounting acclaim and a well-earned reputation for musical excellence. The majority of the season had fewer large works; the fall and spring collaborations with the redoubtable Mount Holyoke Glee Club had a single large work in joint performance—Samuel Barber's *Reincarnations*. There was also no Harvard festival, the series ending after 1978 with the departure of Harvard conductor F. John Adams. But the spring Renaissance concert featured performances of a mass setting and other works by Cipriano de Rore alongside motets by Adrian Willaert. And after graduation, the Glee Club hit the international touring circuit again, this time making their farthest trip to date: a tour of Soviet Russia and Sweden. Equally unusually, the tour was undertaken jointly with the Mount Holyoke Glee Club.

The partnership between Holyoke and Virginia was among the most frequent women's college collaborations at this time, with three seasons in the 1970s featuring joint performances or rolls. But 1978–1979 was the high-water mark of the collaboration, with the clubs performing at each other's schools in fall and spring before embarking on the tour together. The program featured a blend of American and European composers, with works by Copland, Irving Fine, Kirke Mechem, Stravinsky, and Stephen Schwartz—as well as a set of African American spirituals—joining the Barber *Reincarnations*. The itinerary included performances in Moscow, Leningrad, Petrodvorets (Peter the Great's palace, now called Peterhof), and Stockholm, where they performed at a cultural festival.

While the clubs found the audiences welcoming, the reception was not unmixed. Matthew Koch, who would serve as president of the Glee Club the following season, recalls:

> During the Moscow performances, the Glee Club performed a couple of Russian folk songs, for which I was a soloist. One of the songs was a nonsense song; during the performance, the Soviet audience started laughing. The Holyoke women were very concerned, and feared that the audience had been laughing at me. I assured them that it was a good thing that the audience was laughing, as that meant that the audience understood what I was singing.
>
> The dynamic of the 1979 tour was different from other Club tours in which I had participated. While I spoke Russian, had visited the USSR, and knew what I was getting into,

for most of the participants the USSR appeared an alien (and seemingly hostile) environment. Although the people were very friendly, the Soviet Union itself, with anti-American propaganda at every turn, was not a warm and fuzzy place.

The realities of touring during the Cold War were made even more apparent in a border mishap. The clubs traveled by train from Leningrad to Helsinki en route to their final stop in Sweden. At a brief stop on the Soviet side of the border, the students were allowed to disembark and stretch their legs before being called to reboard. Koch describes what happened next:

> Our guys did our head count, the women assured me they were all present and accounted for, and we then headed off into Finnish territory—only to soon hear the women crying out that one of their number had been left behind in the USSR. There was nothing we could do. At the Helsinki airport, I went to the SAS airline desk, explained that one of our group was back in the USSR, and asked them to honor her ticket to Stockholm when (if?) she made it to the Helsinki airport. In addition, the Swedish student from Holyoke called her father, so there was some helpful support from the Swedish Parliament as well. The lost Holyoke student caught up with us in Stockholm a day and a half later, none the worse for wear—and with a great story to tell.[12]

FIGURE 19. Virginia Glee Club members with Mount Holyoke Glee Club women, tour of Russia and Sweden, 1979. Photo courtesy Anthony Gal.

FIGURE 20. Virginia and Mount Holyoke Glee Clubs, on the steps of Petrodvorets, 1978. Photo courtesy Mount Holyoke Glee Club.

The 1979–1980 season, the final season of the 1970s, featured three women's chorus collaborations at Goucher College, Wellesley, and Harvard/Radcliffe, along with the customary Christmas, Finals, and Lawn concerts. It also featured another shot fired in the battle of the Glee Club to claim a greater share of student activity fee allocations. Stung by low or no appropriations in the late 1970s despite their student success, the group pulled out all the stops in February 1980, publishing a bound "annual report" that ran to more than a hundred pages, including James Ballowe's 1977 history of the group, season reports, letters from Loach and the club president, and detailed organization budgets. The group optimistically sent copies to the allocations committee and to Ernest "Boots" Mead, its faculty sponsor. The greatest significance of the report was that it marked the transition of the Glee Club Tour Fund into an actual endowment at Alumni Hall, an event led by business manager Thomas Potter with the substantial assistance of Alumni Hall's Gilly Sullivan.[13]

The Glee Club that exited the 1970s was anything but ordinary. Having completed four international tours in seven years, the group was performing at the highest level among collegiate choirs. And those of the membership who were graduating were extraordinary as well, including Louis Burkot, the Glee Club's assistant conductor (and soloist on "Nachthelle" at the Harvard Festival), who went on to direct the Dartmouth Glee Club from 1981 to 2018 and to establish the Dartmouth Opera Workshop, and James Richardson (1951–1997), accompanist extraordinaire, who cofounded and conducted the Gay Men's Chorus of Washington, DC.

But despite the high level of performance, the caliber of the members, the curricular basis of the group, and Loach's secure position on the McIntire

Music Department faculty, there was still a long way to go to build the institutions of the group. The tour fund, the club's sole capital reserve, had been transformed into a formal endowment in 1979, but it harbored only $6,497 in funds.[14] There was little direct financial support from the University. And the 1980s were to make the prospects for international touring more complicated.

1 Donald Loach, email to the author, May 21, 2021.
2 Wilbur Skeels, "Franz Biebl's *Ave Maria* (*Angelus Domini*)" (program note), https://web.archive.org/web/20110719132345/http:/cantusquercus.com/ave.htm, accessed July 8, 2010.
3 Don Loach, interview, 2016.
4 Douglass List, Virginia Glee Club Wiki, March 29, 2010. List further noted, "The entire tour may have been nothing but a ruse to get the Club to where we could tour the Moet cellars in Reims and test the samples"; https://virginiagleeclub.fandom.com/wiki/Glee_Club_1976-1977_season.
5 Barry Germany, "The French Tour: A Wonderful Experience," *University Glee Club Bulletin* 6, no. 1 (Fall 1977): 1ff.
6 Donald Loach, email to the author, May 10, 2019.
7 Donald Loach, email to the author, May 21, 2021.
8 Peter Brehm, "Glee Club Invited Back to Harvard," *University Glee Club Bulletin* 6, no. 1 (Fall 1977): 3.
9 Donald Loach, email to the author, May 21, 2021.
10 George Gerachis and Nancy Kreiling, "What Record Label Are You On?" *Cavalier Daily*, October 31, 1978, 22–24. Gerachis was a third-year Glee Club member at the time of the Harvard tour, sang with the group for part of his time in law school, and was a Lawn resident and a member of the Virginia Gentlemen.
11 "Craig Wright," Yale University Department of Music, https://yalemusic.yale.edu/people/craig-wright, accessed May 22, 2019.
12 Matthew Koch, email to the author, July 2014.
13 Matthew P. Freeman, interview, February 29, 2020.
14 "Endowment," *University Glee Club Bulletin* 11, no. 2 (Spring 1984): 4.

 **THE 1980S: CHANGING TIMES**

The first full season of the 1980s opened much as the previous few had: a football concert with the Rutgers Glee Club (and a loss the following day to Rutgers, 17–19); collaborations on the road and at home with the Agnes Scott College Glee Club; Christmas, Lawn, and Finals concerts.[1] But there were two additions: a performance at the 1980 Virginia Music Educators Convention in Richmond on November 14, 1980, and the Glee Club's first Renaissance Festival, held March 27–29, 1981.

According to a note from Donald Loach printed at the beginning of the program, the Renaissance Festival was a direct result of the Harvard Festival of Men's Choruses. After F. John Adams's retirement, Loach decided to revive the idea of collaborations with men's choruses, focusing the repertoire on music of the French Burgundian and Tudor English courts. The festival was not to be a direct re-creation of the Harvard experience, however, due to the strong interdisciplinary aspects:

> We have wanted to make our Renaissance Festival something
> more than simply a gathering of men's choruses, and so to
> this end we will present instrumental ensembles, madrigal
> groups, dancers, sword fighters, and lecturers on various as-
> pects of the Renaissance. Within our limited means we hope
> to recreate, for the participants as well as the audience, the
> Renaissance Experience.[2]

Speakers for the event included Fred Hardin, a University of Virginia professor and art historian who had been a Monuments Man in World War II, and Craig Wright, the Yale professor who had asked Loach about his group's recording capabilities just a few years prior at the second Harvard Festival of Men's Choruses. Business manager Matthew Freeman recalls, "Kip Purcell and I went to pick up Craig Wright at the airport. Kip was trying to choose between law school at Harvard—Wright was appropriately congratulatory, if muted—or Yale—and here the professor just lit up. The rivalry between the schools was alive and well."[3]

The original plan for the weekend was to include the glee clubs of both Harvard University and Davidson College, but Davidson College was unable to attend. The Harvard Glee Club, conducted by Jameson Marvin, was the sole guest group. The concert format followed the formula established by the Harvard Festival, with the groups alternating sets each concert followed by a joint performance.

Freeman helped to organize the festival. He recalls:

> The idea for this started because of Loach's particular expertise and because the Glee Club had developed a specialty. It was sort of a branding exercise for us and for Loach as well. We recruited Harvard to come because we had sung in the past and because of their reputation. I talked to their Business Manager Dave Wellborn in the fall semester of 1980 and ended up feeling like I got fleeced because we paid their costs to come down but they never paid us. . . .
>
> This concert was the first time that I had ever done a true media stunt. On the Thursday before the festival, we recruited the society for Creative Anachronism to stage a sword fight on the Lawn and got the CD [*Cavalier Daily*] to come and take pictures of it for some earned media coverage.[4]

The festival was apparently a success, leading to the Glee Club's second recognition by the secretive Seven Society. On Founder's Day in 1981, the Glee Club was awarded the annual James Earle Sargeant Award, given to "an organization that makes major contributions to the University community." The award came with a donation of $777.77. Freeman recalls, "It was disclosed when he passed away that Ernest Mead was a Seven, and I was in a meeting with him and [prior business manager Thomas] Potter that seemed to have no obvious purpose but it must have been connected to the award."[5]

April 17, 1981

Mr. Herbert L. Picket
University Treasurer
Carruthers Hall
The University

Dear Mr. Picket,

On Monday, April 13, during the Founder's Day ceremonies, the Seven Society awarded the University Men's Glee Club with the 1981 James E. Sargeant Award. As part of this award, the Seven Society would like to donate $777.77 to this deserving group.

The Seven Society would appreciate your kind assistance in transferring the above amount to the Glee Club. This donation may be mailed to the following address:

The Men's Glee Club
attn: Mr. Donald Loach
Old Cabell Hall

The Seven Society thanks you for your attention in this matter.

Sincerely,

The Seven Society

FIGURE 21. Letter from the Seven Society to Herbert Picket, University treasurer, regarding the Glee Club's James Earle Sargeant Award.

Members of the Glee Club were busy outside its auspices at this time as well. In the early 1980s, Glee Club members Russell "Rusty" Speidel, Michael Goggin, and Thomas Goodrich, with Michael Lille, formed the band Speidel, Goodrich, Goggin, and Lille. Better known as SGGL, the band remained popular throughout the 1980s and is still performing today.

The following season, 1981–1982, was a tour year. The fall was relatively sedate, featuring the kickoff concert with the Sweet Briar College Choir (followed shortly by a weekend trip there to return the favor) and the Christmas concert. But the spring was unusually busy. The Glee Club went on a spring break tour, beginning with three Massachusetts women's colleges, performing at Wellesley, Smith, and Mount Holyoke on three successive days before finishing at Rutgers University on the fourth. Following the spring concert, which featured the Wellesley College Choir, and the Finals concert, the club returned yet again to the international tour circuit, this time in partnership with the University Singers.

The tour, called the Gira Española by tour manager Rafe Madan, began two days after the Finals concert. Departing on May 22, the groups performed in Seville, Córdoba, Madrid, Toledo, León, and Santiago de Compostela. The program featured works by Hassler, Josquin, Brahms, Poulenc, and Ned Rorem, as well as a set of African American spirituals and (for the first time since 1977) the Biebl "Ave Maria."

The tour, by all accounts a success, continued the Glee Club's streak; they began planning at once for another tour in 1983–1984. But first came a "home" season, complete with challenges from the University itself.

The season began auspiciously enough. In January 1982, the Board of Visitors had appointed Loach as chair of the McIntire Department of Music, beginning in September 1982 for a three-year period.[6] For the first time, the Glee Club not only had faculty support but had it at the highest level.

The Glee Club poured itself into a normal "off-tour year" schedule, opening with a football concert on October 29 (with guests from Washington and Lee rather than the next day's opponent, Virginia Military Institute) followed by a road opener with Mount Holyoke on November 9. Following Christmas and the *Messiah* Sing-In, the spring performances began with a rare orchestral performance with the Glee Club and the men of the University Singers joining the Charlottesville University and Community Symphony Orchestra in a performance of the *Requiem in D Minor* of Luigi Cherubini in March 1983.

Unfortunately, not all the Glee Club's needs from the University were

FIGURE 22. Donald Loach, Old Cabell Hall, Fall 1982. Photo courtesy Jim Tavenner.

within the scope of the music department's control. This became apparent with the following concert on March 26, a performance of Mendelssohn's *Die erste Walpurgisnacht* and other works with Mount Holyoke in Old Cabell Hall. The concert, planned for a year, suffered in attendance after University Union scheduled a concert by Joe Jackson in University Hall on the same night. The conflict would normally have been straightened out in the University's Activity Coordinating Committee, but the show had been booked by the time the conflict was realized. Glee Club president Rafe Madan negotiated compensation from University Union, including paid advertisements in the *Daily Progress*, reimbursement of up to $350 in lost revenue, and notices in the *Cavalier Daily* and *University Journal* that put the facts of the dispute in the public eye. Madan stated his concern that the Joe Jackson concert would not only impact revenue from student ticket sales but might also affect the Glee Club's long-term membership prospects by reducing the number of prospective new members who would attend a concert.[7]

No sooner was this issue settled than the Appropriations Committee announced funding recipients for the following year. Beginning a pattern that would be repeated over coming seasons, the Glee Club's business manager Tucker Echols submitted a budget for $4,041, to cover events, including another Renaissance Festival, but was only granted $836. Echols commented, "We were a bit afraid that our request this year was looked at from the merits of past years and not what we plan to do this year." Appropriations Committee member Rudy Beverly commented that the committee "does look at what a group has done in the past [to determine if] the group's increase in activities is necessary."[8] Though the club would go forward with a Renaissance Festival in 1984, the allocation was another point of strain in the Glee Club's financial model.

Echols was president for the 1983–1984 season. The season featured collaborations with and performances at Wellesley, Hood College, Skidmore College, and Smith; a choral prelude to the Sunday morning service at Washington National Cathedral; and the Glee Club's second Renaissance Festival, featuring an outdoor Renaissance Fair in the McIntire Amphitheatre, lectures, and performances by the Glee Club, the Christ Church Men and Boys Choir, the University of Virginia Collegium Musicum (an instrumental ensemble), and the Harvard Glee Club. The year's Concert on the Lawn included the Glee Club's first documented alumni reunion since 1936, in honor of Loach's twentieth anniversary as the Glee Club's conductor.

The capstone to the season was to be a joint tour of the Soviet Union with the University Singers. As of the spring 1984 Glee Club Bulletin, the plans were afoot to tour, and the endowment had bloomed, having grown from $21,000 in 1983 to $25,170 in 1984. However, this tour was different, with the University Singers taking the lead and the Glee Club playing a supporting role in the trip.

One major change in the world of collegiate choirs was the slow disappearance of women's choruses. As more and more institutions became coeducational—Madison College, now James Madison University, in 1966; Mary Washington in 1972; Longwood College in 1976; Goucher College in 1986—the number of opportunities for collaborations that included the traditional combination of musical and social interactions dwindled. This made the club's traditional domestic tours more challenging, since it now had to manage lodging logistics and costs in addition to transportation costs.

Further, where fall performances might have included collaborations with Virginia colleges, increasingly the Glee Club's collaborations were with the Massachusetts sister schools or with other Virginia choruses. Specifically, by 1984–1985 the Glee Club had performed eighteen concerts featuring guest choruses, including twelve with Massachusetts collegiate choirs, three with University groups, and five with other guests, only two of which were women's choruses. In particular, the 1984–1985 season featured two collaborations with Mount Holyoke and a joint performance of the Handel *Dettingen Te Deum* with the Virginia Women's Chorus in association with the Charlottesville Symphony.

Loach was also busy in 1984–1985 on the professional front. On January 25, 1985, the Board of Visitors voted to reappoint Loach as chair of the music department for another three-year term, to expire in June 1988.

The 1985–1986 season was intended as an international tour season, with another collaboration with the University Singers and a planned trip to West Germany, Austria, the Netherlands, and Sweden. Many of the customary extra activities, including domestic touring, were curtailed, leaving a season with only six events (the fall concert with Smith, the Christmas and spring concerts, a concert of early music, the Concert on the Lawn, and the Finals concert) for the first time since Loach took over as director. However, on April 15, 1986, amid rising incidents of international terrorism, President Reagan ordered the bombing of Libya. This led to additional threats of terrorism, and on April 20, the University Singers and the Glee Club voted to postpone the tour. Glee Club's foreign tour manager Stephen Harrison said the groups were "worried about being sitting ducks," since they were flying in and out of the Frankfurt and Amsterdam airports.[9] The tour would ultimately take place a year later than planned, in 1987, with twenty-six members of the two groups touring in Germany, Switzerland, and Austria. It proved to be the end of the streak of international tours that had seen the Glee Club, with and without accompanying groups, perform in Spain, the Soviet Union, Sweden, France, Yugoslavia, Hungary, Czechoslovakia, Switzerland, Austria, and Italy over a period of fourteen years; the next international tour did not take place for another thirteen years.

The rest of the 1986–1987 season included collaborations with Mount Holyoke and the College of William and Mary, along with a third collaboration with the Charlottesville University and Community Symphony Orchestra, a joint performance of Orff's *Carmina Burana* with the Virginia Women's Chorus. The Glee Club's experiences with these collaborations balanced music and social activity, as described in a contemporary newsletter article:

As is the custom, each year the Glee Club bids farewell to UVA and the rolling hills of Virginia to venture northward in search of wine, women, and song. This year was no exception for over the weekend of November 7 the Glee Club traveled to the sleepy New England town of South Hadley, Massachusetts, to visit the women of Mount Holyoke College for three fun-filled days of social intercourse climaxing with a spectacular Sunday afternoon concert. Making their departure on Friday morning, our band of hearty adventurers boarded their bus (equipped with stereo, VCR, and wet bar) for the rugged eleven hour trip that awaited. Arriving late that night, the Glee Club was met by an enthusiastic Mount Holyoke group and proceeded immediately to get better acquainted with their sister Glee Club.[10]

As can be seen, by this time the Glee Club experience was beginning to place greater emphasis on social activities. In the same newsletter, president Charles ("Charlie") Wise said, "It has been a longstanding belief of the Glee Club that in order to succeed as a cohesive musical ensemble, the members must first feel unified as a collection of friends.... While singing is the ultimate ends [sic] of the Glee Club, it is much more than just a singing group. It is also a social society, a fraternity, with a longstanding tradition and unlimited potential for success, adding much to the college experience of its members."[11]

The 1987 *Carmina* performances featured the birth of a Glee Club mascot. The "Ego sum abbas" solo of the abbot of Cockaigne memorably features the text:

et qui mane me quaesierit in taberna
post vesperam nudus egredietur,
et sic denudatus veste clamabit:
Wafna, wafna! quid fecisti, Sors turpissima?
nostrae vitae gaudia
abstulisti omnia!

and whoever seeks me early in the tavern
will leave naked after vespers,
and stripped of his clothing he will cry:
Wafna, wafna! What have you done, Luck most foul?
You have taken away all the joys of our life!

When members of the group adopted a pink lawn flamingo as a mascot, Wafna became its name. The new mascot immediately become part of the Glee Club's brand, appearing in the poster for the 1987 Concert on the Lawn weeks after her christening.

During this period the club continued to build its endowment as well, reporting the growth of the endowment's balance from $27,000 in 1985 to $37,000 in 1986, outpacing the growth of the Dow Jones Industrial Average in that year.[12]

The 1987–1988 season followed closely the pattern of the previous seasons, with collaborations with Smith and Wellesley and an appearance with the Charlottesville Symphony performing the Brahms's *Alto Rhapsody* and Schoenberg's *A Survivor from Warsaw*. The Wellesley performance was the Glee Club's final appearance onstage with F. John Adams, conductor of the Wellesley Glee Club and originator of the Harvard Festival during his time as the Harvard Glee Club's conductor.

Also in 1987–1988, the number of a cappella vocal groups at the University quietly went from two to three. The Virginia Gentlemen had been a fixture since 1953, and the Virginia Belles had been founded by Katherine Mitchell in 1977 from the nascent Virginia Women's Chorus. But a rising tide of interest in collegiate a cappella had led a number of Virginia students to seek performing a cappella who could not or would not participate in the Glee Club or Women's Chorus, or who were rejected from the existing groups. Among these was Glee Club member Halsted Sullivan (class of 1989). Sullivan tried out for the Virginia Gentlemen twice and was rejected twice, and he decided in the fall of 1987 to create his own group. A cappella historian Mickey Rapkin writes that Sullivan "placed an announcement in . . . *The Cavalier Daily* . . . that read, simply, CAN YOU SING IN THE SHOWER? The ad stressed the fact that, unlike the Virginia Gentlemen, this new a cappella group wouldn't require its members to join the glee club. In fact, reading music would be strictly optional."[13] The Hullabahoos' birth was the beginning of an explosion in a cappella groups at the University. Within a few years the number of groups would blossom to five, with the addition of the female Sil'Hooettes and the mixed-voice New Dominions; then to six with the Academical Village People; and then to dozens over the next twenty years.

In the early years, the new groups benefited the established Glee Club by raising the profile of public singing at the University. While the B'Hoos may have started out with "Glee Club membership optional" as a recruiting cry, several members remained in the Glee Club, including their second music director, Chris Walker, who was described by Rapkin as a prodigy.[14] But they also definitively broke the relationship between the established a cappella groups and the Glee Club; the Virginia Gentlemen soon stopped requiring Glee Club membership as well, ending a formal relationship that had lasted the first thirty-five years of their existence.

The relationship between a cappella groups and college choirs is complicated. On the one hand, prospective a cappella group members must start somewhere, and since unknown first years are less likely to pass an audition than singers who have already earned a reputation on Grounds, some may choose membership in a chorus to keep singing—or to make their reputation for the next year's auditions. Other, more serious musicians may choose both, either for broader repertoire or to keep their voices in shape. Leaders of the group might choose to remain in a chorus as an effective way to get a line on prospective talent.

But then there is the flip side: some students find that they enjoy the pop repertoire more than the traditional chorus repertoire after a year. Others find the time commitment of membership in two groups intolerable, especially if they are serious about academics. And as the number of groups increases, the attractiveness of any individual group, even a choral group that's been around for more than 130 years, decreases for the same reason that viewership of the Big Three television networks dropped as more and more rivals launched network TV–style programming on cable and the internet.

In 1987–1988, though, the arrival of the Hullabahoos meant only that the Virginia Gentlemen had competition and that there were now two men's a cappella groups showing that singing could be a path to on-Grounds fame—or, as Robin Williams's John Keating in the next year's hit movie *Dead Poets Society* put it, a way "to woo women."[15]

Perhaps most interestingly, the example of the Hullabahoos opened a path for vocal performance on Grounds that had *nothing whatsoever* to do with the McIntire Department of Music or any professor or curricular inclination. If students wanted to take the responsibility of managing a singing group into their own hands, they could. By the late 1980s, in fact, there were spirits in the air that supported, even encouraged, independent student activity—spirits legal, institutional, and philosophical.

On the legal side, in the mid-1980s the University moved to formalize the relationship of the many student organizations on Grounds to the University itself. Following instances of student injury and other potential liability while involved in activities sponsored by student-run groups, the University declared that all groups formed by students had to become a contracted independent organization (CIO). The CIO agreement was a legal document that established the group as an entity separate from the University, effectively limiting the University's liability and minimizing the CIO's ability to use the University's name and symbols. Over time, the master agreement also established that student groups could not ride on the University's tax-exempt status, and it subjected the group to terms regarding discrimination, sexual harassment, and hazing. In exchange, the student groups were eligible to use University facilities and to receive student activity funds.[16] While many groups found the CIO application process cumbersome—the "Hoover" comic strip in the *Cavalier Daily* in the mid-1980s caricatured University president Robert O'Neil as a Gollum-like creature sitting in the shadows of Carr's Hill and moaning about liability—by creating a legal framework that clarified the relationship between the University and student groups, it became much easier to access University resources. By the early 1990s, it was possible to establish a CIO and access student activity funds simply by filling out and signing a form.

Beyond the legal structure, there was a powerful institutional support structure at Alumni Hall. The UVA Alumni Association, in addition to maintaining relationships with graduates through newsletters, magazines, and reunions, was by the late 1980s the custodian of the UVA Fund, the single largest endowment of any Virginia educational institution.[17] The fund functioned as the parent of many individual student organization endowments, including the Glee Club's.

Philosophically, there was by the late 1980s a byword at the University: *student self-governance.* The concept had its earliest roots in the University community's reaction to John A. G. Davis's murder and the idea that the only way for the student body to move beyond the bedlam of the first twenty years of the University was for students to govern themselves, including establishing codes of conduct that they enforced themselves. Beyond the Honor and Judiciary Committees, there was a broader implication to the notion: that students were responsible for their own destiny, and in fact could make it.

So in 1988–1989, the Glee Club was at another turning point. The rise of the a cappella groups had sapped some of its distinctiveness even as they provided reason for more talented singers to attend the University of Virginia and join the Glee Club. The University had established a set of supporting concepts, principles, and processes that enabled student groups to function well on their own without support from the academic machinery of the University. The Glee Club had built an endowment that neared $45,000.[18] And Loach, coming off a six-year term as chair of the department of music, was about to celebrate his twenty-fifth season as director of the Glee Club, a longer term than any of his predecessors by some thirteen years. Little could have prepared the group for what was to happen next.

1   "All Time Results," Virginia Sports, https://web.archive.org/web/20180626142326/http://www.virginiasports.com/sports/m-footbl/spec-rel/all-time-results.html, accessed June 19, 2018.
2   Don Loach, Introduction, Renaissance Festival Program (1981), 4.
3   Matthew P. Freeman, interview, February 29, 2020.
4   Ibid.
5   Ibid.
6   University of Virginia Board of Visitors minutes, January 30, 1982.
7   Steve Werner, "Union Gets OK for Concert," Cavalier Daily, March 22, 1983, 1.
8   Linda MacColl, "BSA and Glee Club to Appeal Council Appropriations Decision," Cavalier Daily, April 12, 1983, 1.
9   Katie Long, "Concern over Trips Voiced," Cavalier Daily, April 21, 1986, 1.
10   "Glee Club Weekends with Mount Holyoke," University Glee Club Bulletin 14, no. 1 (Spring 1987): 2–3.
11   Charles Wise, "Letter from the President," University Glee Club Bulletin 14, no. 1 (Spring 1987): 3.
12   "Endowment," University Glee Club Bulletin 14, no. 1 (Spring 1987): 4.
13   Mickey Rapkin, Pitch Perfect: The Quest for Collegiate A Capella Glory (New York: Penguin, 2008), 100.
14   Ibid., 104.
15   He was talking about poetry, which is not quite the same as choral singing but closely related, especially for many eighteen- to twenty-one-year-old University men.
16   UVA Student Council, "Agreement for a Contracted Independent Organization, 2018–2019," https://studentengagement.virginia.edu/sites/studentactivities.virginia.edu/files/2018-2019_CIO_Agreement.pdf, accessed September 28, 2021.
17   In FY 2018, the University of Virginia endowment was valued at $6.9 billion, more than the endowments of the next three largest Virginia schools (University of Richmond, Virginia Commonwealth University, and Washington and Lee University) combined. For reference, Virginia Tech's endowment stood at $1.14 billion, and

William and Mary's at $935,000; "U.S. and Canadian Institutions Listed by Fiscal Year (FY) 2018 Endowment Market Value and Change in Endowment Market Value from FY 2017 to FY 2018," National Association of College and University Business Officers and Commonfund Institute, https://www.nacubo.org/-/media/Nacubo/Documents/EndowmentFiles/2019-Endowment-Market-Values--Final-Feb-10.ashx (PDF), accessed April 8, 2019.

18 "Glee Club Endowment" (graph), *Virginia Glee Club Bulletin* 15, no. 1 (Spring 1989): 4.

 AN ECHO AND INDEPENDENCE

The 1988–1989 season started like many others had in the preceding ten years. The fall concert (now branded the Kickoff Concert) featured the Mary Baldwin College Choir and advertised the forty-eighth annual Christmas concert, a spring performance with the College of William and Mary, a new Renaissance Festival, a Concert on the Lawn, and a Finals concert. The Kickoff program was lighter, with Thomas Weelkes's "Hark, All Ye Lovely Saints" and other light works on the first half, and Britten's *The Ballad of Little Musgrave and Lady Barnard* alongside Richard Genée's opera parody "Insalata Italiana" and a Gilbert and Sullivan collaboration with Mary Baldwin on the second half. The light program stood in stark contrast to the 1987 opener with Smith, which had included Handel's *Zadok the Priest*, works by Sweelinck and Poulenc, and a return of Randall Thompson's *Tarantella* and David Davis's *Summer Songs*.

In retrospect, it's tempting to read the 1987 program as a recapitulation of past Glee Club glories and the 1988 as a capitulation to popular tastes. It is possible that the two programs simply reflected the relative skill levels of the two choirs. But the 1988 program also calls to mind Loach's remarks from ten years prior in the "What Record Label Are You On?" interview: "The selection of music for all-male chorus is limited, and 'we found ourselves having to repeat the same pieces every four years or so,' says Loach." With this program did the Glee Club turn a corner toward lighter repertoire or was it the end of the line for Loach and men's choruses?

It is impossible to know with certainty what Loach might have intended at the beginning of the season while programming the Kickoff Concert, but we do know that in the fall of 1988, an ad hoc committee of the McIntire Department of Music convened to restructure the University's choral groups. The committee's full membership included Donald Loach, then current department chair Marita McClymonds, and other members of the faculty.[1] It did not include Katherine Mitchell-Parker, the director of the Virginia Women's Chorus, or any student representatives.[2]

The first inkling of what was to follow came in the form of a three-by-five-inch index card. Mailed to the homes of the Glee Club officers over Thanksgiving weekend, the cards invited them to a meeting with Loach following the Christmas concerts that year. "It was sort of cryptic," recalls Larry Mueller, then serving as vice president.[3]

The Glee Club gave its forty-eighth annual Christmas concerts on Friday and Saturday, December 2–3, 1988. The following Wednesday, shortly before Finals, the music department's ad hoc committee announced its plan to reorganize the choral programs. Under the plan, the existing Virginia Glee Club, Virginia Women's Chorus, and University Singers would be realigned into two mixed-voice ensembles. The larger group, planned as an eighty-voice chorus, would consist of the Glee Club and Women's Chorus membership, while the University Singers would be reduced in size to a forty-voice chamber ensemble. The music department said in its announcement:

> The primary point by far is the desire of the music faculty to
> improve its educational mission. It is . . . important for capa-
> ble performers to come to grips with some of the significant
> works from the vastly superior repertoire for mixed voices.[4]

There would be no more single-sex choruses at the University. The change hit like a punch to the gut. This was *their group*, and it was being taken away without any consultation. The officers were dumbfounded by the proposal, particularly the part that suggested that two mixed choruses would be "more economical" and would fund a part-time jazz instructor. Was this really about faculty salaries? Why were they hearing about this change as a finished decision—why hadn't the students who ran the groups been consulted? And was this now the end of 117 years of musical tradition?

The Glee Club officers were stunned to realize that Loach had been part of the committee that made the recommendations. Reaching out to other faculty, they found little support. Professor Thomas MacCracken responded on December 12 to their appeal for help with a letter in which he wrote:

> In my opinion, the crucial point to keep in mind about the music department's decision to reorganize the choral program is that this is a curricular matter. It is therefore appropriate that such a decision be made by the faculty rather than by the students enrolled (or otherwise participating) in the courses affected by it. I find it essentially analogous to another recent decision whereby the number of semesters of music history required for the music major was increased from two to three.[5]

There were other considerations at work beyond the "educational mission," which became clear when the first responses from the music department were published following the winter break. An article in the *Cavalier Daily* on January 24, 1989, quoted McClymonds as calling into question the feasibility of single-sex groups at all:

> McClymonds said the University is one of the last institutions to keep choral groups segregated by sex. "Mixed choral groups are the natural and normal structure, especially since [the University] is now mixed," she said.[6]

In this, McClymonds was partly correct. As noted above, many women's choruses had been eliminated or become mixed-voice as formerly single-sex institutions went coed. Of the oldest men's glee clubs in the United States, Yale (founded in 1861) had gone coed in 1970 shortly after beginning to admit women, and Wesleyan and Princeton followed suit. However, many more schools retained single-sex choruses, including Harvard, University of Michigan, University of Pennsylvania, Amherst, Cornell, Union College, and Lehigh (all founded prior to 1871), all surviving until the present day. In retrospect, the extinction of men's glee clubs looks less inevitable.

The December 7 communication presented the change as a *fait accompli*. After all, Loach said of the committee's work that "we felt we were dealing with a curricular thing."[7] But the announcement was met with deep resistance by the officers of both groups. The Glee Club in particular was aware of its history and its legacy of male choral performance, and it was fiercely proud of its student leadership. Bruce Kothmann, who was the unlucky president of the group, wrote in an editorial in January 1989:

> The current choral groups are almost entirely student-run. Students handle correspondence, prepare budgets, arrange for printing of programs and posters, prepare for concerts, manage both foreign and domestic tours and perform countless other tasks which allow these groups to exist . . .
>
> Students were never consulted in the decision-making process. It is clear that these groups are run primarily by students and, in the case of the Glee Club, existed for 100 years independent of the music department.[8]

While much of the student resistance to the changes can be read in the context of organizational pride, an equal share likely accrues to student self-governance. Put simply, the student leaders and members of the Glee Club and Women's Chorus felt that they had a substantial say in the destiny of their singing groups by virtue of the sweat equity they built in running them.

Students put forward a counterproposal that was basically the status quo: keep the University Singers as a mixed chorus option, maintain the historical single-sex groups, and continue the joint concerts between them to give more opportunities for the members to experience the mixed chorus repertoire. Business manager Steve Billcheck told the *Cavalier Daily*, "We agree with the department's position and what they're trying to do" (in deepening the educational opportunities), but "our goal is to remain in the music department, but as separate groups."[9]

Whatever the cause, the students acted quickly to ensure that the music department's plan would not be accomplished without further consideration. They did so by focusing on four areas: the library, student opinion, institutional support, and the endowment.

The first mission was the riskiest. The Glee Club's library of men's choral music resided in a closet adjacent to their rehearsal space in room B-012 in Old Cabell Hall. Without the music, the group would have had a steep hill to climb to remain an independent performing entity. So late one night, an anonymous group of club members entered the building and moved the library to a secret location, with the thought that at least they could keep their options open a little longer.

Student opinion required more direct action, across a variety of fronts. Kothmann and Andrea Kahn, the Women's Chorus president, manned tables on the Lawn, asking students to sign petitions to maintain the "existing choral organizations," an effort they dubbed "ECHO." The petition drive both raised awareness and garnered hundreds of signatures in favor of ECHO. And Kothmann wrote an editorial that appeared in the *Cavalier Daily* making the case for ECHO and asking students to support the effort.

The groups' executive officers combined the student outreach with appeals to other stakeholders on Grounds. The officers appealed to the assistant dean of students, Mary Alice Sullivan, who noted, "Many students feel that there has not been enough cooperation between the administration and the students. We're here to work with [students] and discuss issues that affect them." The students also reached out to Alumni Hall, reconnecting with Gilbert "Gilly" J. Sullivan, who had been the director of the Alumni Association since 1958 and who had helped them establish the endowment in 1979. The students found Gilly sympathetic to their arguments, and he became an important supporter over the next few months.

The most significant support provided by Alumni Hall was its defense of the Glee Club's endowment. The fund, valued at that time around $45,000, was targeted by both sides. The music department argued that the fund belonged to them since it was raised to support a curricular group. The Glee Club countered that the fund had been specifically donated to support the University of Virginia Glee Club, since most of the money had been raised and donated for student tour support.

Ultimately Gilly and the others in Alumni Hall, including Alumni Fund associate director Bonnie Ford, found the Glee Club's argument more compelling, partly because they did more research. They were able to confirm that the Glee Club had not been an official curricular option until the 1970s, having many years of student-led history. They refused the music department's claim on the funds.

By the time the students were granted a meeting with the ad hoc committee on January 25, the tide had shifted in favor of the students. They had confirmed ownership of their music and their endowment; the associate dean of students and Alumni Hall were publicly supportive; and the student council had unanimously passed a resolution supporting ECHO.[10] All this momentum likely influenced the final compromise, which was announced in mid-February.

The single-sex groups would keep their identities but lose their curricular status within the music department. A new, small, mixed-voice ensemble, Coro Virginia, would be formed, allowing the University Singers to remain the larger mixed-voice ensemble. The Glee Club and the Women's Chorus could retain their CIO status and apply for student activity fee fund allocations but would receive no more investment from the music department. McClymonds stated that "to enrich, upgrade and maintain the single-sex organizations would delay the realization of other plans that are part of the departmental priorities." Under the terms of the CIO agreement, the groups could no longer use "University of Virginia" in their official names; the Glee Club would now simply be known as the Virginia Glee Club. Kothmann noted that the compromise did not guarantee them access to practice or performance space, which would be a priority. He also stated that "the Glee Club will remain a viable organization. We're ready to take whatever steps we have to [to] make sure the Glee Club stays around the University."[11]

So the groups maintained their independence, their identities, traditions, and endowments. They had the support of the University community and had upheld the importance of student self-governance. The Glee Club had a clear path forward.

Unfortunately, what they didn't have was a director.

There is little contemporary documentation of Loach's state of mind regarding the controversy, aside from his admission considering the amount of student input in the decision that "we might have thought about it a little more."[12] But it was quite clear that Loach was done with conducting a men's chorus, one way or the other. The reduction in depth of the Glee Club schedule from the early 1980s through 1988 suggests that Loach's ambitions now lay elsewhere, as did the increased inclusion of the University Singers in international touring. At any rate, he took a leave of absence in the spring of 1989, and so the issue was forced: there had to be a new conductor.

The group had to scramble to find musical leadership, for the first time since 1921. Fortunately there were candidates close at hand. The conducting duties for the spring semester were shared by University professor Scott De-Veaux, normally a specialist in American music and jazz, and Loach's assistant conductor Michael Butterman. Butterman, by now a graduate student in the music department, had been an executive officer of the group as an undergrad, serving as secretary and vice president, and had inhabited 5 West Lawn in 1987–1988. His course schedule would not permit him to take sole charge of the club, but with help from DeVeaux in the spring of 1989 and fellow graduate student Cheryl Brown-West in the fall of the following season, he was able to provide some much-needed continuity. His familiarity with the club's traditional repertoire and his already well-developed conducting skills were significant assets, as was his identity as a "Glee Club guy," which was important for settling the hurt feelings of the membership as they transitioned to independence.[13] Also important, as a graduate student he maintained some connection to the department and was able to ensure the club's continued access to rehearsal and performance facilities, though not always without compromises.

The club was able, with DeVeaux's and Butterman's leadership, to finish out the 1988–1989 season, including mounting the third (and final) Renaissance Festival. It took some diplomacy to ensure that the guest groups, which included the Yale Collegium Musicum under the direction of Paul Walker, would continue to participate after the Glee Club's change in status. The Glee Club's repertoire was respectable, including Byrd's *Mass for Three Voices* and "Ave Verum Corpus," a set of other English Renaissance anthems, madrigals, and chansons by Orlando di Lasso and Clément Janequin. The Glee Club still had a part of their budget for the year from the music department and spent a good amount of it on catering, programs, and posters for the event.

The Virginia Women's Chorus was less fortunate. With a fraction of the endowment enjoyed by Glee Club, they had no capacity to continue to pay a music director, and so reluctantly the Women's Chorus performed its final 1989 spring concert before ceasing operations.

So ended the year of separation, with one chorus on indefinite hiatus and one still standing but facing a continuous struggle to find its feet. For the first time in sixty-eight years, the Glee Club had no faculty conductor and no association with the music department. But one good thing did come of the year's events: though the choruses remained separate, Bruce Kothmann married Andrea Kahn in 1991. Their daughter served as business manager of the Virginia Women's Chorus in 2017–2018.[14]

The Glee Club's members during this season were at least as important as its student and musical leadership in keeping the organization going. The challenge of going up against the music department and, if not winning, then at least fighting to a draw and an undeniable victory for student self-governance forged bonds of brotherhood among the members. It was no accident that the fall of 1989 saw a group of club guys band together to rent a house at 505 Valley Road; for the first time in many years, the club had a place to call home. The clubhouse underwent continuous occupancy through 2011, and club returned after some long-overdue renovation.

New and recently developed traditions and in-jokes abounded. Wafna remained a beloved mascot. The club even gained a motto, albeit through adversity. There was a fall "roll" to the northeast to sing at Harvard that didn't go well; the Radcliffe chorus didn't realize they were getting a student-run group with no faculty supervision.[15] The bus ride home was long. In the middle of it, in the dead of night, a very frazzled Chris Walker, possibly worse for the wear, who was by now Butterman's assistant conductor as well as the driving musical force behind the Hullabahoos, got on the microphone. What followed was a long, heartfelt, and astonishingly profane monologue about the ingratitude of the host group and the fortitude of the Glee Club. Those who were there remember few details of what was said, but they do recall the motto they seized from Walker's rambling, or at least its initials: VMHLB. In later years the club would publicly embrace the motto in unabbreviated form as "Virginia's Messengers of Harmony, Love and Brotherhood," but in its early years it was a secret token, a combination of handshake and Greek letter to identify member to member.

The 1990–1991 season saw the club embrace something like normalcy, but still with an intense feeling of brotherhood. Butterman, who had completed his coursework for his master's the year before, was able to take on full-time directorship of the club while he worked on auditioning for his next career move. Butterman combined familiar and new works in the first season's programming. One returning work was "Poor Wayfaring Stranger," in an arrangement by American composer Douglas Moore with amendments by Donald Loach. Loach had programmed the piece on the 1974–1975 European tour; Butterman pulled it out for the Glee Club's first rehearsal night. After the group sang through "Poor Wayfaring Stranger," Donald Webb, a first-year student who had joined the rehearsal just in time for that piece, stood up and addressed the group. He said his father had passed away the year before, but that "Poor Wayfaring Stranger" reminded him that he had not left but gone home. He also declared that the group was now his family.

The leadership of the group planned fall and spring trips and hosted women's chorus collaborations at home in the fall and the spring. The fall trip wasn't without incident: arriving at Goucher College for a multigroup collaboration with the Goucher Women's Chorus and the chorus of College of Notre-Dame in Baltimore, the men of the Glee Club stayed in empty dorm rooms at Goucher but managed to almost get into a fight with drunken, belligerent Goucher men (who had been admitted to the former women's college only a few years previously). Club member Jim Wiser was near the altercation, which began when a Goucher man accused a club guy of trying to steal "their" girls. Wiser went to reason with the Goucher man and learned that he was a Naval ROTC recruit. Since Wiser—also an ROTC man—outranked the Goucher freshman, the incident was resolved without violence.

The real high point of the year was undoubtedly the Fiftieth Annual Christmas Concerts. The club performed three shows, two Friday night performances at St. Paul's Episcopal Church and a Saturday show at Old Cabell Hall. The performances featured accompaniment from Yvaine Duisit on organ and a small string ensemble. Seizing on the opportunity of the significant anniversary, club president Stephen Sweeney reached out to the governor of Virginia, L. Douglas Wilder, who responded with a certificate of recognition:

> WHEREAS, the Virginia Glee Club of the University of Virginia is proud to host its 50th annual Christmas Concerts on December 7 and December 8, 1990; and
>
> WHEREAS, 1990 marks the 120th season of concert performance by the Virginia Glee Club at the University of Virginia; and
>
> WHEREAS, the music and talents of the Virginia Glee Club inspire those who attend the concerts; and
>
> WHEREAS, the songs and melodies sung by the Virginia Glee Club express the magic of the holidays and carry the message of joy to the world;
>
> NOW, THEREFORE, I, Lawrence Douglas Wilder, Governor, do hereby recognize the VIRGINIA GLEE CLUB, congratulate the members who are dedicated to the traditions celebrated during this 120th season, and send to each my very best wishes for a memorable 50th Christmas Concert series.

Most significantly, the concert was recorded and released on cassette, marking the first Glee Club recording offered for sale since 1972 and *A Shadow's*

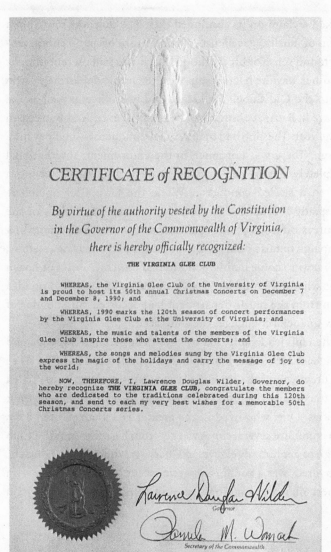

FIGURE 23. Glee Club Certificate of Recognition for the Fiftieth Annual Christmas Concerts, signed by Virginia governor L. Douglas Wilder.

on the Sundial. All told, the concerts did a considerable amount to raise the profile of the Glee Club in the community, and perhaps more importantly to lift the group's collective self-image. Rounding out the season, the spring featured collaborations at home and in Massachusetts with the Wellesley College Choir, performing the Bach cantata "Gott ist mein König."

So the club had found its footing after its separation from the music department and staked a claim on its continued existence that was rooted in a continued tradition of musical excellence, a long history of men's choral repertoire, and a newfound sense of brotherhood. But it was still on tenterhooks in virtually every other way. Its relationship with the music department, who controlled access to the Old Cabell Hall stage and box office as well as the club's rehearsal space in B-012, continued to be frosty as ever. And Butterman left at the end of the year. The club had to find a new conductor—and pay him.

Pay was the rub. There was not much in the endowment; international touring was completely out of the question, to say nothing of paying a reasonable salary to a skilled conductor. While the Glee Club members had developed a steady routine for fundraising, availing themselves of the Alumni Hall resources offered by Gilly Sullivan to contact their alums in a fall telephone campaign to raise funds and to publish twice-yearly newsletters, alumni money was slow to come in. Many alums had fond memories of Loach and no context for what the group had just been through; some had no idea that the separation from the music department had occurred, and no idea of the staggering new financial challenges the club faced.

Undaunted, the club leadership, led by president Stephen Sweeney and president-elect Michael McCullough, mounted a conductor search, the Glee Club's first ever. It drew a number of qualified candidates, and two were invited to Charlottesville to conduct the group in rehearsals to get a feeling for their skills and capabilities. One, who lived in the greater DC metropolitan area, would have had to commute several times weekly from his other gig; the Club couldn't pay enough to get him to relocate to Charlottesville full time. But the other, whom Club hired, was a young, energetic recent college graduate with an affinity for Robert Shaw and a sardonic sense of humor. His name was John Robert Liepold.

---

1 McClymonds had been appointed chair of the music department by the Board of Visitors; University of Virginia Board of Visitors minutes, March 18, 1988.
2 Mitchell-Parker, as an undergraduate, had founded the Virginia Belles. She would remain engaged with the Virginia Women's Chorus, returning in the 2000s to direct the group. (She now is also known as KaeRenae Mitchell.)
3 Interview with Larry Mueller, June 8, 2019.

4   Cited in Bruce Kothmann, "ECHO Fighting to Keep Existing Choral Groups," *Cavalier Daily*, January 24, 1989, 3.

5   Thomas MacCracken, letter to the officers of the choral groups, December 12, 1988.

6   Marita McClymonds, quoted in Karl Fitzgerald, "Choirs, Faculty to Meet," *Cavalier Daily*, January 24, 1989, 1ff.

7   Donald Loach, quoted in ibid.

8   Kothmann, "ECHO Fighting."

9   Steve Billcheck, quoted in Fitzgerald, "Choirs, Faculty to Meet."

10   Jennifer Bermant, "Student Council Passes Two Proposals," *Cavalier Daily*, January 25, 1989, 1.

11   Michelle Mabe, "Compromise Reached on Choral Issue," *Cavalier Daily*, February 15, 1989, 1.

12   Loach, quoted in Fitzgerald, "Choirs, Faculty to Meet."

13   Butterman is now a professional symphonic conductor and, as of 2019, is music director of the Boulder Philharmonic Orchestra, the Shreveport Symphony, and the Pennsylvania Philharmonic. He was a diploma laureate in the Prokofiev International Conducting Competition and a recipient of a Seiji Ozawa Fellowship, studying at Tanglewood with Robert Spano, Jorma Panula, and Maestro Ozawa.

14   "Alumna Spotlight: Andrea Kahn-Kothmann," *Virginia Women's Chorus Newsletter*, Winter 2018.

15   The Glee Club has called its weekend trips to perform at other colleges "rolls" since at least the 1980s, and maybe longer, both to distinguish them from weeklong tours and in homage to the many hours spent in buses and other motor vehicles along the way.

23 L-L-LIEPOLD!

John Liepold was not much older than the fourth-year Glee Club members who hired him. Having finished his undergraduate education at Wesleyan University in 1988, he came to the Glee Club with a wealth of choral experience. He studied at Wesleyan under Neely Bruce and, perhaps more important, spent time at choral conducting workshops with Robert Shaw, who had by this time become a dean of American choral leadership.[1] Liepold brought his techniques as well as his philosophy—and some of his programming—to the Virginia Glee Club.

Liepold also brought energy, entrepreneurship, and a keen sense of promotion and of the importance of maintaining University connections for the Glee Club. Within the first week of the club's return to school, they performed at University president John Casteen's welcoming reception for incoming first-year students, and if the repertoire was light ("Come Again, Sweet Love" and the Virginia songs), it was still an early exposure to the University community. A similar gig followed in early October at Woodberry Forest School, a nearby prep school that had been attended by Glee Club member John Vick, then in his second year—and which had been Liepold's first postgraduation job. An appearance at the annual dinner of the Lawn Society, a group of University donors, followed a few days later.

By the time the Glee Club gave its first official concert of the season, the Kickoff Concert in Old Cabell Hall on October 19, the group had dug into its repertoire for the season. After a set from their guest group, the Glee Club began with Maurice Duruflé's "Ubi Caritas" and "Tota Pulchra Es," then performed the first half of the Tallis *Lamentations of Jeremiah*.

They then premiered "Come, Heavy Sleep," a newly commissioned work by composer (and Liepold's classmate) Benjamin Broening. The work, which Liepold announced as the first in the Virginia Glee Club Series for Men's Voices, is a setting of madrigal text by John Dowland that moves from a chant-influenced passage in minor mode into a more polychromatic setting that borders on dissonance, flirting with major tonality, and finally concludes on a unison in octaves.[2] The work, significantly more modern than most of the Glee Club's repertoire to that point, sounded a newly adventurous note in their programming, as did the promise of more commissioned works to come.

The effect of the Broening was striking, especially after Liepold announced that, in the tradition of newly premiered works, the Glee Club would now perform it a second time so the audience could listen to it more closely. This came as a surprise to audience and singers alike, and the second performance, as heard on the recording of the performance, has an edge and intensity that startles.[3] The set closed with two spirituals: "Poor Wayfaring Stranger," which had taken on a yearning, plaintive quality over the course of six weeks of rehearsals, and "Soon-ah Will Be Done." Liepold conducted "Soon-ah" as a study in spiritual apocalypse, with the refrain sung quickly, quietly, and fiercely and the verses sung with a booming forte. Liepold asked for a slightly covered quality in the quiet parts, an affect that Robert Shaw called "hooty," and the effect was otherworldly. To observers, the performance was electric. It was clear that Liepold was putting his own artistic stamp on the group—and getting results.

The concert was followed by a trip to Villanova and a collaboration with the Villanova Voices. En route the bus driver got lost and drove in the wrong direction for some time until Glee Club member Nathan Moore reoriented them by sighting Polaris. This earned Moore the nickname "Pathfinder," which he embraced with periodic newsletters that were titled "Notes from the Path"; this eventually became the title of the official Glee Club newsletter.

The Christmas concerts that followed the Kickoff Concert featured a full program, with settings of "O Magnum Mysterium" by Victoria, Gabrieli, and Poulenc, a reprise of the Duruflé "Deux Motets," and two large-scale works, Duruflé's *Messe "Cum Jubilo"* and Rutter's *Gloria*. The latter, in a symbolic gesture, was performed together with the University Singers under Donald Loach's baton. The University Singers had remained a sizable group, but at this point in their history much of their male membership overlapped with the Glee Club, raising challenges for Christmas concert programming. The joint concert was meant to ease tensions while pointing to the very real challenge that sharing Old Cabell Hall would bring.

The second half of the concert also included an appearance by the Virginia Gentlemen and a set of winter songs and carols. But first came the already infamous audience-participation rendition of "The Twelve Days of Christmas." As in years past, Glee Club fans positioned themselves for the battle of the three French hens versus everyone else, but this year the Glee Club itself stole the show. On the final rundown of twelve days of gifts, the Glee Club members rushed forward and surrounded Liepold, holding the final note of "five golden rings" in four-part harmony as Glee Club vice president Paul Stancil walked on stage with a silver tray holding a bottle of champagne and two flutes.[4] Stancil then opened the bottle and toasted with Liepold, whereupon the Glee Club returned to the risers to conclude the concert. It was a dramatic, funny, and slightly unhinged moment that brought the house down.

There was one more significant moment in the concert. In the final set of songs and carols, Liepold programmed an old song made famous by Dartmouth College, Frederic Field Bullard's "Winter Song." Prior to the Fifty-First Annual Christmas Concert, the work had only been performed once in a Virginia Glee Club concert, by the University of Pittsburgh Glee Club in 1968. As performed by the Virginia group, it was a hit. The lyrics, which speak of "the cup [at] the lip / in the pledge of fellowship," caught the new sentiment of the Glee Club, which blended musicianship and fraternity in more or less equal measures.

One significant aspect of the group's musicianship was Liepold's use of Shaw's distinctive conducting techniques. These included musical exercises, such as singing the text with short pitches on nonsense syllables (staccato on *doo*) and *count singing*, in which the singers sing the beat number in place of the text ("one and two and tee and four"), with the substitution of "tee" for "three" so that the consonant cluster would not slow the singers down. Liepold also echoed Shaw's persuasive speeches. A favorite was a Shaw saying about the power of choral performance being akin to the arrival of the Holy Spirit, provided that the singers had done the necessary hard work to be ready: "If you want the Dove to descend, you have to clean out the birdcage."

The bolder profile of the Glee Club was reflected in a new graphical identity, driven largely by Liepold and assisted by the vice president, who was responsible for the Glee Club's publicity.[5] There had not really been a distinctive graphic identity for the Glee Club prior to the mid-1960s. While it's hard to say for sure—posters and other large printed ephemera are rarer than programs in the historian's archives—all the printed matter before 1965 is simple, generally consistently typeset, probably in a University house style. This started to change once Loach took over leadership of the group. As early as Christmas 1965, and maybe earlier, the Y conductor glyph started to appear on Glee Club printed matter. Designed in the International Style, the icon was clear and recognizable, and it put a new graphic element into the club's printed materials. The Y conductor glyph appears often through the 1960s and 1970s, most strikingly as the central design element in the poster for the 1971 Concert on the Lawn. But it was not used consistently, and by the mid-1970s it had largely disappeared in favor of graphic elements intended to reinforce the theme of each individual concert: woodcuts for concerts of medieval and Renaissance music, sheet music for a concert of Viennese works, silhouettes of Jefferson and images of the Lawn for University functions.

By the 1980s, a hand-drawn style had begun to emerge. The iconic Christmas wreath, as shown on the cover of the Christmas program from 1982, is colorful, rendered by hand, and generally less formal than the 1970s programs. The Kickoff Concert program cover from 1988 is even less formal, looking sketchy and even cartoonish. Use of both of these designs would persist into the early 1990s. Liepold took a hands-on approach to the design of programs, letterhead, and other printed matter. He designed a distinctive new logotype, set in bold Palatino, the word *the* in small caps with a thick rule beneath, always either black on white or white on black. He also increased the use of photography in publicity materials, including the first use of a group photograph in a poster.

The bolder branding appeared beginning in the spring of 1992 with the materials for the Tour of the South. The itinerary took the group to destinations throughout the southern states, including Chapel Hill, Atlanta, Athens, Georgia, and New Orleans. The repertoire for the tour included much of the fall concert material, including the Tallis *Lamentations* and "Come, Heavy Sleep." New for the group was "De profundis" by Estonian composer Arvo Pärt, a slow-moving, chant-inspired work with organ and percussion accompaniment. It could be performed at only a few stops on the tour given the requirement for an organ, and the group had to bring a gong with them on the bus—possibly a first for a Glee Club tour.

THE VIRGINIA GLEE CLUB

JOHN LIEPOLD, CONDUCTOR

with

THE SMITH COLLEGE GLEE CLUB
Lucinda Thayer, Conductor

and

THE VIRGINIA GLEE CLUB CHAMBER ORCHESTRA

BACH Cantata BWV 4, "Christ lag in Todesbanden" • BRUCKNER Motets
Works by Elliott Carter, Pablo Casals, Arvo Pärt, Thomas Tallis, Tomás Luis de Victoria and others

8:15 PM • Saturday, March 28, 1992
Old Cabell Hall • University of Virginia
Tickets: $5 General / $3 Students and Senior Citizens
Box Office: (804) 924-3984 • Information: (804) 296-4852

FIGURE 24. Spring 1992 concert poster.

Another new work that entered the Glee Club's repertoire at this time was a familiar melody in a new arrangement. The Glee Club had previously sung the folk tune "Shenandoah" in arrangements by Harvard Glee Club conductor Archibald T. Davison (during the Loach years) or Yale Glee Club conductor Marshall Bartholomew (as far back as 1953). But Liepold had heard a new arrangement of the work for SATB voices and commissioned its arranger, University of Richmond choir and glee club director James Erb, to create a version for five-part men's chorus. The result was both more exposed, beginning with the first verse sung as a solo line by the tenors, and richer, featuring echoic writing in two and three parts before resolving to a high, quiet coda signaling the river's disappearance in the distance. The commission became a staple of the Glee Club's repertoire, appearing on seven out of the eleven recordings produced by the Glee Club since 1992.

The tour itinerary for the Tour of the South was a combination of planning and happenstance. In early 1992, Liepold got a call from a man with a thick southern accent, who identified himself as "Hah Bran," and who asked if the Glee Club still performed "*the* Ave Maria." Assured that they did, the man, who turned out to be Mississippi state senator Wendell Hobdy Bryan II, invited the group to perform at the state house in Jackson.[6]

On the first day of spring break, the club members piled onto the tour bus, a charter from Leisure Unlimited Vacations, wearing their newly manufactured white Glee Club ball caps embroidered with "VMHLB." The first four days of the tour on the LUV bus were relatively uneventful, with the performances in Chapel Hill, Atlanta, and Athens all uneventful. All the performances on the tour were hosted in churches, with the Atlanta stop actually part of the Sunday worship service. Following Athens, the group traveled to Oxford, Mississippi, arriving around eight p.m., only to find that the town's one bar closed at nine. The group opted for other entertainment, with a number of them decamping for a moonlight visit to Rowan Oak, the former house of William Faulkner.[7]

The following day, the group traveled to Jackson, where they entered the Mississippi State Senate Chambers just before lunch and performed the Biebl "Ave Maria" and the customary medley of "Virginia, Hail, All Hail" and "The Good Old Song." They immediately got back on the bus and rode another three hours to Loyola University in New Orleans, the group's energy flagging somewhat as they faced the prospect of their fifth performance in three days. Jim Heaney, the Glee Club's business manager, got on the microphone and announced to the group that they had arrived in New Orleans on St. Patrick's

Day and proceeded to teach them utterances in "Cajun Irish," including "Airoosh Spreeng! Frashuncleen as a weesol!"

Despite the comic relief, the mood was grim, and the first half of the evening's concert at the Loyola Chapel, consisting of the "Alle psallite" processional, Duruflé's "Ubi Caritas," settings of "O vos omnes" by Victoria and Casals, and the Tallis *Lamentations*, was challenging and suffered a few pitch problems. At intermission, the group retreated to their impromptu green room, a hot chamber off the rear balcony near the organ, and vented their frustrations. Tyler Magill then addressed the group and exhorted them to better performance, saying, "This is our opportunity for the Dove to descend." The second half of the performance, including "Come, Heavy Sleep," madrigals and spirituals, Erb's "Shenandoah," and the Biebl "Ave Maria," was spirited and energetic, yielding the group a standing ovation at the end. The performances were recorded and later issued on cassette under the title "A Dove in the House."

The jubilant Glee Club members were hosted by the local University of Virginia alumni chapter for a short reception, and then they spilled out to a nearby takeout bar, where they acquainted themselves with New Orleans's lax open container laws but otherwise were relatively well behaved. The following day, the only day of the tour that did not involve travel or a concert performance, was a slightly different story. It started off promisingly enough, with club members experiencing many of the attractions of the city, including fried alligator bites, beignets, the voodoo cemeteries, and more. There were moments of musical ambassadorship. Brian Menard recalls:

> I was on the trolley heading down St. Charles with a group
> of Glee Clubbers and someone had the grand idea of singing
> "Nunc Dimittis" while we rode. We had at least four others,
> covering all five parts, though I think there were more. Might
> have had any or all of Kevin Dixon, Nathan Moore, John
> Vick, Matt Benko and Jim Heaney there, as well as any others. Anyway, as hoarse as we were from so many concerts, we
> started singing and the trolley got quiet as we shared some of
> the VMHLB Dove with fellow trolley travelers for a couple
> minutes of metropolitan commute.[8]

After dinner and various stops, including Preservation Hall, many club members convened at Pat O'Brien's Piano Lounge, where they asked the pianist to play "Auld Lang Syne" so that they could perform "The Good Old Song." For some, the night lasted for many hours afterward.

The reckoning came the next morning, as bleary club members piled into bus and van for a performance at a prep school on the other side of Lake Pontchartrain. The group's vocal quality was impaired by lack of sleep, with the *Lamentations of Jeremiah* going flat by as much as a minor third. After the performance, sitting on the middle school–sized seats in the cafeteria for lunch, one normally quiet member broke into hysterical, uncontrollable laughter, with others trying but failing to console him. Later, after the group was back on the bus and on the way home, someone asked him what had made him lose his composure. "Those poor kids," he replied.

On their return the Glee Club still had three more performances for the season. The spring concert featured a joint performance with the Smith College Glee Club including the Bach cantata "Christ lag in Todesbanden." The Concert on the Lawn included some familiar elements from the Loach and Butterman years, including "Old McDonald Had a Farm," but also featured a men's chorus arrangement of "Free Bird" by graduating Virginia Gentlemen member and arranger David Fouché.[9] Following a beach week trip to South Carolina, the Finals concert concluded the season.

FIGURE 25. The Virginia Glee Club performing Biebl's "Ave Maria," in the Mississippi State Senate Chambers, March 16, 1992.

Also following the tour, the Glee Club held officers' elections. An annual feature, by the early 1990s the elections had evolved into multiple-hour events featuring preplanned and spontaneous orations and heated debate on the pros and cons of the different candidates. The 1992 elections, held in a classroom in Wilson Hall, were notable for a speech from club member and Virginia Gentleman John Wright, who in describing the unique attributes of the Glee Club called it a "fraternity of talent." Although Wright was not elected, his use of the phrase (originally uttered by Brogan Sullivan) stuck and became part of the Glee Club's vocabulary for its invocation of both musicianship and brotherhood.

Both musicianship and brotherhood were significant themes of Liepold's first season, with the Tour of the South and the club's performances both serving as advertisements of the Glee Club's capabilities. The next season, though an off year for touring, would offer an even broader stage for the group's activities.

FIGURE 26. The Virginia Glee Club at the Mississippi state house in Jackson with state senator Hob Bryan, March 16, 1992.

1 "About," John Robert Liepold, Conductor, https://johnrobertliepold.com/, accessed June 2, 2019.

2 Liepold intended that the commission would be the first of a long series of commissioned works for men's voices; the group commissioned at least one new work per year for the following five years.

3 "Kickoff Concert" (recording), October 19, 1991, https://search.lib.virginia.edu/sources/uva_library/items/u1884198.

4 Likely, this was not French champagne. The Glee Club social managers had found that supplying cases of sparkling wine for the Christmas concert parties required a more modest budget. Stancil joked that the bottle they served, André, was "the Pepsi of Champagnes."

5 By this time, the Glee Club was designing and producing all their posters in-house, thanks to the desktop publishing revolution. The vice president would typically either design the posters, flyers, and programs himself or recruit a club volunteer, known as the "Computer Guy," to do it.

6 Hob Bryan (born 1952, elected to the Mississippi state senate for the seventh district since 1984), who had become acquainted with the Glee Club as a University of Virginia law student in the late 1970s, remains an active supporter and friend of the Virginia Glee Club and has served as a member of the Virginia Glee Club Alumni and Friends Association.

7 Other members of the group, opting for more traditional collegiate pursuits, invented the Glee Club's version of Beer Olympics (hammered throw, shotgun put, and so on) in their hotel room.

8 Brian Menard, in a comment on social media, July 11, 2019.

9 The "Foosh" arrangement opened with a plainchant that translated into Latin the line, "If I leave here tomorrow, will you still remember me?"

"THE FAVORITE PASSION OF MY SOUL": JEFFERSON'S 250TH

The 1992–1993 season started auspiciously enough. Morale was still high from the Tour of the South, and the membership had swelled to almost sixty members, up from forty-four in the 1990–1991 season. Over midsummer weekend, president Jim Heaney and the other executives had met with Liepold to plan the season, and it was a doozy.

The fall had a more or less normal schedule: a Kickoff Concert with the Radford University Chorale, a trip to Smith and Holyoke, the Fifty-Second Annual Christmas Concerts. The new year would prove much more unusual. April 13, 1993, marked Thomas Jefferson's 250th birthday, and a variety of celebrations had been planned to commemorate the occasion at the University, including an elaborate Founder's Day ceremony that would feature former Soviet premier Mikhail Gorbachev as the keynote speaker. The group explored the logistics of the day: Would the University like to have the Glee Club perform during the ceremony? Unfortunately, tensions with the music department were still high even five years after the Glee Club's separation, fueled by what the students perceived as unfair treatment and unequal access to resources. Whatever the reason, the Glee Club was not offered the performance spot, which was instead extended to the University Singers.

Liepold realized, however, that this opened other opportunities for the group to participate in the celebration of the day and found not one but three alternative performance venues: Monticello, the Jefferson Memorial, and the

Jefferson Hotel in Richmond. In typical Glee Club fashion, the group decided to take on all of them, on the same day.

But first came the fall performances. The repertoire was to be a variation on the theme of the prior year, with multiple settings of the story of David's lamentation for his son Absalom as the anchor for the Glee Club's set, along with a Parker/Shaw arrangement ("What Shall We Do with the Drunken Sailor?"), and Erb's "Shenandoah." The "David" set reached ambitiously from Josquin to Thomas Tomkins, to a shape-note setting by William Billings, to the premiere of a new setting of the Tomkins text, "When David Heard," by returning composer Benjamin Broening.[1] To get the Glee Club members properly motivated for their performance of the Billings, Liepold played them a cassette recording of a Sacred Harp convention singing the piece. The loud, fiercely independent polyphony was as compelling as the rural diction was faintly comical, but the club was able to capture something of the muscular strength of the Sacred Harp singers in their own performances.

The odd man out on the program was Paul Patterson's *Time Piece*. Once again Liepold's quirky programming had placed a complete curveball of a work alongside the carefully selected program. *Time Piece*, commissioned and performed by the King's Singers, was a meditation on the creation of clocks and time by God. It featured formless cosmic humming, a more conventional choral section, and an insanely complex fugue on the "ticks and tocks" that included vocal percussion, chimes, ringing alarms, phone operator quotes ("At the sound of the tone . . ."), free interjections of "Hurry up, please, it's time," ultimately brought to a halt by the voice of God (portrayed in the Glee Club's performance by new member Brett Posten) yelling "STOP!" The choral moment that followed ("Stop," said God, holding his head / "Clocks are bad news") became a byword that year. The piece brought down the house in Cabell Hall and received an enthusiastic, if also puzzled, reaction at Smith College, where the group performed it on tour.

There were also the customary collaborative performances; this year's selection was *Chichester Psalms*. The home concert collaboration with the Radford University Chorale featured a countertenor solo in the second movement, as Glee Club member Kevin Dixon had sung the work in his boy soprano days, but the part was sung by an alto member of the Smith College Glee Club on the road.

Christmas featured the customary mix of high art and seasonal cheer, including the club's performance of the "Gloria" from the *Missa Mater Patris* of

Josquin and a pair of "Ave Maria" settings, including one by Glee Club member Nathan Moore. This was the first of several compositions by current Glee Club members to appear in performance over the next several years. It also featured John Tavener's haunting setting of William Blake's "The Lamb."

The Christmas concerts also featured the arrival of a unique (and fictional) Glee Club member. Vihem Aeschlbie, who had been named the previous summer by Heaney after the Club's VMHLB motto, first "performed" as a first tenor, was inserted in the roster as an in-joke by Liepold and vice president Tim Jarrett so that the four sections would appear visually balanced. Aeschlbie would make other appearances in programs to balance out whichever section appeared shortest, and even got his own T-shirt the following year, courtesy of new member Lars Bjorn.

At the end of the winter break, the Glee Club made its first Jeffersonian performance of 1993 with an appearance in a ceremony at the Jefferson Memorial. The January 16 outdoor performance, an event sponsored by the Council for America's First Freedom and commemorating National Religious Freedom Day, was brief.[2] Assistant conductor Matt Benko led the group in Erb's "Shenandoah" and "America the Beautiful," Liepold being unavailable that weekend. Cameras from both MTV and HomeTeam Sports were there, though no footage has survived.[3] The gig was perhaps most noteworthy for a moment of silent reflection at Jefferson's statue before the performance, broken by Tyler Magill exclaiming, "No wonder he was able to accomplish so much! He was eighteen feet tall!"

The following weekend, the club went to River Road Church, Baptist, in Richmond, Virginia, for its spring semester rehearsal weekend. The performance at the end of the weekend, issued on cassette as *Music for a Noble Acoustic*, captures the fall repertoire of the group—the David set, the Josquin "Gloria," the "Ave Maria" set including the Biebl and Moore settings, "Shenandoah," and "Drunken Sailor"—in addition to one new piece, William Henry Smith's setting of "Ride the Chariot."

The other significant piece of new repertoire for the group was premiered at the spring concert and was the most ambitious commission yet. Liepold engaged his undergraduate mentor Neely Bruce, a professor of music at Wesleyan University, to write the work. Bruce looked for texts to set but found too many cases where Jefferson's own writing, while elegant on paper, proved unsuitable for choral settings.[4] The solution came in Jefferson's literary commonplace book, begun in his student years and maintained until his marriage.

In the book he wrote texts, poems, and passages from other writers that in-spired him, offering a unique perspective on the formation of Jefferson's mind. The resulting composition, *Young T.J.*, paired Jefferson's favorite quotations from Shakespeare, Nicholas Rowe, Edward Young, Congreve, Homer (in the Alexander Pope translation), and others with music inspired by early Ameri-can composers. Bruce had made a study of Billings's forthright harmonies and contrapuntal writing, and *Young T.J.* reflects both in ten short movements.

The Glee Club premiered *Young T.J.* at their spring concert, alongside the now-familiar "David" set, a new setting of the Neruda poem "Me gustas cuan-do callas" by graduating fourth-year student Burt Kann, and *The Testament of Freedom*.[5] The guest group, the University of Georgia Women's Glee Club, performed Peter J. Wilhousky's "Battle Hymn of the Republic" with Virginia. Vihem Aeschlbie sang second bass.

Eighteen days later, the group hopped aboard the LUV bus at 4:50 in the morning, bound for Monticello. The *Today Show* cast, including Matt Lauer, Willard Scott, and University of Virginia alum Katie Couric, was broadcast-ing from Monticello in commemoration of Jefferson's 250th birthday. In the predawn darkness the group assembled the risers on Mr. Jefferson's front lawn

FIGURE 27. Glee Club members with Katie Couric on the set of the *Today Show* at Monticello, April 13, 1993. From left: D. R. Tyler Magill, Mitch Harris, Scott Mohajeri Norris, Couric, Paul Stancil, Denis McNamara. Photo courtesy Paul Stancil.

and during the cuts to commercials sang "What Stronger Breastplate" and "Let There Be Music" from *Young T.J.* for the cameras. The director of the show asked them to remain in case they were needed for additional performances, so they quietly watched Katie Couric chatting with Matt Lauer. Several members recall an awkward but jovial conversation with Willard Scott in the Monticello men's room.

When they were finally released after a show-ending performance of Erb's "Shenandoah," they scrambled back onto the bus. Liepold gave the driver, Ray, instructions to "floor it." They were cutting it close for the arrival at their next destination, the Jefferson Memorial and a performance for President Clinton at the official celebration of Jefferson's birthday in the nation's capital. Exacerbating the tight connection, the driver got a little lost. Liepold awakened club secretary John McLaughlin and asked him, "We missed a turn. Can you find the fastest way to the monument?"

McLaughlin wrote in the club's newsletter the following fall:

> [As] a native Washingtonian, that wasn't so hard. Slightly more taxing, however, was the sprint from the exit ramp through the gate—smiling graciously at the 400 or so persons whose places we took in line as we were ushered through security clearance—to the waterside of the Memorial. On those steps, looking out over the wreath of cherry blossoms that surrounded the water, we sang six movements of *Young T.J.* . . . In his address, Mr. Clinton remarked that he enjoyed

FIGURE 28. Vihem Aeschlbie T-shirt, circa 1993, designed by Lars Bjorn, based on an illustration from the *Non Sequitur* comic strip by Wiley Miller.

the piece, especially its recognition of Mr. Jefferson's love of freedom.[6]

The club had cut it close indeed, and members nervously joked about the run from the bus, imagining Secret Service snipers with itchy trigger fingers. But the risky schedule paid off, with members not only able to sing for the president but also to shake hands with him and with Hillary Clinton.

The rest of the day's schedule was more relaxed, but not relaxing. The members climbed aboard the LUV bus once more and drove to Richmond to sing at a third Jefferson celebration, this time in the Jefferson Hotel. Performing *Young T.J.* and the final movement of *The Testament of Freedom*, they closed out a very long day in triumph.

Returning to the University that night, they compared notes with their colleagues in the University Singers who had sung for Gorbachev. Asked about the work they had sung, a setting of the Declaration of Independence by Judith Shatin, they merely shook their heads. "Jefferson wasn't a poet," one said. But the poetry of the works he preserved in his commonplace book would receive

FIGURE 29. Thomas Nassif (center) shaking hands with President Bill Clinton at the Jefferson Memorial, April 13, 1993.

one more performance, a taping for *Voice of America*. Just as with *Testament* fifty years earlier, *Young T.J.* would be broadcast far beyond Charlottesville.

The rest of the season saw the Glee Club moving beyond the Jeffersonian world. The Concert on the Lawn featured the usual off-kilter spring repertoire, including a men's chorus arrangement of the Rolling Stones' "You Can't Always Get What You Want," courtesy of graduating Virginia Gentlemen musical director John Navarrete. And members of the Glee Club joined other choirs at George Mason University in a performance of Orff's *Carmina Burana*, introducing a new generation of men to the inspiration for Wafna.

The following season began with a plan, hatched over brunch during the Midsummers party weekend in 1993: it was time for a recording.[7] And not just any recording. Liepold had planned the next season's repertoire around a rarely performed, never before recorded work by Cristóbal de Morales, his *Missa Ave Maria*. The programs would be filled out with other Marian settings, both familiar (Biebl, Mark Keller) and new (a seventeenth-century setting from Adam Gumpelzhaimer and a brand new commission from Alice Parker).

It was an ambitious undertaking. But the Glee Club was both stronger and weaker than it had been at the time of the prior recordings. The group now counted many serious musicians among its members, but it had a large contingent drawn more by the camaraderie than the music making. Increasingly the student-run a cappella groups were drawing away shared members who were unable to commit to two demanding rehearsal and performance schedules or who found the recognition from the fans and the fulfillment of the a cappella groups' yearly recordings more attractive.

The relationship between Liepold and the Glee Club, while still productive, was beginning to show signs of strain. The conductor was a demanding taskmaster in rehearsal and committed the group to a busy series of performances. He was also still in his twenties, only a few years older than the men he conducted, and the line between director and friend was sometimes blurry. The job was also demanding for Liepold; his ambitions for the group meant that, even with considerable help from the club's student executives, he was putting in long hours.

And the pay for those hours was almost laughably small. The group had continued to fundraise each fall with an annual phone campaign, with Larry Mueller, now finishing his graduate work at Darden, leveraging his connections to help the club get access to the phone bank at Alumni Hall. But there was still very little capital in the endowment. Liepold had to take other jobs to fill in the gaps, including conducting the Washington and Lee Glee Club and working part time at the South Street Inn.

The hope behind the planned recording, which the club leadership and Liepold had started calling the "Marian project," was that this would be the payoff for all the hard work. By issuing a compact disc, they thought they could raise the profile of the group to the next level, broaden its appeal, and support outreach to more donors.

The season started well enough, albeit with concerts in a new setting, University Baptist Church in the Corner, a historic area in Charlottesville, due to ongoing renovations to Old Cabell Hall. Liepold had divided the work of learning the mass into smaller segments; the fall concert included performances of the "Kyrie" and "Gloria," alongside "Ave Maria" settings by Gumpelzhaimer and Keller, a reprise of "Poor Wayfaring Stranger," and joint performances of madrigals with the Mary Baldwin College Choir. The performance also included a King's Singers arrangement, "New Day"; the "Inveni David" of Anton Bruckner, with a trombone quartet (Tim Boda, future club president Andrew Breen, current vice president Derek Ramsey, and president Donald Webb); and Eugene Thamon Simpson's powerful spiritual "Hold On." The latter work is better known by the words that the civil rights movement set to its tune, "Keep Your Eyes on the Prize," and its use in the compelling 1986 PBS documentary of the same name.

The inclusion of "Hold On" came at an interesting time in the University's racial evolution. In the fall of 1990, Student Nonviolent Coordinating Committee cofounder and former Georgia state legislator Julian Bond had begun a professorship in history, focusing on the civil rights movement and its impact on the country. University of Virginia students flocked to the class, which combined a deep reading list (including James Farmer's autobiography *Lay Bare the Heart* and James Forman's *The Making of Black Revolutionaries*, alongside more conventional civil rights movement histories) with Bond's compelling personal recollections. Bond incorporated multimedia elements in the lectures, and it was in this spirit that he asked in the fall of 1993 for volunteers to prepare some of the songs of the movement so that the class could hear the works performed. So it was that a group of Glee Club, University Singers, and Virginia Belles members found themselves performing "Eyes on the Prize" and other movement songs for Bond and their classmates.

That fall the club took its "Ave Maria" set, along with "Inveni David," "New Day," and "Wayfaring Stranger," to Harvard for a performance with the

Radcliffe Choral Society. Joint works included Bruckner's "Os Justi" and Jacob Handl's "Ascendit Deus." An additional joint work, Bruckner's "Christus factus est," had to be scrapped when Liepold and Radcliffe conductor Bev Taylor decided that the groups weren't ready to perform it.

In particular, the Virginia Glee Club was unready. The Morales mass was absorbing practice time at an apparently never-ending rate, as the group was working on learning the remaining movements by Christmas. The programming, indeed, seemed to some members to have become monotonous. Unfortunately, the group did not yet have the Morales up to a recording-ready level, so the work continued.

Christmas came and the group performed the entire *Missa Ave Maria* for the first time; indeed, the performance consumed almost half the concert, together with two more "Ave Maria" settings—by Mark Keller and (in its premiere) Alice Parker. The second half incorporated a wider range of traditions, including two Hanukkah pieces and the Wendell Whalum/Via Olatunji collaboration "Betelehemu." Perhaps because of its novelty, the Glee Club threw themselves into "Betelehemu," learning polyrhythmic drumming and embracing vocal improvisation on the solos. The work made an impression, with one Nigerian undergrad congratulating the soloists on the clear diction in the improvised parts. Unusually, the concert did not feature "The Twelve Days of Christmas," as the club executives were concerned their Baptist hosts might not look kindly on the "Five Golden Rings" champagne toast, which had become a tradition.

After winter break, the Glee Club turned its attention to the upcoming spring tour. Officially, this was the Tour of the Northeast, but as more than one club member observed, "This is the first time Knoxville has been a northeast city." The club had been invited to Knoxville, Tennessee, to perform in the southern division of the American Choral Directors Association, the only group from Virginia to perform that year. The rest of the itinerary included stops at Mount Holyoke and West Hartford, Connecticut—on the same day!— Boston, Stamford, Philadelphia, New York City, and Washington, DC.

The program featured most of the works from the fall, together with a reprise of *Young T.J.* In the spirit of the Pärt "De Profundis," which had been performed on the 1992 tour, Liepold also intended to have the club present Steve Reich's 1972 composition "Clapping Music," written for clapping hands without any other musical accompaniment. However, the Glee Club proved unable to master the shifting rhythm of the work, in which one part claps on a fixed rhythm throughout the piece while the second part steadily shifts the pattern by an eighth note until it comes back in sync after twelve repetitions. Student assistant conductor Shawn Felton, one of the few African American members of the group at the time, noted wryly that it might have been asking too much to expect a group of mostly white college boys to clap in rhythm.

The American Choral Directors Association performance went well, despite the eight-hour drive to get there (once again aboard the LUV bus, which thanks to tour manager Eric Rothwell's acumen came at a $500 discount).[8] Now the tour began in earnest, with a long drive punctuated with a hotel stay in Tennessee and another in Delaware. The bus pulled up to the Asylum Avenue Baptist Church in Hartford, Connecticut, where they were greeted by none other than Neely Bruce, who was on hand to conduct *Young T.J.* at the tour stops. They rehearsed Neely's work and Fauré's *Requiem*, dusty from languishing unrehearsed for several weeks, to pull it back into shape before their meeting with Mount Holyoke later that day.

After a rocky rehearsal and an evening's worth of celebration in the local dorm—punctuated by the arrival of the Public Safety officer (the campus police) due to the late-night loud music—the groups finally performed together the following afternoon. The Virginia group opened with its tour set, with one difference—the dedication of "Hold On" to their bus driver, Ray, whose mother had passed away the night before. The Holyoke group debuted a brief composition by Clifton J. Noble, and the combined groups followed with a workmanlike performance of the Fauré.

After a brief bus ride, the men, still in concert dress, found themselves in West Hartford in the resonant acoustics of St. James's Episcopal Church. Thus far on the road, the long bus journeys had kept the group from performing at its best, but that night, on their first full concert of the trip, the group pulled it together, delivering a solid first half before raising the audience's proverbial hair with *Young T.J.* In the closing, when Liepold asked if any past members were in the audience, three septuagenarian men joined in singing "Virginia, Hail, All Hail" and "The Good Old Song."

The next morning, the men rolled to Torrington High School for a morning concert and then to the town's middle school for an afternoon performance, interrupted only by the stomach difficulties of several of the men after days of road food. Then it was on to Boston for the northernmost stop on the trip, in the Gothic Revival architecture of the Old South Church. The performance went well for a sizable crowd, including current University of Virginia students and alums; the local alumni group hosted a reception after the concert in the Tower Room, up five tall flights of stairs, where the club sang "Happy Birthday" to one of the current students.

Then it was on to Harvard University, where Radcliffe had once again volunteered to host the men, although their schedules had not permitted a joint concert on this leg of the tour. A mostly quiet night passed, notwithstanding a visit to the famous Hong Kong Chinese restaurant in Harvard Square, where some of the members enjoyed "Strange Flavor Chicken" and "Delight of Two."

The following day, the group headed once again back down into Connecticut. Their destination: the Basilica of St. John the Evangelist in Stamford. They were greeted by an elaborate wooden sign, with white letters on a red background proclaiming, "THE UNIVERSITY OF VIRGINIA MEN'S GLEE CLUB, TUESDAY, MARCH 15, 8:00 PM IN CONCERT."

The club took advantage of their lengthy break before the concert for a private rehearsal in the church's chapel to woodshed the "Credo," which had been rocky since the beginning of the tour. Liepold returned to the Robert Shaw playbook, having the men rehearse the movement in sections, then in a circle as a group singing and marching in rhythm. He also spoke to them a few minutes about the impact that their performance would have on the listeners, seeking to dispel road fatigue with inspiration from Robert Shaw. When they returned to the sanctuary, they discovered the most welcoming acoustics of any venue on the tour. They also discovered one of the club's two architecture grad students, Denis McNamara, who had been absent from the early road stops due to academic commitments. He introduced them to the priest and provided an impromptu lecture on the construction and symbolism of the church based on his thesis research.

The concert itself was not only free of incident but included a visit from the Dove, as the acoustics added to the emotional impact of the Biebl, leaving audience and singers alike with tears in their eyes. The group's performance was strong overall, with "New Day," *Young T.J.*, and "Hold On" all having an impact. The audience, including alumni and parishioners, sought them out for pictures at the reception afterward, and the group broke into spontaneous song while changing into their civilian clothes. A small group returned to the chapel to sing Duruflé's "Ubi Caritas" in the now empty acoustic space.

Finally, the men piled into the bus, along with the red and white sign (which went with the group with the priest's knowledge and blessing). They were entertained by Neely Bruce and his wife in their colonial era home before bunking for the night in Fayerweather Gym at nearby Wesleyan University. The next morning they headed to Philadelphia, where they performed a concert for a small audience in the small Church of St. Martin-in-the-Fields. The next morning, the bus failed to start in the frigid spring air, and they had to wait for a jump before heading to New York.

New York, the penultimate stop of the tour, started on the wrong foot. As the bus stopped in front of the Church of St. Mary the Virgin on 46th Street, Liepold quieted the group for some advice. Jeff Slutzky remembers:

> Liepold asked everyone to quiet down. He had once lived here, and he had some advice. New York City, he said, was not a place where one could walk around wide-eyed like a small-town tourist (which some of the members of the Glee Club actually were). You have to keep your wits about you, he said, never let down your guard. New York was a wonderful place, he continued, but it could be dangerous if you didn't watch yourself. That was true with the first steps off the comforting Luv bus: the Glee Club walked right out the door and right into oncoming traffic.

The group warmed up in the incredibly resonant acoustics while the sound man who was recording the concert checked levels. Slutzky remembers, "The experienced recording artist listened and gave some technical advice in order to elicit the best sound possible. He also told them something else. He said that he had heard many groups sing the Biebl before, but that this was one of the best renditions he had ever heard."

Before the concert, the misadventures continued, with a sharp thief convincing two club members that they needed to let him "inspect" their cash to ensure that it wasn't counterfeit. But the performance was solid, if not the best of the tour, and the sound was spectacular. On a happy note, the Glee Club's other architecture grad student, J. Craig Fennell, was able to join them; like Denis McNamara, his grad school obligations had kept him out of the tour so far. Unfortunately, the bad news continued—the van had been burglarized during the concert, and only Lucky, the driver, had kept thieves from breaking into the bus.

At least the club had a day (mostly) off in New York. A subset of the group went to Grand Central Station to sing in the early evening, and then the members separated, some to Broadway shows, some to see Eric Bogosian's one-man off-Broadway performance, "Pounding Nails in the Floor with My Forehead."

The last day of the trip was consumed by a bus ride to Washington, DC, and the final rounds of a weeklong Spades tournament. When they arrived at the Cathedral of St. Matthew the Apostle, after a much needed warm-up they made their way upstairs to the sanctuary. There, in front of a full audience of music aficionados, friends, and alumni, they gave one of the strongest performances of the tour, marred only when Chris Newman fainted on the risers during the "Sanctus" of the Morales mass. The group was welcomed by a reception put together by Mike McCullough and the DC alumni chapter, and then they fanned out across Georgetown to various venues, including a detachment to Au Pied de Cochon, home of inexpensive French bistro food and famed site of Soviet defector Vitaly Yurchenko's escape from his CIA handler prior to redefecting to the Soviets. The group finally arrived home in Charlottesville at four a.m. The Spades tournament, interrupted by the arrival at St. Matthew's, was never concluded.

But the season wasn't over. The following weekend saw Mount Holyoke roll down to Charlottesville for the Glee Club's spring concert. The encounter with campus police a week earlier had not been forgotten, and there was a tense executive summit between the student leaders of the two groups on Saturday morning. Ultimately they came to an understanding, and that night the two groups delivered a strong reprise of the tour program, including the Duruflé collaboration. The evening was marred only at the beginning, when the outgoing executives took extra time before going on stage to deliver farewell speeches to the club. When they filed on, an irate voice from the crowd shouted, "You're twelve minutes late!" Tyler Magill responded, "Sorry, we were having a group hug."

There followed the usual spring activities, with the Concert on the Lawn, with special guests the New Dominions, conducted by their music director and Glee Club member Curt Alt, and featuring a show-closing men's chorus arrangement of Lynyrd Skynyrd's classic rock anthem "Free Bird." The Finals concert saw the return to the repertoire of "Ubi Caritas" and "Poor Wayfaring Stranger," as well as Grieg's "The Great White Host" from the graduating members' first concert in 1992.

The year and its ten-day tour had seen the club make its way through significantly larger venues and crowds than the Tour of the South just two years before. The repertoire ambitions were higher, as was the level of preparation;

the recording of the Morales in New York was proof that the group was determined to perform on a higher plane. But the tour also laid bare some tensions in the group—between schoolwork and performance, rigor and fun, and even the group's party side and its collaborations. Several members opted out of the tour due to the pressures of their coursework, with a few leaving the club altogether. The quest for high standards was beginning to exert a toll on the "fraternity of talent."

<hr />

1 This season was the Glee Club's second performance in its history of Billings's "David's Lamentation." The first was almost forty years earlier, in a joint performance with the Goucher College Glee Club in 1955.

2 President George H. W. Bush proclaimed January 16 National Religious Freedom Day in commemoration of the anniversary of the passing of Jefferson's Virginia Statute for Religious Freedom.

3 Scott Norris, "A Season of Celebration," *Virginia Glee Club Newsletter*, Spring 1993, 1ff.

4 For example, the final movement of Thompson's *Testament of Freedom*: "And even should the cloud of barbarism and despotism again obscure the science and liberties of Europe . . ."

5 Kann was also the founding musical director of the New Dominions, the University's first coed a cappella group. Several of the male "NewDos" in the early and mid 1990s were Glee Club members, including Kevin Dixon, Curt Alt, John "JP" Park, John Vick, Todd Simkin, Parker Hudnut, Farrell Kelly, John Duncan, and Eric Meade.

6 John J. McLaughlin, "Happy Birthday, Mr. Jefferson," *Virginia Glee Club Newsletter*, Fall 1993, 1ff.

7 Midsummers is one of the University of Virginia's "party weekends." With roots in dance weekends organized at various times in the school calendar as early as the late nineteenth century, the modern University calendar included Midwinters, Easters, and Midsummers, until the Easters party weekend was permanently canceled by University president Frank Hereford in the early 1980s.

8 I am indebted to Jeff Slutzky's contemporaneous history of the 1994 trip for this and other details.

 # FROM CHANTICLEER TO KANSAS CITY

f Liepold heard any of the concerns from the membership about the pace of the group, the 1994–1995 season betrayed no signs of slowing down. The season, in fact, started with something of a programming coup: on October 10, 1994, the Glee Club hosted a concert by Chanticleer at University Baptist Church in Charlottesville.

By 1994, Chanticleer, an a cappella men's choral ensemble founded by Louis Botto in 1978, had become nationally famous. Uniquely among recorded, professional music ensembles of the time, they featured not only traditional bass/baritone and tenor voices but also male countertenors, both altos and sopranos. The all-male lineup of between eight and twelve singers developed a reputation for exciting performances of a varied repertoire for men's voices that included Renaissance composers, spirituals, jazz, and gospel music. They also toured relentlessly; the season tour announcement for 1994–1995 listed thirty-four performances between September and December across the United States and Germany, and the full season included seventy-one performances plus an Asian tour. The group's reputation was further spread by its recordings, released on its own label, and by the fall of 1994 it was seen as an artistic touchstone for men's choral performance.

Liepold contacted the group and arranged not only for a performance in Charlottesville (alas, not at the University; Old Cabell Hall was still closed for renovations) but for the members to give the men of the Virginia Glee Club a vocal clinic. The performance drew participants from across the University and Charlottesville, and afterward some of the Glee Club members retreated up the street to the newly opened Michael's Bistro, which had developed a reputation for its intersection of musical performance (the owner was a jazz fan) and unusually good beer selections.

Frank Albinder, who was a member of Chanticleer at the time, recalls what happened after several rounds of drinks:

> The club guys were great hosts . . . so when they asked if we were singing the Biebl and I said no, they were disappointed. They told me how much the song meant to them, so I asked Joe if we could add it to the program or substitute it for something else. It would have been a very easy change, but Joe said no . . . there was nothing I could do. At the dinner at Michael's, one of the club guys came over and asked if we'd join in if they started singing it. We said sure, and eleven of us got up and we circled the room with the club guys and sang away. Would that there had been cell phone cameras back then![1]

The first official concert (as opposed to the informal gigs, which included a first-year orientation performance, a set at President John Casteen's house, and a church performance, which began the season) was a fall performance with the Wellesley College Choir in which the two groups jointly performed Handel's *Dixit Dominus*. Unusually for the Glee Club, they only performed four other works, but they were momentous: the Palestrina "Sicut cervus," Fenno Heath's arrangement of "Sometimes I Feel Like a Motherless Child" (for the first time since 1968), a reprise of Arvo Pärt's "De profundis" from 1990–1991, and the Perotin *Viderunt Omnes*. The latter work, in its first performance by the Glee Club, was memorable—over ten minutes of twelfth-century French polyphony, with the title as the only text.

The juxtaposition of the two works together suggests a source for Liepold's programming inspiration. Both "De profundis" and *Viderunt Omnes* had appeared on recordings in the late 1980s by the Hilliard Ensemble, a men's early music and contemporary classical ensemble originally directed by Paul Hillier.[2] In some of Liepold's programming choices—the juxtaposition of new commissions with medieval and Renaissance works, the addition of works with limited or unusual instrumentation such as the percussion in "De profundis"—there are echoes of Hillier's style.

Whatever the origin of the unusual program, only some of it was repeated when the club traveled to Wellesley; the Glee Club performed "Sicut cervus" and "De profundis" only, perhaps to make room for a Handel *Concerto Grosso* that opened the concert. However it happened, it was an unusual trip. The night before, Virginia football threatened to disrupt club attendance. Andrew Breen remembers:

> Virginia's historic win over Florida St[ate] happened on 11/2/95. Thursday night. Club was leaving on a weekend roll . . . the next morning at crack-of-ass o'clock. I think I speak for nearly all of us when I say that I slept ZERO that night, showed up to the bus . . . and then enjoyed watching the VHS of the game several times on the bus on the way up I-95.[3]

Another unusual feature of the performance at Wellesley: the use of professional soloists, many of whom had performed with the Boston Symphony, for the *Dixit Dominus*. At Virginia, members of the student groups, including John Craig Fennell, Jayson Throckmorton, and Morgan Whitfield, provided the solos. Despite the replacement of the student soloists, their spirits were high after the performance, with some members of the Glee Club jumping in nearby Lake Waban later that night (presumably not wearing their tuxedos).

After Wellesley, a month elapsed before the Fifty-Fourth Annual Christmas Concerts. *Viderunt Omnes* made a repeat appearance, as did a new set of works dedicated to the Virgin Mary, this time based on the "Salve Regina" plainchant. After performing the chant, the Glee Club sang settings of the "Salve Regina" text by Josquin, Francesco Cavalli (accompanied by cello and harpsichord), and a full mass setting by Jean Langlais, with the Virginia Glee Club Brass Ensemble and members of the Virginia Women's Chorus.

The Virginia Women's Chorus had been dormant for over five years, ever since the music department made the decision to eliminate single-sex choral groups from the curriculum. However, in August 1994, Elizabeth Noseworthy, Wynne Krause, Esta Jarrett, and Christine Burt met in a student-rented house on Cherry Street to discuss their desire for an all-female chorus. Noseworthy and Krause, who had been longtime members of the University Singers, invited Jarrett (who they knew from Coro Virginia) and Burt to join the effort. They reconstituted the group and recruited Kathy Mitchell-Parker, née Katherine Mitchell, as their conductor. That fall, they recruited members and began rehearsals; the Christmas concert included fifteen singers, of whom about a third were University Singers members of the New Dominions; the rest had not performed with other University choruses. Mitchell-Parker was not able to continue as the permanent director but was able to provide continuity and, importantly, a library of music from the group's first incarnation, as well as arranging for the purchase of more works from Washington and Lee choral director Gordon Spice.[4] The following spring the Virginia Women's Chorus hired Donna Plasket as its new full-time conductor.

The *Missa Salve Regina,* in which the newly re-formed group joined the Glee Club, was the latest incarnation of a project that had underpinned Liepold's programming since his second year of directorship. The project, consisting of settings of chant-based songs of praise to the Virgin Mary from Renaissance and contemporary composers, turned from "Ave Maria" settings to other Marian texts. The 1994 Christmas concert, for instance, included not only the "Salve Regina" settings but also an arrangement of the Kievan chant "Bogoroditse Devo" (Rejoice, O Virgin), and the 1995 spring concert saw the premiere of a setting of "Virgo Virginum Praeclara," another Marian chant, by Benjamin Broening. Liepold had ambitions of securing a proper release for the recordings on a major label, and recordings of Mary-based works continued during the 1994–1995 season.

In addition to the Broening commission, the spring concert featured a performance of the Lotti *Crucifixus* for eight voices in a men's voice arrangement, conducted by assistant conductor Craig Fennell. Fennell, who had completed his graduate studies in landscape architecture in the spring of 1994, was still living in Charlottesville. Having sung in an a cappella group at Rutgers University as an undergraduate, he had joined the Virginia Gentlemen in 1993–1994 and had become their music director following John Navarette in the 1994–1995 season. His clear tenor and skilled arrangements were behind one of the Virginia Gentlemen's most durable recordings, "Insomniac" (originally by folk rock duo Billy Pilgrim), which premiered on the 1995 Virginia Gentlemen recording *Seven and Seven*.[5] The Lotti work, in its arrangement for four-part men's chorus by Harvard Glee Club conductor Archibald T. Davison, had been first performed by the Virginia Glee Club in 1935 and again at the 50th Anniversary Concert in 1936, but had disappeared from the repertoire until this concert.

In addition to the Lotti, the concert also featured a joint performance of the Duruflé *Requiem* with the UNC Greensboro Women's Choir under the direction of Richard Cox. The program was repeated the following day at the University of North Carolina–Greensboro. And an unusual *third* spring concert followed two weeks later at St. Andrew's Catholic Church in Roanoke, featuring repertoire from throughout the season.

The annual Concert on the Lawn was notable for the Glee Club's revival, after forty years, of Donald MacInnis's arrangement of Tom Lehrer's "The Hunting Song," as well as for the performance of another work by graduating Glee Club assistant conductor Shawn Felton, "The Elegy of Spring," and an appearance by the newly reconstituted Virginia Women's Chorus.[6] The year concluded with the annual Finals concert, held one last time at University Baptist Church as renovations of Old Cabell Hall were still underway.

By this time, the Glee Club had entered a rhythm in which major touring seasons alternated with home seasons. The home seasons (e.g., 1990–1991, 1992–1993, 1994–1995) might feature substantial weekend engagements away from the University but were generally held close to home. As can be seen by the 1994–1995 season, this did not mean that the Club was idle or less ambitious in its programming, but at this stage the Glee Club was still constrained by the availability of funds to support broader touring. In 1993, the group anticipated spending 26 percent of its annual budget on the spring tour of the Northeast, slightly more than the annual salary paid to Liepold.[7]

In recognition of the club's need to grow its endowment, the leadership of the group had asked Larry Mueller for assistance in beginning a major development project, an outgrowth of the Glee Club Advisory Board that first met in 1994. Mueller had developed a fundraising plan for the Glee Club while at Darden, and he believed the time was right to drive a funding appeal with a significant target: $800,000, enough to boost the endowment to the $1 million mark. The development committee, which included Mueller, Advisory Board president Rafe Madan, outgoing Glee Club president Jonathan Finn, Ruben Basantes, and this author, met several times during the spring and early summer of 1995 but only succeeded in establishing a constitution and bylaws for the Advisory Board.

Based on the normal rhythm, 1995–1996 would be a major touring year, and the executive committee together with Liepold decided to head west, with an eye toward tapping into an underserved University of Virginia alumni market and collaborating with other major choruses. The actual event took place somewhat differently, as we will see.

Fall of the 1995–1996 season began with a return to Old Cabell Hall, newly reopened after a two-year renovation, and with the return of the Virginia Women's Chorus, now fully fledged with forty-eight members and under the direction of Plasket. Glee Club membership was up as well, with fifty-three members (not including Vihem Aeschlbie, who could not participate in the Kickoff Concert but who returned for Christmas). Repertoire for the Kickoff Concert was lighter, as it was a true joint concert, with the two groups sharing the program almost equally. The Glee Club's repertoire was meaty, however, with the last two movements of *Quatre Petites Prières de Saint François d'Assise* by Poulenc in the first half, and Samuel Barber's "A Stopwatch and an Ordnance Map" in the second. The other theme woven through the concert was the hall itself, with joint performances of Bruckner's "Locus Iste" opening the concert and Lukas Foss's "Behold, I build an house" closing.[8] In between, the Glee Club added a Hebrew work, "El yivneh hagalil" ("The Lord will build Galilee"), reinforcing the theme. After the Kickoff Concert, the group hit the road for Mount Holyoke College, resuming the collaboration that had last taken place in 1994 with the Tour of the Northeast.

If the Kickoff Concert had been a deviation from Liepold's Marian works, the Christmas concert brought a return to more ambitious repertoire. The concert alternated three movements from the Monteverdi *Vespers of 1610* (also known as *Vespro della Beata Virgine*, the "Vespers of the Blessed Virgin") with works by Bach, Taverner, and a full performance of the Poulenc *Quatre Petites Prières*. The second half brought more traditional fare, and also a newly composed piece by Felton ("Tintinnabulation") and a reprise of "El yivneh hagalil." The Hebrew work was a surprise. Announced from the stage simply as "Remix," the work began as normal, but after the first iteration of the chant Eric Rothwell added vocal percussion, transforming the chant into something reminiscent of electronic dance music.[9] The crowd audibly lost its mind.

"Remix" was not the first time the Glee Club had played with audience expectations on stage. At one spring concert a year or two previously, the club surprised the audience, and Liepold, by bursting into "Helan Går," a Swedish drinking song that had been taught to them by club member Marcus Hagegård. And the by then established tradition of including a choral arrangement of a popular song in the Concert on the Lawn had originated as a practical joke with Dave Fouché and John Liepold in 1992. But "Remix," with its combination of high art and hijinks, set a standard for the club's emerging brand of musical mischief.

At the same time, the relationship between Liepold and the club's leadership was fraying. Liepold continued to push for higher musical standards, but his relentlessness was starting to cause turnover among the membership. Part of the challenge may have been his age. Only a few years older than the grad students who sang in the group, it may have been challenging for them to treat him with authority and respect when they would also hang out and have a beer with him at the Glee Club House.

Another factor in the strained relations, on Liepold's side, was financial. Due to the club's strapped finances, they could only afford to pay him a pittance, and he took on a variety of other jobs to make ends meet. Because the McIntire Department of Music didn't offer many teaching opportunities for nonaffiliated instructors, he had to seek employment elsewhere and was faced with taking nonmusical jobs in Charlottesville (including a stint working at the South Street Inn) or musical jobs farther afield. In 1993–1994, in fact, he was also the director of the men's glee club at Hampden-Sydney. But he poured the lion's share of his energy into the Virginia Glee Club, not only conducting and planning the programs but devising collaborations, planning tours, designing stationery, writing press releases and program notes, and many other activities that kept him busy with little fiscal reimbursement.

Liepold knew the relationship was straining but didn't know what to do. In an interview in late 1995, he pointed out, "I report to the student executives, who haven't managed employees before. I haven't had a performance review since I began the job in 1991, and it's challenging when I know there are issues but can't address them."[10]

Ultimately matters came to a head in the planning for the tour. Some members stopped coming to rehearsals out of frustration with the rigorous schedule; Liepold asked the executives to bar them from the tour. An argument ensued and ultimately Liepold resigned as musical director.

The timing was perilous. Not only was this the eve of the tour, but Liepold had planned many of the stops, including one in his hometown. A compromise was worked out: he would conduct in Kansas City, but the musical leadership for the rest of the tour stops fell to Fennell, with assistance from John Stanzione and Tom Nassif. As Dan Roche, in recalling the tour, notes, "The replacement conductors for the week, in the tradition of student self-governance, came from the ranks of Club itself. John Stanzione was barely 20, a second-year computer genius with a larger-than-life personality who loved to sing everywhere. Tom Nassif was a fourth year Chemistry major. John Craig Fennell was 26. He had completed a master's program in Architecture the year before, and sang with Club largely to keep connected to the community and a hobby he loved."[11]

Once musical leadership was confirmed, a dozen more issues had to be addressed. Roche recalls: "[The officers] met late into the night in Cabell B12, picking up the pieces, assigning and re-assigning logistical tasks. They made long distance phone calls, ironing details, recommitting to prior commitments. Yes, the Virginia Glee Club had a new director. Yes, we would be appearing to perform as scheduled. No, no reason for concern."

The tour got off to an inauspicious start. Lars Bjorn recalls that the "roll to the Midwest began in a snowstorm [and] took fifteen hours to reach Louisville." Stanzione notes that "the bus problems started on the way to Louisville with ice forming on the inside of the windows. Or that may have just been Hell freezing over."[12]

The group performed in Louisville and then headed on to Kansas City, Missouri, where Liepold waited. Somehow the group made it through the performance and then headed on the next day to St. Louis. From there the bus headed north to Chicago and, in the tradition of Glee Club tours, broke down along the way. Bjorn notes that "somehow, [Glee Club president] Andrew Breen didn't strangle anyone."[13] Eventually the group made it to Chicago and a performance at Quigley Seminary. Of that performance, Farrell Kelly recalls,

> we made a joyful noise unlike anything else I've ever been a part of. [After] singing under our former director in Kansas City, [we] were really under our own steam. That night, (for me, it was while singing Poulenc under Nassif's direction), we knew we were able, through our shared work, to make it work—greater than the sum of any parts. That's one of the few times the dove was made manifest, more than a metaphor or an ideal to aspire to. When we left Charlottesville, we hadn't been sure what we would come home to; after Quigley, we knew what home we wanted to build.
>
> And then, of course, the absurdity afterward, when just after Quigley a bunch of us got mocked in the street by *Wheel of Fortune*'s Pat Sajak for spending Spring Break in tuxedos in frigid Chicago instead of at the beach like "real" college students. How could Pat Sajak have known what we had just spelled together?[14]

Kelly separately recalled that "we also stayed at the same Best Western in downtown Chicago as guests of the Jenny Jones show, which made for interesting elevator interactions."[15]

From Chicago, the group headed on to Ann Arbor, Michigan, and a performance at the University of Michigan. Roche recalls the episode in detail:

Midway through the tour, the Club pulled into Ann Arbor, Michigan to perform with the fabled University of Michigan Men's Glee Club. In the moment, the contrast between the two groups could not have been starker. The Michigan Club was (and is) the second oldest collegiate chorus in the United States. It enjoyed dedicated proposal and administrative space in the University Student Union building. Their conductor was paid-for by the University. They had a crest, a "house" on a nearby street, and were known for forming a perfectly seriffed and aligned "M" in official photographs. Most members were music majors in the University's esteemed conservatory. The Virginia Glee Club, by comparison, had two music majors.

The Michigan men welcomed Virginia to town at a happy hour in a restaurant on University Avenue. The host group was well groomed and trimmed. They wore clean, pressed pants with professional-looking button-down shirts, tucked in tight with collars sharp. They were performers, on and off stage. Virginia, in contrast, were halfway through a bus trip. They were tired and unkempt. Few had showered that day or even the day before.

The President of the Michigan Glee Club shook hands all around. He was a music major who played two different instruments in addition to singing, or so the group was helpfully informed. John Craig Fennell emerged from the bus, binders in hand, pencils in pocket. The tall Michigan student extended his hand. "Ah, you're John Craig Fennell," he sneered, "the landscape architect."

Others recall what happened next. One member of the Michigan Glee Club said, "Now let's show these Virginia boys how to drink." Stanzione says, "I distinctly remember kicking several of the kegs at that place. The Michigan guys really didn't understand they were dealing with professionals."

Through it all, it was only the assurance and professionalism of the officers and musical leaders of the group that kept things going. Kelly notes, "I don't think the amount of chaos, uncertainty, and eventual empowerment that was wrapped up in that trip can be overstated. Craig's calm and self-effacing leadership set an example for all of us (one that some of us still aspire to), but I don't think we can discount the importance of folks like Andrew, and the rest of the exec, who did the legwork and, despite any personal fears or misgivings, set a tone for adventure and fun that kept the rest of us from panicking."

At the end of the trip, Roche recalls:

> The Club arrived home in Charlottesville late on a Sunday, shell-shocked but proud. John Craig Fennell reported to work the next day at his architectural firm. They practiced the day after that in Cabell B12, Fennell taking the podium and preparing for the next round of performances before graduation.
>
> Later that week the Club executive board presented Fennell with a token of appreciation for what he had done, how he had stepped up to lead the group and hold the perimeters on student self-governance for another day. It was a small, cheap trophy, painted gold over plastic on a small wooden frame, mahogany veneer taped over a cheaper wood. Much like the Virginia Glee Club, it was scrappy. Fighting over its weight. Making due with what it had and in the process doing the work of something much more expensive and pretentious. The front wore a personalized nameplate:
>
> "John Craig Fennell—Landscape Architect."

Somehow, against all odds, the group had survived the trip. And somehow, after the tour, the Glee Club hosted its first large-scale reunion weekend in recent memory. The 125th Anniversary Weekend featured a performance by the club and allowed alums to catch up with each other.

During this period, the Glee Club's officers issued the group's first recording on compact disc. *Notes from the Path*, named for an infrequent newsletter that was written by Nathan "Pathfinder" Moore (class of 1993), featured concert recordings from 1994 to 1996, including the first CD recordings of much of the lighter repertoire from these years. It did not include any of the Marian recordings (*Missa Ave Maria* and the "Ave Maria" commissions) that the group had worked to record during Liepold's time.[16]

The officers were also grappling with the vagaries of the student activity fee appropriations process. At this point what little income there was from the endowment was still a tiny fraction of the club's operating expenses, so even the pittance from the appropriations could help. Business managers typically spent many hours constructing formal budget documents to argue for student council funding. But often, as in 1996, the results fell far short of expectations. Stephanie Kendall, president of the Virginia Women's Chorus at the time, wrote a formal letter of complaint to the Student Council, cc'ing several deans, after a hearing involving the Virginia Women's Chorus and the Glee Club in which the committee displayed highly unprofessional behavior:

> the [committee] members' state of mind detracted from a properly serious consideration of the matters at hand . . . more than one member admitted to taking stimulants such as Vivarin (one member swallowed pills during the proceedings). All members were affected to the point of giddiness from lack of sleep, stress, and caffeine. These conditions impaired their memory and ability to deal with the situation. For instance, during one discussion the members had an argument about who had been present at certain other deliberations, since each individual could not remember which ones he had seen. . . . One member commented "My eyes are closing by themselves" . . . One member lay on the floor for the majority of the deliberations. . . . Members frequently screamed at each other—as a matter of fact, most of the proceedings could be termed a shouting match. The members allowed their personal grievances to interfere with their rational abilities, using incessant profanities and personal attacks. The phrase "I hate you," directed from one Committee member to another, was used more than once.[17]

Behind the scenes, though, a council of past officers was called to discuss what to do about the conductor challenge. The Glee Club Advisory Board's fundraising efforts would have to wait; stabilizing the leadership of the group took immediate priority. While the Glee Club under Fennell's direction finished the 1995–1996 season, the challenge was to find permanent musical leadership. That leadership was soon to arrive, in the form of a new faculty member: Bruce Tammen.

1 Frank Albinder, email to the author, October 11, 2019. "Joe" was Chanticleer's director at the time, Joseph Jennings.

2 According to Discogs (discogs.com), an online database of recorded music, the Perotin first appeared on a recording in 1964, then in a subsequent 1975 release by the Early Music Consort of London under the direction of David Munrow, in which three of the members of the 1989 Hilliard Ensemble recording also appeared. Like the Hilliard Ensemble recording, Liepold performed the work entirely a cappella. "De profundis" received its recorded premiere under Hillier's direction on the Hilliard Ensemble's *Arbos* in 1987.

3 Andrew Breen, Facebook comment, July 12, 2019.

4 Esta Jarrett, letter to Gordon Spice, February 27, 1995.

5 "Insomniac" was singled out for inclusion on a volume of the *Best of Contemporary a Cappella* (BOCA) anthology, and also appeared on the 2014 *Best of BOCA: The First 20 Years*.

6 Although the Lehrer piece disappeared from the concert repertoire of the Glee Club, it was taken up by the Virginia Gentlemen sometime in the 1970s and was still performed in the 1980s, according to Virginia Gentleman and Glee Club member Ellis Butler.

7 Jonathan Finn, "Phone-a-Thon, Oct. 25–27: Glee Club Needs Money to Meet Operating Budget," *Virginia Glee Club Newsletter* 20, no. 1 (Fall 1993): 1ff.

8 Bruckner wrote this motet, based on the Latin gradual "*Locus iste a Deo factus est*" ("This place was made by God"), for the dedication of a votive chapel in the New Cathedral in Linz, Austria, where he was an organist. And as noted by Liepold in the program notes for the concert, Foss wrote "Behold, I Build a House" for the 1950 dedication of Marsh Chapel at Boston University. The chapel, which serves as the official place of worship for the university, is today the home of choral performances by its own chapel choir and many choral groups around Boston. It may be better remembered as the home of the Marsh Chapel Experiment, a double-blind experiment in which human volunteers were given either psilocybin or a placebo to see if the psychedelic substance could induce a religious experience.

9 The Christmas 1995 performance of "Remix," and the crowd reaction, appears as a bonus track on *Notes from the Path*.

10 Interview with John Liepold, fall 1995.

11 Dan Roche, July 12, 2019. This and the direct quotes on the following pages are from a lengthy Facebook thread with the quoted participants in the summer of 2019.

12 Lars Bjorn and John Stanzione, July 12, 2019.

13 Lars Bjorn, July 12, 2019.

14 Farrell Kelly, July 12, 2019.

15 Farrell Kelly, July 10, 2019.

16 The master recording for this still-unissued project is in the University of Virginia Library under the title "Marian Echoes."

17 Stephanie Kendall, letter to the Student Council Appropriations Committee, April 8, 1996.

26 BRUCE TAMMEN AND A NEW PROFESSIONALISM

Bruce K. Tammen was unusual in some ways, compared to the preceding Virginia Glee Club directors. He shared a few traits with his predecessor John Liepold: both were products of the American Midwest; both had studied and performed under Robert Shaw. But the similarities ended there. Tammen was entering the third decade of his career, having led the University of Chicago's Motet and Rockefeller Chapel Choirs from 1984 to 1996. His choral background was more Lutheran than Renaissance, with credentials including a stint with the Oregon Bach Festival under Helmuth Rilling. And, importantly for the Glee Club officers embarking on a new director search, he was *faculty*, having followed his wife, Old Testament scholar Esther Menn, to the University, where he taught voice.[1] In a word, he was perfect for a group shaken by the uncertainty of the preceding months.

After meeting the group in the fall of 1996, Tammen agreed to take over officially for the spring semester. That left John Craig Fennell to conduct the fall and Christmas concerts, and in so doing he reintroduced the group to a work that remained in its repertoire for years after, Ralph Vaughan Williams's setting of "Loch Lomond."[2]

When Tammen took over in the spring of 1997, he promptly set his stamp on the group. The spring featured a concert largely dedicated to the works of German composers, a first since Donald Loach's tenure, which included the works of Felix Mendelssohn, Anton Bruckner, Johannes Brahms, and Franz Schubert. Perhaps equally importantly, the concert featured several members of the group as soloists, allowing Tammen to showcase individuals as well as the group's sound.

Tammen's rapport with the singers helped them over an important hurdle: recognizing that they needed to improve their performance. A year later, in spring 1998, president Drew Cogswell looked back over the preceding year and announced from the stage, "We thank our conductor, Bruce Tammen. We've improved *a lot* over the past year." Tammen's easy way of helping the group grow their sound was observed by a University of Chicago writer, who in 2006 recorded the following Tammen utterances during a rehearsal of Bach's *Mass in B Minor*: "'Your pianissimo must be a living, passionate thing, a furry animal inside you.' 'Behold! He is coming to save you! You can't believe it! Be more incredulously joyful!' 'You are bouncing on a celestial trampoline!'"[3]

The following year—Tammen's first full season with the group—found them embracing both the rigorous performance focus of their new conductor and an expanded musical palette. The fall concert, a collaboration with the Virginia Women's Chorus, opened with a typically serious set from the Glee Club including Fauré's "Cantique de Jean Racine," selections from William Byrd's *Mass for Three Voices*, Tammen's arrangement of Max Janowski's "Avinu Malkeynu" (a vocal feature for Michael Belinkie), and Alexander Gretchaninoff's "Nunc Dimittis" ("Lord, Now Lettest Thou Thy Servant"), which the group now performed in the original Church Slavonic. After the women's set, the group returned with lighter repertoire, but only by comparison, opening with Mendelssohn's "Liebe und wein," followed by Colonel Mellish's venerable "Drink to Me Only with Thine Eyes," Marshall Bartholomew's arrangement of "Little Innocent Lamb," and, unexpectedly, Jerome Kern's "All the Things You Are," featuring Bill Bennett as the soloist.[4] The Glee Club's trademark combination of highbrow works for men's voices and crowd-pleasing numbers was intact, but Tammen's approach was bringing a broader scope to the group's repertoire and heightening their performance skills.

Both of Tammen's soloists would go on to musical careers. Belinkie, attending law school at George Mason after graduating from Virginia in 1998, sent an audition tape to the United States Navy Sea Chanters after learning about the group's touring; he was accepted, enlisted, headed to boot camp, and was still performing with the group at the time of this writing.[5] Bennett studied music at DePaul University in Chicago and performed with opera companies in the area as well as starting a music technology company.[6]

Following a trip to Wellesley and a joint performance of the Mozart *Requiem*, the Christmas concert continued along the same lines, with the Byrd, Gretchaninoff, and "Little Innocent Lamb" returning alongside Grieg's "Ave Maris Stella," "Winter Song," the Biebl "Ave Maria," and a set of spirituals and hymns, including Peter Cornelius, "The Three Kings." The piece by Cornelius, a feature for Bill Bennett, would continue to feature in the group's performances over the next few years.

The next step was a tour. Continuing to tour neighboring states during even years, the club went south in 1998, heading to Charlotte, North Carolina; Atlanta; Panama City, Florida; New Orleans; Memphis; and (after returning to Charlottesville for the spring concert) Washington, DC. The tour was the Glee Club's first performance in Florida and only its second in Memphis, more than a century after their performance there on the 1894–1895 tour.

The spring concert, somewhat unusually, did not include a guest group, but its program, drawn from the tour repertoire, introduced a few new songs to the Charlottesville audience, including the "Chorus of Returning Pilgrims" from Wagner's *Tannhäuser*, Ralph Vaughan Williams's arrangement of "The Turtle Dove" (a feature for Fennell), and the return of Jacob Handl's "Ascendit Deus" (last sung under Donald Loach) and James Erb's arrangement of "Shenandoah." The group brought this repertoire to the Concert on the Lawn and the Finals concert as well.

Having honed the season's repertoire to a high standard, the Glee Club issued its second compact disc, *Brothers, Sing On!* A compilation of recordings from the 1997–1998 season, this sent a message that the group was serious about continuing to expand its musical legacy under its new conductor, even as its cover photo, showing the group posed in performance tuxedos in front of the Rotunda, echoed publicity photos taken for the group's previous tours under Liepold.

The following fall began atypically with a trip to New York City, where the Glee Club performed at the Yale Club on October 23 and sang a service at St. Patrick's Cathedral the following day. The season continued with the annual Kickoff Concert, showcasing a renewed collaboration with Wellesley and a joint performance of Bruckner's "Os Justi." The club's repertoire included works by Tomás Luis de Victoria, Gretchaninoff, and Bruckner's "Ave Maria," as well as the return of Randall Thompson's "Alleluia," James Erb's "Shenandoah," and "All the Things You Are," now joined by J. Fred Coots's "You Go to My Head." Tammen's arrangement of the 1938 *Great American Songbook* entry brought out the similarities between the work and the folk song melodies—"Shenandoah" and Sibelius's "Norden."

"You Go to My Head" also suggested a new musical direction for the group, whose secular repertoire had previously looked back to madrigals or spirituals. If part of the reasoning behind the McIntire Department of Music's

The Virginia Glee Club
Bruce Tammen, Conductor

Brothers, Sing On!

FIGURE 30. *Brothers, Sing On!* album cover, 1998.

attempt to merge the Glee Club and the Women's Chorus was a lack of significant repertoire for men's voices, Tammen's new direction seemed to suggest that they simply weren't looking hard enough.

The Christmas concert brought more German repertoire, both ancient and modern, with Bach's "Break Forth, O Beauteous Heavenly Light" sitting alongside Hugo Wolf's "Nun wandre, Maria" and Jacob Handl's "O Magnum Mysterium." The season continued with an unusual February event, a Valentine's Day Concert with the Glee Club, the Women's Chorus, and singers from Tammen's Opera Workshop. The spring season continued with a concert at Old Cabell Hall with the Smith College Choir and a performance of Bach's *Magnificat*, followed a week later by a concert with the Mount Holyoke College

Glee Club at Thomas Aquinas Church. The Mount Holyoke concert included performances of Benjamin Britten's "Rejoice in the Lamb," Fauré's "Cantique de Jean Racine," and Haydn's "The Heavens Are Telling."

A few weeks later, on April 23, the Glee Club performed at New York Avenue Presbyterian Church in Washington, DC. This performance was done in lieu of the Concert on the Lawn, and in fact marked the demise of that tradition. There were a couple of reasons for the change. One was a conscious decision that the club's time would be better spent reaching out to its alumni. While the effort to mount a formal capital campaign had petered out between the normal organizational challenges of fundraising and the confusion around the departure of Liepold, the group remained painfully aware that they needed to build a stable financial base, and performing in the epicenter of the alumni base seemed an appropriate way to do it. The other reason was artistic: Tammen had repeatedly expressed his dissatisfaction with the acoustic experience of the outdoor performances. So ended a tradition that had its roots in the 1936 season and was nurtured by David Davis, Donald Loach, and John Liepold.

If 1998–1999 was relatively conventional, the following season was unprecedented in the club's recent history: there would be an international tour, a return to Europe. The first international tour in eighteen years and the first performances in France since 1977, the tour consumed much of the group's energy and time for the season. This is not to say that no other performances took place; in addition to the Christmas and Finals concerts, the season began with what would become a new tradition, the Family Weekend Choral Showcase. An opportunity for parents to hear the choral groups of the University, the October performance included the University Singers, the Virginia Women's Chorus, and the Glee Club. The event provided an opportunity for the groups to hear each other, and perhaps a small competitive nudge; it also marked the end of the Glee Club's standalone Kickoff Concerts, since it was hard to schedule two October concerts in Old Cabell Hall. Christmas and a winter concert with the Vassar Women's Chorus marked the winter season, while a concert in Washington, DC, at Gonzaga College High School and the Finals concert rounded out the spring.

The group that boarded the plane for Paris was entirely transformed from the uncertain, rebellious group that toured the Midwest four years previously. The repertoire built by Tammen over the preceding three years included deepened explorations of Renaissance music, including Victoria's "Duo seraphim" and Cipriano de Rore's "O crux benedicta," twentieth-century works by Alan Hovhaness and Jean Berger, a set of early American songs, including Tammen's setting of "The Morning Trumpet" and Shaw's "Amazing Grace," both originally published in *The Southern Harmony and Musical Companion*, and a set from the *Great American Songbook*, including "You Go to My Head," "All the Things You Are," and Cole Porter's "Night and Day." The audiences in Paris, Montluçon, Anzy-le-Duc, Le Val, Marseille, Pourrières, Ouveillon, and Peillon responded favorably to the students, especially to the group's incoming president, Bert Steindorff, an Alabamian who spoke fluent enough French to serve as the Glee Club's program guide. Steindorff and the audience's response can be heard on *Tour de France*, the recording compiled from the best performances of the tour.

FIGURE 31. Virginia Glee Club with Bruce Tammen at Anzy le Duc, *Tour de France*, 2000. Courtesy Flickr user Wayfarer 88.

The following season was a home season and as such was considerably less travel-intensive, if not less ambitious. The season opened with the Virginia Choral Showcase and the Christmas concert, split by a trip to Mount Holyoke to perform the Duruflé *Requiem* with the Mount Holyoke Glee Club and an orchestra. Spring featured collaborations with two different women's choruses. In February, the Glee Club held a February concert with the visiting Mount

FIG 32. Virginia Glee Club in concert at Peillon, *Tour de France*, 2000. Courtesy Flickr user Wayfarer 88.

Holyoke Glee Club, performing the Duruflé with National Symphony organist William Neil. And the spring concert in March featured a visit from the Radcliffe Choral Society under the direction of Constance DeFotis, performing works of Brahms and Mendelssohn.

The season was also Tammen's final one as the director of the Glee Club.

Having arrived in Charlottesville when Esther Menn joined the University of Virginia faculty, his departure was triggered by her acceptance of a faculty position at the Lutheran School of Theology at Chicago.[7] His departure, after a last Finals concert, left the Glee Club in much better shape than he had found it. The rebellious, raw group of students who hired him were now a mature ensemble capable of mounting an international tour. The second and final recording from Tammen's tenure, *Tour de France*, features one of the most well-developed choral sounds that the Glee Club had yet put to disc.

But there was still institutional risk. The endowment was still modest, and the major fundraising originally planned for the late 1990s had not taken place, perhaps because of the reduced urgency inspired by five years with a conductor who was part of the faculty and accordingly was less dependent on the club for income. And with his rather sudden departure, the group was unprepared to mount a search for his replacement. So once again, they turned to someone from within.

---

1   Brooke E. O'Neill, "Blood, Bach and Bruce," *University of Chicago Magazine* 98, no. 4 (April 2006). https://magazine.uchicago.edu/0604/peer/tammen.shtml.
2   The Glee Club had previously performed Vaughan Williams's "Loch Lomond" in the fall of 1974 under the direction of Donald Loach. Though the work appeared on Glee Club programs only about ten or fifteen times since 1996, it appears on two of their recordings and is one of a handful of songs that are performed from memory at various informal performances, particularly at the Glee Club House.
3   O'Neill, "Blood, Bach and Bruce."
4   The performances of "Liebe und wein," a drinking song comparing the pain of love and the joys of intoxication, became a favorite of the group and its audiences, especially the recitation of the English translation of the work beforehand.
5   Ed Crews, "Singing Sailor: Michael Belinkie (Col. '98) Finds His Voice in the Navy Sea Chanters," *Virginia Magazine,* October 13, 2010, https://uvamagazine.org/articles/singing_sailor.
6   "About," Velvet Singer, accessed August 4, 2016, http://web.archive.org/web/20160804204230/http://www.velvetsinger.com/about/.
7   O'Neill, "Blood, Bach and Bruce."

27 SEASONS WITH THE VIRGINIA GLEE CLUB

urke Morton was a member of the Virginia Glee Club in 2000–2001, but he was not a student at the University of Virginia. Morton had graduated from the University of Chicago in 1995, where he had sung in the Rockefeller Chapel Choir under Bruce Tammen; he had rejoined his old conductor while working in Charlottesville as a wine salesman. The incoming executives turned to Morton to hold the Glee Club together as its interim musical director while they conducted a search.

The executives for 2001–2002 included Jared Q. Libet, business manager; Tristan Van Tine, secretary; Willis Shawver, vice president; Mike Galdo, publicity manager; and Thomas Deal, president. They knew from talking to Glee Club alumni that the search process had been challenging in the past, and that it would likely take a full year to identify a new director. They accordingly took out a display ad in the *Choral Journal*:

> The Virginia Glee Club seeks an experienced choral conductor to direct a select ensemble of approximately fifty men. This part-time position begins August 2002. An established record of musical excellence is required, and an advanced musical degree is preferred. . . .
>
> The Virginia Glee Club typically presents six full concerts of classical repertoire in Charlottesville and performs

in two or three other cities on the East Coast each year. The group regularly performs collaborative works with women's choirs from the Northeast and tours internationally every few years.[1]

The tone of the advertisement was pure Thomas Deal. Deal, who came to the University from Norfolk, Virginia, would complete a law degree and would serve as president, unusually, for both 2001–2002 and the following season. He was an imposing young man with a dry wit, a love of words, and high ambitions for the Glee Club.

While the club sorted through the responses to the ad, they were not idle. The 2001–2002 season recruited a large class, with a total membership of fifty-five members, and saw the group put on three nearly sold-out Christmas concerts, a trip to New York City, and two concerts in the spring: the homecoming concert in March in collaboration with the Virginia Women's Chorus and a joint concert with the chamber ensemble Scaramouche at the Thomas Jefferson Memorial Church in April, at which they performed Brahms's *Alto Rhapsody*. They somehow also found time to record a Christmas album, *A Season with the Virginia Glee Club*. And they connected with the professor who became their conductor the following season: Michael Slon.

Slon was hired by the Board of Visitors in August 2001 as an assistant professor in the McIntire Department of Music.[2] He came to the University of Virginia from graduate work at Indiana University's School of Music, and before that from Cornell University, where he was deeply involved with the Cornell Glee Club.[3] He was hired as the director of choral music for the University, following the retirement of Donald Loach in 1998.

Slon's season with the Glee Club featured strong performances of a major masterwork as well as the Choral Showcase and the Christmas concerts. The spring saw a trip to Smith College, with a stop in New York City; the Glee Club performed Mozart's *Requiem* with the Smith College Glee Club, in New York City, at Gonzaga College High School in Washington, DC, and in Old Cabell Hall.

The following season, 2003–2004, saw the return to Charlottesville of someone who had last visited with Chanticleer in 1994: Frank Albinder.

Albinder had been busy in the intervening nine years. He remained a member of Chanticleer through the end of the 1990s, appearing on twenty of the group's recordings, and was the associate conductor and artistic director for Chanticleer's 1999 album *Colors of Love*, which won a Grammy Award for Best Small Ensemble Performance at the Forty-Second Annual Grammy Awards in February 2000. But Chanticleer was only part of his choral resume. While in graduate school in Boston he had sung in the Boston Camerata under the direction of Joel Cohen, where he appeared on several of the group's albums on the Nonesuch Records label. Like John Liepold and Bruce Tammen before him, he had also sung with Robert Shaw. He left Chanticleer to move to Washington, DC, where he became the music director of the Washington Men's Camerata in 1999 and of the Woodley Ensemble in 2000.

Due to his musical connections and his Grammy, there was an air of glamour about Albinder. Notes found in the Glee Club library made by an anonymous Glee Club member, presumably during the discussion about hiring him, had freely associated words written down next to his name: "Kennedy Center, pizazz, Lincoln Center."[4]

The group started the fall of 2003 under Albinder's baton, beginning as had become customary with the Choral Showcase in November. For the first time, the showcase featured both past and present Glee Club conductors, as Slon's University Singers were also on the program along with the Virginia Women's Chorus. The season was otherwise unremarkable, with a fall trip, Christmas concerts, and spring concert rounding out the activities. The following season was much the same, with the Haydn's *Lord Nelson Mass*, performed in April 2005, providing the requisite major work in performances with the Wellesley College Choir, both at Wellesley and in Old Cabell Hall.

The 2005–2006 season, however, would change the course of the Glee Club substantially. In the most substantial shift in the group's organization since the departure from the music department in 1989, the spring of 2006 saw the formation of the Virginia Glee Club Alumni and Friends Association (AFA). Conceived originally as something like an alumni association for Glee Club members paired with a board of directors to oversee alumni volunteer activities in support of the group, the Virginia Glee Club AFA provided a structured way for the alumni community to engage and help a Glee Club that, while once more under the direction of a full-time conductor, was still precarious financially. Past efforts to establish a board and start fundraising had foundered due to the difficulty of organizing busy alumni, as well as the Glee Club's own shifting priorities as their musical direction changed through the late 1990s.

This time was different. A few key ingredients made the new effort more promising: energetic board members, a broader effort to bring alumni into the fold, and the support of the University of Virginia Alumni Association, which was beginning to formalize programming—and funding—for alumni interest groups as a way to keep alumni engaged with the University and giving to the UVA Fund.

From the beginning, the new leadership of the board was highly motivated. Thomas Deal had come through the two years of his Glee Club presidency with an appreciation for the importance of stability in the club's governance. He took on the role of president of the AFA. He was joined by like-minded alumni, including Douglass List as chairman and Fred Kaspick as "ambassador." That the officers of the board included heavy representation from the 1970s alumni was a deliberate choice to reach out to older alumni who still remembered their time with "Coach Loach" fondly. The full board also included Liepold era alumni Jonathan Finn and George Shirley, who cochaired the capital campaign. Both brought deep experience to their role and both were certified financial professionals; Shirley had ten years of experience as a financial adviser, while Finn was a hedge fund manager and consultant. But they also provided a draw for alumni from later eras to join and participate. Indeed, part of the original messaging appeal of the AFA launch was a call for alums to become life members of the association, and Kaspick and others led a broad outreach to draw in participants.[5]

The association was formally inaugurated with a Rotunda Dinner held March 11, 2006. In addition to the launch of the AFA, the event also marked the first presentation of the Gilbert J. Sullivan Distinguished Service Award, in recognition of "an individual whose tireless efforts, selfless dedication, and continuing support have contributed in a significant way to the success of the Virginia Glee Club." The first recipient was none other than Bonnie Ford, who alongside Gilly Sullivan had supported the club's efforts for independence and who at the time was the associate director of the UVA Fund.

For its part, the Glee Club was starting to raise its musical sights on more ambitious targets. In his second and third seasons, Albinder commissioned two works for the club, the first new commissions since Liepold's departure almost ten years previously. The works could not have been more different. Judith Shatin's "The Jabberwocky," a setting of the Lewis Carroll poem, was rollicking and ambitious, and as far from the club's normal repertoire as could be imagined. Shatin's compositional background was eclectic; a student of Milton Babbitt, she had founded the Virginia Center for Computer Music and had written a folk oratorio, *COAL*, about the life of West Virginia miners, as well as the April 1993 setting of the Declaration of Independence, "We Hold

These Truths," which was performed on the Lawn by the University Singers while the Glee Club performed *Young T.J.* on the *Today Show* and at the Jefferson Memorial.[6] In the following season, 2006–2007, Lee Hoiby's "Last Letter Home," also known as "Private First Class Jesse Givens," set the text of Givens's letters home from Iraq prior to his death in a 2003 tank accident. Hoiby, a student of Gian Carlo Menotti, specialized in vocal music and composed both operas and songs, including numerous settings of the poetry of Elizabeth Bishop.

Alongside the commissioned works, the club's repertoire overall was diversifying. While the Christmas repertoire in 2006 would have been unremarkable under Tammen or Loach, the 2007 Founder's Day concert featured not only the premiere of the Hoiby work but also performances of the South African freedom song "Tshotsholoza," a medley of "Coney Island Baby" and "We All Fall," portions of *The Testament of Freedom*, the Biebl, and—for the first time in several years—the "Virginia Yell Song" and "Vir-ir-gin-i-a," the latter conducted by Loach in his first concert appearance with the Glee Club in seventeen years.

The season also saw a strong start to the activities of the AFA. The Glee Club capital campaign was officially launched at a dinner led by the AFA, with a lofty target of $1 million and over $100,000 already raised from board members and other donors, including $50,000 from an anonymous donor. The goal was simple: financial stability and an endowment big enough to pay the Glee Club's expenses. The spring newsletter reported that, after only ten months, the campaign balance stood at over $196,000, 20 percent of the goal. At this early stage, most of the growth was fueled by significant gifts, with only sixty named donors.

The following season featured more ambitious undertakings, including a fall concert at the Yale Club in New York City, a trip to Massachusetts to perform Bach's *Magnificat* with the Wellesley College Choir at First Congregational Church, Cambridge, and a new commission from composer Steven Sametz that set the poetry of Walt Whitman ("Not Heat Flames Up and Consumes," from the collection *We Two*). But the season might have been more significant for the groundwork it laid for the future, in the form of a $15,000 award from the Jefferson Trust to fund "recording an album that will be comprised of music that was once popular at the University but has since been forgotten."

The project, as researched by Albinder and Glee Club members, sought to expand the working repertoire of Virginiana beyond the few pieces that had survived, like the "Virginia Yell Song," "Hike, Virginia," and others. Ultimately, *Songs of Virginia*, the album financed by the project, served as the only recording for more than a dozen songs (out of two dozen total tracks) that had been published a hundred years previously in the book *Songs of the University of Virginia*. The grant and the recording returned the Glee Club to one of its earliest missions: recording the history of student song at the University.

The recording was mostly a cappella and mostly true to the songs' original arrangements, presenting arrangements by Fickénscher and even earlier arrangements from *Songs of the University of Virginia* instead of the more familiar, more recent arrangements by MacInnis and Loach. The selections were not all a hundred years old, however; composer Christopher Marshall contributed arrangements of several songs, including an impressionistic take on "Oh, Carolina." The album also included the newest addition to the University song repertoire, Loach's arrangement of Arthur Kyle Davis's "Vir-ir-gin-i-a." A few of the tunes were presented in "live" performances of the Glee Club with the University Band, just as they were on the 1950 *Songs of the University of Virginia*. Alongside the recording, Albinder provided liner notes that discussed the histories of the compositions. The booklet provided the first printed background of some of the lesser known tunes.

While the club researched and recorded, they were not idle. The spring of 2009 saw an alumni reunion featuring an alumni chorus, a concert at which the *Songs of Virginia* material was debuted, and a banquet, at which the association awarded the second Gilbert J. Sullivan Award to Larry Mueller for his role in helping to steer the club toward independence and his support as an alumnus, including his early fundraising and his work on the Virginia Glee Club Advisory Board, the forerunner to the AFA.

Songs of Virginia was ultimately released in the fall of 2009, nearly seven years after the club's previous album, *A Season with the Virginia Glee Club*. To make up for the long drought, Albinder and the officers released two *other* albums at the same time, both drawn from live concert recordings. *Virginia Glee Club Live!* featured recordings of the club's commissioned works "Last Letter Home" and "The Jabberwocky" alongside other repertoire, and *Christmas with the Virginia Glee Club* compiled recordings from the Christmas concerts from 2004 through 2008.

The album releases coincided with a tour year, and president Jeff McKenzie and his officers, Steven Kern, Jimmy Ko, David Crouch, and Kevin Brown, used the season's tour to take the *Songs of Virginia* material on the road for the 2010 Tour of the Northeast to Doylestown, Pennsylvania; Smith and Wellesley in Massachusetts; Madison Avenue Presbyterian Church in New York; New York Avenue Presbyterian Church in Washington, DC; Williamsburg and Roanoke, Virginia; and then, as an exclamation point, to Ann Arbor, Michigan.

The officers had not lost their minds, nor were they trying to emphasize the "north" part of the Northeast. Rather, while planning the tour, an invitation came to Frank Albinder from Paul Rardin, conductor of the University of Michigan Glee Club. The Michigan group was celebrating the 150th anniversary of its founding that year, and they thought it might be fun to celebrate with other groups of a similar vintage. The Harvard Glee Club under Jameson Marvin was planning to join them; might Virginia as well?

It didn't hurt that Ann Arbor held another attraction in the presence of Teresa Sullivan, the provost of the University of Michigan, a sociologist who had collaborated with Jay Lawrence Westbrook and Elizabeth Warren on groundbreaking work on consumer bankruptcy—and who had, on January 11, 2010, been elected by the Board of Visitors as the next president of the University of Virginia. Not only would this trip be a rare collaboration with other top-notch Glee Clubs, it would also be a once in a lifetime opportunity to make an important friend.

So the club's itinerary was set. They made stops in Pennsylvania, Massachusetts, and New York; met Congressman Tom Perriello (son of Vito A. Perriello Jr., Glee Club 1958–1960, who had passed away the prior year) and sang illicitly from House Speaker Nancy Pelosi's balcony until being shushed by a Capitol guard in Washington, DC; performed in Williamsburg, where they brought up to the stage Bonnie Ford, who would retire at the end of that year, to thank her; and collaborated with Jeffrey Sandborg's Oriana Singers in Roanoke—only their second collaboration with Sandborg since their experience with Mahler's Second Symphony sixteen years previously.

Then, after a full week on the road, the club and their director drove nine hours north from Roanoke to Ann Arbor. The three glee clubs, with a collective 440 years' experience under their belts (Michigan, 150 years; Harvard, 151 years; and Virginia, the relative newcomer at 139 years), presented a program drawn from their respective spring tour repertoire. Virginia alumni in the Michigan area got a relatively rare chance to hear the club perform. And the club members got to meet the University of Virginia's future president, Teresa Sullivan, at the preconcert reception.

The season saw one other "first"—the formation of a new a cappella group that performed as a subset of the Glee Club. In February 2010, the Glee Club sponsored a concert called Singfest, featuring a cappella performances by the Glee Club, the Sil'Hooettes, Remix, the New Dominions . . . and a new group called the Gleemen. Albinder and the officers identified the need for an a cappella group associated with the Glee Club as they saw an increase in loss of members to the other a cappella groups and a steady decline in the number of members who remained in the Glee Club after joining another group. By this time, there were about twenty groups in existence at the University, and competition for singers had grown fierce; creating the Gleemen gave the Glee Club a voice at a cappella events like Singfest and provided a way for club members to experience a cappella performance without the need to join another group.

The competition for singers was a real problem by this time, both for the more traditional choruses and the other a cappella groups. A few years previously, in Mickey Rapkin's book *Pitch Perfect* in which the Hullabahoos were profiled as part of a larger study of collegiate a cappella, he noted about the University of Virginia scene that "competition for fresh meat is fierce among the a cappella groups."[7] But it was far more challenging for the Glee Club, the Women's Chorus, and the University Singers, who now had to compete for members with groups who performed better known repertoire—and had greater sex appeal.

The psychology of college activities had changed dramatically since the founding of the Virginia Gentlemen. In the 1950s, one could feasibly be a member of both the Glee Club and the Virginia Gentlemen and still have time to pledge a fraternity, join an honor society, and serve as head cheerleader for the football team.[8] Even in the late 1980s, when the Virginia Gentlemen separated from the Glee Club, members still participated in both groups. But now students found juggling their studies and the rehearsal schedules for multiple groups extremely challenging, to the point that there were virtually no members of the Glee Club who were simultaneously active members of an a cappella group. The introduction of the Gleemen was an attempt to stave off this challenge to the membership—essentially, to offer both kinds of performance without requiring two full rehearsal and performance schedules.

It might seem unusual for a group of students who had historically managed by the seats of their tuxedo trousers to be thinking strategically about long-term membership trends. But, as the club headed into its 140th anniversary year, the leadership had begun to mature institutionally, due to two factors: the addition of a full-time administrator who could provide some institutional memory from year to year, and the twice-yearly meetings with the board of the Virginia Glee Club AFA. As the capital campaign neared its goal, conversations with the board were increasingly directed toward the future.

1 *Choral Journal 42*, no. 4 (November 2001): 37.

2 University of Virginia Board of Visitors Minutes, January 25, 2002.

3 In 1998, he published *Songs from the Hill: A History of the Cornell Glee Club*, which might be said to be the spiritual cousin of this book.

4 Manuscript notes on the back of a vocal score, found April 26, 2020, in the Virginia Glee Club library.

5 The outreach was broad indeed. Thomas Deal called me and asked me to join the VGCAFA as its historian after coming across my early research into the club's history on a Google search, which led him to my blog.

6 See "Judith Shatin, Composer," Wendigo Music, accessed June 21, 2020, https://www.judithshatin.com/.

7 Mickey Rapkin, *Pitch Perfect: The Quest for Collegiate A Cappella Glory* (New York: Penguin, 2008).

8 Kermit Lowry Jr., class of 1955 and a founding member of the Virginia Gentlemen, was an exemplar.

28 140 AND BEYOND

Entering the 2010–2011 season, the focus of both board and club was on the 140th anniversary. On the Glee Club's side, the group planned for a master-works reunion concert with orchestra and guest choir on a grand scale. The board had two initiatives going into the season: a successful 140th Anniversary Reunion and bringing the capital campaign to a close. They were able to achieve one of those outcomes and celebrate substantial progress toward the second.

The reunion was planned as a grand event on the Grounds of the University of Virginia. With the 2009 reunion under their belts, the board and volunteers knew what they wanted for the weekend: opportunities to sing, socialize, and listen to the club, along with visits from honored guests. They also wanted to declare victory on the capital campaign. From its starting point, the dogged fundraisers had managed to grow the endowment substantially. The 2008 recession had blunted the growth of the endowment a bit, but by the time of the reunion in the spring of 2011, the collected moneys had grown to almost $900,000—not the million-dollar mark the board was aiming for, but incredible progress nonetheless. Board president Thomas Deal and chair Douglass List wanted to use the weekend to help push the endowment over the top.

The reunion also marked the first major event planned with the assistance of new Glee Club administrator Jessica Wiseman. The position of administrator was originally established for the purpose of reporting to the Alumni and

Friends Association, but it quickly became clear that the club would benefit far more from having a full-time administrator. Wiseman, who had a background in choral music and arts administration, took over from Jennifer Brecht, who had served in the post for the first few years of the association's existence. Wiseman immediately proved to be popular with the club, where she played the role of den mother as well as a consistent point of contact for the officers of the association.

The reunion wasn't the only alumni engagement event for the year. That fall, the club inaugurated a new tradition, a Rotunda Dinner that drew alumni, parents, club members, and special guests—this time including Donald Loach, Ernest Mead, and Henry Morgan, who had recently retired in Charlottesville and reconnected with the Glee Club through Loach. After Frank Albinder's address and toasts led by Loach, the gathering conferred the Gilbert J. Sullivan Distinguished Service Award to Loach and Mead.

Performing a masterworks concert with a guest group proved more challenging than in years past, simply because the number of women's choruses was starting to dwindle. Ultimately the redoubtable Jeffrey Sandborg and his Roanoke College Oriana Singers were tapped to join the club in a performance of the Mozart *Requiem*. Another old friend returned to perform the tenor solo, Bill Bennett. Selections from the group's repertoire, including material from the *Songs of Virginia* project, compositions by Palestrina, Pavel Chesnokov, and Sibelius, and the alma maters, would round out the repertoire, which also featured a piece Frank Albinder planned to premiere first at the 2010 Christmas concerts and which would unexpectedly land the Glee Club smack amid the culture wars.

Albinder had connected with composer and arranger Ethan Sperry, who was the director of choral activities at Portland State University, some years prior through the American Choral Directors Association. Sperry specialized in arrangements of world music, editing the Global Rhythms series for Earthsongs, and was a frequent collaborator with film composer A. R. Rahman, winner of two Academy Awards for his score to *Slumdog Millionaire* in 2009. Sperry had arranged Rahman's song "Zikr," from the soundtrack to the 2004 biopic *Netaji Subhas Chandra Bose: The Forgotten Hero*, for men's chorus. The song functioned as a hymn of praise to Allah in the Sufi tradition; Albinder, interested in adding world perspectives to the annual Christmas concert, programmed the work for Christmas.

The Glee Club performed the work alongside Chesnokov's *Spaséniye sodelal,* Palestrina's "Sicut Cervus," the South African anthem "Tshotsholoza," and a host of more traditional Christmas carols, in two performances: December 3, 2010, in Old Cabell Hall, and December 10 at the Paramount Theater in downtown Charlottesville. Eight days later, the Charlottesville *Daily Progress* printed a letter from Jean Price decrying the inclusion of "Zikr":

> The program was advertised as a Christmas concert, so we were surprised to see one of his selections, "Zikr." This song has nothing to do with Christmas. It is a Muslim chant to their God. I think it is disingenuous to insert an Islamic chant, however good and exciting the music, which is the antithesis of Christian music.
>
> Zikr reminds Muslims to remember their God—Allah, who is not the God of the Christians. We celebrate at Christmas the biblical view of God—that he is one in three persons: God the Father, God the Son (Jesus Christ), and God the Holy Spirit. To give recognition to the Muslim's God by putting this devotional chant along side Christian songs is totally inappropriate. Would a Ramadan celebration include a Christmas song?
>
> The God of the Koran does not recognize Jesus Christ as the Son of God the Father who came to earth to save us from our sins. Was this chant included for the purpose of political correctness?[1]

That might have been the end of it, except that the letter was picked up by a series of right-wing blogs, who bewailed the "political correctness" of Albinder's programming choice. Albinder responded in his own letter to the *Progress*:

> The Arabic word for God, Allah, predates the establishment of the Islamic faith by generations. To call God "Allah" is no more remarkable than to call God "Adonai," "Jehovah," "Yahweh," "Dieu" or any of God's many other names. Islam, like Christianity and Judaism, is one of the three foundational Abrahamic faiths. All three religions worship the same God the Father.
>
> I intended no political message. Every fall, the Glee Club

learns several general occasion sacred pieces to perform at UVa's Family Weekend concert. I then include these pieces on our Christmas program.

Because the Glee Club is made up of students, I feel responsible to program a wide variety of music to expose them to beliefs and cultures that might not be their own as part of their broader education. The university's founder, Thomas Jefferson, owned a large quantity of religious texts including a prized copy of the Quran. I would hope that he would be supportive of just such an approach to programming.[2]

The attention of the right-wing blogosphere having moved on by March, there were no comments about the reprise of the work for the 140th Anniversary Concert, again alongside "Tshotsholoza" and *Spaséniye*.

The actual reunion weekend was far less controversial but substantially exciting. On Friday, March 18, Glee Club alumni gathered in the Colonnade Club for a reception and a chance to talk to AFA members about the progress of the capital campaign, before heading down the Lawn for the concert and the performance of the Mozart *Requiem*. The following morning, the alumni headed back to Old Cabell Hall for an alumni sing, this time under the direction of Albinder, Loach, John Liepold, and Bruce Tammen. They performed a set of works together, including Dowland's "Come Again, Sweet Love," "Winter Song," "Sometimes I Feel Like a Motherless Child," "Love Is a Green Girl," "A Shadow's on the Sundial," "Hark All Ye Lovely Saints," "Shenandoah," and the Biebl "Ave Maria."

The alums then headed up the Lawn to the Rotunda for group photos. It was one of those rare spring days in Charlottesville: sunny and crystal clear, not too hot, and quiet. A group of younger alums started singing as they mounted the upper terraces of the Lawn, forming a circle that drew in more and more participants until some thirty stood at the foot of the Rotunda, performing "Loch Lomond." The collected alumni, a hundred strong, sang "Virginia, Hail, All Hail" and "The Good Old Song" from the top of the Rotunda steps.

That night, at the banquet, Lloyd Stamy (class of 1973) introduced former University of Virginia president John Casteen, who spoke warmly of the contributions of the Glee Club to University life. He was followed by Deal, who spoke about the state of the capital campaign and the association, and by Patrick Lynn Garner (class of 1972), who spoke about the recording of *A*

FIGURE 33. Glee Club alumni and friends, Rotunda Steps, March 19, 2011. Visible (from left): John Liepold, George Wu, Chris Tuggey, David Temple Jr., Thomas Deal, Greg Dodson, Drew Cogswell, Bryan Strickland, Eric Sall, Larry Mueller.

Shadow's on the Sundial as a fundraiser for the 1972 European tour. Garner said, "I understand that they asked several other people to talk about [the recording], and no one could remember, so no one can challenge me: we worked very hard on the recording and we had fun on the tour." At the conclusion of the banquet, List gave newly remastered CD copies of *A Shadow's on the Sundial* to the 1970s attendees to jog their memories.

With the reunion in its rearview mirror, the Glee Club took its new repertoire on the road, performing the Mozart *Requiem* with the Oriana Singers in Roanoke on April 9 and at Wellesley College the following weekend. The performances were a fitting cap to a monumental season.

While the 2011–2012 season had no reunion, it had a much more ambitious tour: the Tour of the West Coast took the Glee Club to Seattle and Vancouver, Washington; Sacramento; Orinda and Claremont, California; Las Vegas; and Long Beach, California, where they collaborated along the way with Seattle Pacific University Men's Choir, Portland State University Men's Choir (under the direction of Ethan Sperry), Pomona College Men's Blue and White, and the UNLV Varsity Men's Glee Club, concluding in Long Beach at the March Madness Choral Festival. The first Glee Club tour of the West

Coast brought out alumni who hadn't seen the Glee Club in years, including Mark Jander (class of 1954) and Al Prichard, Glee Club president in 1956 and founding member of the Virginia Gentlemen.

The experience of singing with the West Coast choirs brought the club's music to a new audience, who shared their appreciation—sometimes (as in the March Madness Choral Festival) in writing. Albinder wrote in his tour blog, "Some of the comments we got were, 'Beautiful resonance!' 'Beautiful balance of parts.' 'Beautiful tone.' 'You are a fine ensemble.' 'Magical ending!' (to the Wesley) 'Gorgeous! Great shape and intensity.' 'I am melting in this tone!'"[3]

The next few seasons followed this pattern. As Albinder noted, there were fewer opportunities to collaborate with women's choruses on weekend tours; longer and more frequent spring break tours allowed the Glee Club to travel farther and reach larger audiences. In 2013 this touring philosophy took them to Northampton, Massachusetts, to collaborate with Smith College; then to Millersville and Natrona Heights (Pittsburgh), Pennsylvania; Ypsilanti, Michigan; Westlake, Ohio; and Chicago. The 2014 tour took them to the Intercollegiate Men's Choruses National Seminar and stops in Pittsburgh; Oxford, Ohio; Louisville; Knoxville; and Roanoke (the "Tour to Avoid West Virginia"). On the 2014 tour, the group went way back to its roots while visiting Vanderbilt, where they serenaded Stamy's daughter, at his request, with Virginia songs so that she might think twice about her choice to attend Vanderbilt rather than Virginia. (Albinder reported that "she seemed sort of nonplussed by the whole thing.")

Things were changing at the University, as well. At the end of the 2011–2012 academic year, just three weeks after the Glee Club's Finals concert in the University Chapel, University rector Helen Dragas announced that Teresa Sullivan would resign as the University's president, just two years into her five-year contract. Subsequently, it became clear that Dragas and vice rector Mark Kington had engineered a recommendation by the Board of Visitors that Sullivan resign, citing her reluctance to take exceptional measures, such as eliminating the Classics Department, to address what they saw as an impending crisis in higher education funding. Sullivan agreed to resign, feeling that she had lost the support of the board. But as news spread about Sullivan's ouster, it became clear that the board's support for Dragas was far from unanimous and that Sullivan's support among the faculty and students was far stronger than anyone had realized.

On Monday, June 18, Sullivan returned to the Rotunda to address the Board of Visitors. She was greeted by a rally on the Lawn that had begun at 2:30 p.m. with the arrival of former University president John Casteen, who said to the crowd, "My interest is in having the public's business done in public," urging the board to hold a public meeting on the matter. At the edge of the Lawn, radio station WTJU had set up a broadcast booth manned by Glee Club alumni and DJ Tyler Magill. It was Magill's suggestion that the studio run the broadcast from the Lawn that day in support of a call for "openness and fairness."[4] He held an open mic to any bystander who wanted to share their thoughts on the matter. Siva Vaidhyanathan, the chair of the media studies department, spoke up:

> Mr. Jefferson made this a place to think because he was a modest man who didn't know where the future was going, who didn't know what we were in for as a republic. And he never assumed that he knew what should be studied in the next century. Anyone who pretends that you can prescribe what [a] university like this should and shouldn't be doing from above, or from some yacht off Connecticut's coast, is full of crap.[5]

Ultimately, after a revolt from the faculty—provost John Simon threatened to resign if Sullivan was forced to leave—revelations that Dragas and Kington sought to engineer Sullivan's resignation for months before landing on the excuse of blaming her handling of financial matters, and a threat from embattled Virginia governor Robert McDonnell to remove the entire board if they did not resolve the matter, a new vote of the board unanimously called for Sullivan's reinstatement. She would continue in the role for another six years following the incident.[6]

Amid the excitement, the Glee Club continued a combination of normal and unusual promotional activities. The fall of 2013 marked the release of their recording *In Harmony, Love and Brotherhood*, which featured the Glee Club House prominently on the front cover. The house at 505 Valley Road had returned to the club after a year of non-occupancy in 2011–2012, during which the house was renovated by its owner. On the more unusual side, the group jumped at the chance to perform on ESPN in support of the men's basketball team in the fall of 2012 and to sing the national anthem for the football team.

On the membership side, 2014–2015 saw the culmination of a deliberate effort to increase the group's membership. In 2010–2011, the membership had stood at forty-five; in 2014–2015 the membership hit sixty for the first time in recent memory. Glee Club vice president Andrew "Drew" D'Amato, in an article in the fall 2014 newsletter cheekily entitled "Size Matters," wrote, "While Club increases its presence on Grounds through its member size, Club is able to spread its message of Harmony, Love and Brotherhood to a student body which has not experienced this type of music before. Guys join Club, they grab their friends from their dorms to join and to attend their concerts, and soon you have a vast group of committed friends and loyal families, all of which are strong supporters." D'Amato noted that the increase in group size seemed correlated with results: the 2013–2014 Singfest raised over $2,200 for the area food bank, compared with only $100 in the event's first year, and the club sold out both its Christmas concerts and three standing room only Finals concerts in the Chapel.[7]

The 2015 tour likewise benefited from the increased membership, with members planning stops at the University of Maryland Men's Chorus Invitational; St. Paul's Lutheran Church in Falls Church, Virginia; Paoli United Methodist Church in Paoli, Pennsylvania; Springside Chestnut Hill Academy in Philadelphia; and Bethlehem Lutheran Church in Baldwin, New York. Unfortunately the Maryland appearance was snowed out, but the rest of the tour proceeded as planned, including a day off in New York City.

The acme of this strategy of increased touring and membership came in the following season, the Glee Club's 145th, with another significant milestone: the Glee Club's first international tour since the 2000 Tour de France and only the second since Loach's tenure. For this trip, Albinder and his executive committee, including D'Amato, now president, vice president Kevin Chen, business manager Will Wheaton, secretary Jacob Higgins, and publicity manager Andrew Burrill, went in a somewhat unexpected direction: Argentina. The trip, with performances in Buenos Aires and La Plata, enabled the Glee Club to have a performance workshop with composer and conductor Oscar Escalada as well as to collaborate with Argentinian choirs.

The following month marked the celebration of the 145th anniversary and another reunion. The program was similar to the one from five years earlier, though with no concert—the reunion followed the club's spring concert by a week due to the challenges of scheduling space on Grounds, which had grown substantially over the prior years. The spring concert, a collaboration with

Smith College, performing Rossini's *Petite messe solennelle*, marked another successful joint performance in the most recent of the Glee Club's partnerships with significant women's choruses.

The season marked another milestone: the ending of Deal's tenure as president of the Virginia Glee Club AFA. Under his leadership, the club's various endowments had grown to over $1.2 million, providing a reliable income stream to pay a conductor's salary, and a board of more than thirty alumni, family members, and friends had become an important resource in helping the club's leaders keep the organization on an even keel. Deal noted, in a farewell letter in the newsletter:

> In the spring of 2001, Bruce Tammen instructed me that the only way the Club could consistently recruit and retain a talented conductor was with the support of a robust board of alumni and friends, which at the time did not exist. And all those who were familiar with the Club's situation knew that the lack of consistent annual funding created a potentially fatal vulnerability that could see the Club dissolve or wither in the absence of Herculean efforts by the undergraduate leaders every year, without fail.
>
> Well, it took 15 years, but the task is complete.[8]

Deal's replacement was his vice president, Kevin Ross Davis, who, having served on the board for years, provided continuity in the leadership. The board recognized both Deal and List, who had stepped down as chairman a few years previously, with the Sullivan Award at the reunion.

The 2016–2017 season saw no international tour, but that didn't mean the club was idle. On the contrary, under president Joseph Marchese-Schmitt, their schedule was busier than ever: an appearance at the Women Against Violence Rise Up Concert, a benefit hosted by the Virginia Women's Chorus; the Family Weekend Choral Showcase ; sold-out Christmas concerts; Singfest; the Finals concert; and a tour of the south, a collaboration with three other choruses in a spring concert, and the club's first appearance in Carnegie Hall.

The club had stepped up the frequency of its collaborations with the Virginia Women's Chorus substantially in the preceding few years; indeed, thanks to the fall Choral Showcase concerts and the club's Singfest winter fundraiser concerts, the two groups were typically sharing a stage at least twice a year.

Even with this factor, 2016–2017 stood out due to the additional appearance at the Women Against Violence concert. The concert, organized by the Virginia Women's Chorus as a fundraiser for the Women's Center at the University of Virginia, was intended to raise awareness of resources for sexual assault survivors and to draw attention to the issue of sexual assault on college campuses.

The Women's Chorus planned to return the favor in the spring with an appearance with the Glee Club at their spring concert. Thanks to the touring schedule of two other choruses with long-standing relationships with the club—the Roanoke College Oriana Singers under Sandborg and Chicago Men's A Cappella under Tammen—the concert became more of an impromptu festival. Due to the timing (relatively late in the season) and competition from other spring events, the executives made the decision to open the concert up as a free event. The resulting event, billed as "Four Free," brought a sizable audience to hear the collected groups.

The spring concert was, however, not the first event added to the schedule through serendipity. The Concert for Peace, held in Carnegie Hall on January 14 and commemorating the life and works of Martin Luther King Jr., featured nine other college and high school choirs. The opportunity to join the performance happened late in the fall semester, but the club's student leadership leaped at the chance to perform at the famed New York venue, even if they would only have a short set alongside a joint performance of Ralph Vaughan Williams's "Dona nobis pacem."

With all this, one could be forgiven for forgetting about the spring tour. The tour, however, proved unforgettable, not least of which due to the bus breaking down which caused the group to miss its second gig, a performance at the McCallie School in Chattanooga, Tennessee, and stranded them in Johnson City, where they had performed the night before with the East Tennessee State University BucsWorth Men's Choir. After repairing their transportation, the group made its way through stops in Birmingham and Mobile before reaching Jackson, Mississippi. There the group performed a solo concert at Fondren Church before making an appearance at the Mississippi State Capitol Building, courtesy of state senator Hob Bryan. (The performance did not go unnoticed. Adam Ganucheau, the editor in chief of *Mississippi Today News*, tweeted, "The University of Virginia Glee Club is singing beautifully on Senate floor. Sen. Hob Bryan, notorious UVA grad, is beside himself.") The tour finished in Atlanta with a rehearsal exchange with the Morehouse College Glee Club, but time prohibited an actual joint performance.

All in all, the 2016–2017 season was typical of the 2010s Glee Club routine. Unfortunately, things were about to get very atypical.

The January 2017 Concert for Peace held a double meaning for some members of the Glee Club. The previous November, Donald Trump had been elected president of the United States on a platform that was widely viewed as encouraging division and violence. Following the election, tensions already brewing began to make themselves felt in Charlottesville. The immediate flashpoint was a decision from the Charlottesville City Council to remove the statue of Robert E. Lee from Lee Park, following the massacre of nine African Americans during a bible study at the Emanuel African Methodist Episcopal Church in Charleston, South Carolina, in 2015. The shooter, twenty-one-year-old Dylann Roof, had admired modern White supremacy movements and posted images of the Confederate battle flag; the resulting public debate following the shooting saw widespread reconsideration of the display of Confederate symbols and war memorials.

In Charlottesville, the decision to remove the statue of Lee was met with a strong backlash led, in part, by Charlottesville native and University of Virginia alumnus Jason Kessler. Kessler attempted to force vice mayor Wes Bellamy to resign, circulating a petition calling for his removal from office; while circulating the petition, Kessler was arrested for assault when he punched a man who questioned his motives. Together with White supremacist Richard Spencer, he organized a series of marches beginning in May that drew alt-right protesters from around the country, chanting antisemitic slogans and brandishing lit torches. A separate march by the Ku Klux Klan in protest of the plans for the statue's removal in July 2017 drew 1,000 counterprotesters, who held a nonviolent vigil against racism; after the Klan left, the Charlottesville police declared the counterprotest an "unlawful assembly" and dispersed the group with tear gas. The stage was set for a more violent encounter, one in which two Glee Club alumni would play a significant role.

Kessler joined forces with Spencer and other White supremacists in planning a large gathering in Charlottesville on August 12. Called "Unite the Right," the gathering sought to bring together neo-Nazi fans of the website the Daily Stormer, the National Policy Institute, and members of the component groups of the Nationalist Front; the Klan; the White supremacist group Identity Evropa; and many others. As publicity about the rally grew, a group of counterprotesters made their own plans to attend, including members of the National Council of Churches, Black Lives Matter, the Democratic Socialists of America, and others. Glee Club alumnus Seth Wispelwey, who was serving as clergy in Charlottesville, helped to organize a group of clergy and other leaders, including Cornel West, to march against the alt-right protesters.

The night before the rally, a group of around 300 White nationalists gathered at Nameless Field at 9:30 p.m. and lit torches before marching toward the Lawn, chanting "Blood and Soil," "Jews Will Not Replace Us," and other neo-Nazi slogans. Magill, a Glee Club alumnus, having worked a long day at the University library, saw the gathering and called 911 when he saw the torches. After watching multiple police motorcycle patrols pass the gathering crowd without action, he retreated to the Rotunda, where the marchers walked up the Rotunda steps around him.[9] They headed for a group of twenty-five or thirty counterprotesters at the base of the statue of Jefferson on the north steps. Magill felt the counterprotesters, one of whom was in a wheelchair, were in danger. "I was just thinking, Be with them; maybe my presence will change something . . . I figured if they're willing to kill twenty-five people, maybe they're not willing to kill twenty-six." He linked arms with the counterprotesters, and the marchers charged. Magill remembers smelling lighter fluid and being hit with torches.[10] Eventually the state police arrived and dispersed the brawl.

The following day, the rally saw more violence, with Wispelwey and his clergy rushed by attackers. He recalls, "We met beforehand with Cornel West, whose goal was to engage in nonviolent confrontation with the marchers. 'We want to go to jail,' he said. But when those guys with riot weapons came at us, he turned to me and said, 'Nobody's going to jail today.'"

The rally and its aftermath—the murder of counterprotester Heather Heyer, the beating of preschool teacher DeAndre Harris, and other horrific events—have been well documented. One consequence: after peacefully marching on Saturday, and literally chasing Kessler away from his press conference on Sunday shouting, "Her name is Heather, Jason. Her blood is on your hands," on Tuesday, August 15, Magill suffered a stroke stemming from a partially dissected carotid artery, an injury suffered while defending the students at the statue of Jefferson. He fortunately received immediate medical care and recovered. But his harsh criticism, published as an open letter to Sullivan in the *Washington Post*, of the University's and Sullivan's inaction in the face of the fascist marchers left a shadow on the closing year of her presidency.

It was a shaken Glee Club that returned to Charlottesville that fall. Outwardly, at least, the routine was not disrupted; 2017–2018 was a fairly typical season except for the release of their latest recording. On top of everything else during the 2016–2017 season, somehow the club had found time to record songs for their next album. Released on December 1, 2017, *Songs of the Shenandoah* highlighted some of the club's commissions, including Oscar Escalada's "Hanacpachap" from the Argentinean tour, excerpts from *Summer Songs*, and James Erb's arrangement of "Shenandoah." It also provided the first recording of the Gleemen. The following spring tour saw the members performing material from the album in Washington, DC; Falls Church, Virginia; Chapel Hill, Matthews, and Shallotte, North Carolina (the latter from an invitation from alum Tim Boda); and Roanoke, Virginia.

The season's end saw the Glee Club bid farewell to University president Teresa Sullivan. Though she had suffered criticism for her administration's handling of the August 2017 Unite the Right rally—subsequent investigations showed that the administration had received warnings about the seriousness of the plans but had not acted sufficiently to protect students—the group had managed to create a connection with "Terry" that had not been possible with her predecessors, as evidenced by the many photos that were taken as they serenaded her with Christmas poinsettias or joined her at Carr's Hill to welcome incoming first-year students.

The 2018–2019 season had an active schedule from the very beginning, starting with a joint appearance with the Notre Dame Glee Club in October while they were on their fall tour. A joint appearance at convocation with the redoubtable Virginia Women's Chorus, the Family Weekend Choral Showcase and Christmas concerts, Singfest, a tour, and a pair of concerts with Smith College in Washington, DC, and at Smith followed. The tour, returning to the West Coast, saw the Glee Club performing in Vancouver, Washington; Willamette University in Salem, Oregon; and three destinations around Seattle, including a performance of Beethoven's Ninth Symphony with the Northwest Symphony Orchestra. At the Friday performance at Epiphany Church in Seattle, the club members met voice actress Ellen McLain, who performed the character GLaDOS in the video game *Portal* and was a friend of someone's aunt. In the concert, the Gleemen performed an a cappella arrangement of the character's song, arranged by their longtime director Xuemeng "John" Xia, and McLain joined in, singing the lead.

Yet all was not running smoothly. The membership was back down to somewhere in the thirties, and the club was having trouble retaining members. This led to challenges on the tour, when some of the members, demonstrating customary college student forgetfulness, missed one of the concerts, leaving parts extremely light and exposed on a performance of "Shenandoah," and soul searching about the ability of the group to continue to collaborate at a high level with women's groups. Albinder was particularly frustrated about the collaborations with Smith, where the small numbers of the group left the men's parts exposed on the Haydn *Missa in Angustiis* (Mass in troubled times).

This led into an even smaller group in 2019–2020. Albinder noted in his customary message in the fall newsletter that "we had the smallest number of students audition for Club this year since I came to the Glee Club in 2002. And this in spite of herculean efforts from our Publicity Manager and other members of Club." Albinder blamed the decline on long-term effects of smartphone use and the associated anxiety and distractions. Whatever the cause, the situation occasioned long discussions with the board, but no action was taken.

The smaller club, numbering only thirty members, still managed to begin the season in style, rejoining the Virginia Women's Chorus for a reprise of the Women Against Violence charity concert and performing at the Family Weekend Choral Showcase. Perhaps due to the smaller membership numbers, the club failed to sell out its Christmas concerts, but still mounted memorable performances.

Administratively, the season was the first in almost ten years without Wiseman, who had taken a job at Alumni Hall the preceding spring. Her replacement, Travis Lively, not only took over for Wiseman in helping the club plan the season, but also sat in on first tenor, due to the low numbers in the group. He had his work cut out for him, since the group would execute the second "Tour to Avoid West Virginia" the following spring.

Like the first, the 2020 tour took the group along the inner states of the mid-Atlantic, with planned stops in Pittsburgh and at Miami University (Ohio) and rehearsal exchanges at Ball State University in Muncie, Indiana, and Albion College in Michigan. The final stop was to have been at Roanoke College for a return collaboration with the Roanoke College Choirs under the direction of Sandborg.

The Glee Club's bus left Charlottesville on March 7 and made it to Pittsburgh on March 8, where they were joined by Albinder, who had been presenting at the American Choral Directors Association conference in Rochester. They managed a successful joint concert at Miami University, despite a club member forgetting his tour blazer and having to perform in a denim jacket hastily purchased at a local Walmart. The two glee clubs partied at the Miami University Glee Club House and then hit the road for Indiana on March 9.

In the meantime, however, anxiety was growing all around the country due to the increasingly alarming information coming seemingly from all corners of the globe about a new respiratory illness. Following an unprecedented quarantine order in China on January 23 that had restricted the movements of up to eighteen million people in and around Wuhan, the World Health Organization declared a global health emergency on January 31, followed by a similar declaration in the United States on February 3. But at this stage little was known about the virus's transmission, and many activities, including conferences and concerts, went on as planned.

It all came to a head the week of the Glee Club's tour. They were scheduled to have two rehearsal exchanges, in Indiana and in Michigan. But on March 11, the World Health Organization declared COVID-19 a pandemic, and the University of Virginia moved all courses online for the remainder of the semester, urging students to return to their homes; the rehearsals were canceled, as were the remaining dates in the tour. On March 13, the day the Glee Club was to have concluded their tour in Roanoke, President Trump declared COVID-19 a national emergency and imposed a travel ban affecting European visitors to the United States, and the University of Virginia's administration ordered all students who were able to do so to return to their homes. The Glee Club got off the bus in Charlottesville to a University in lockdown.[11]

Many in the working world were put out of work or forced to telecommute, with parents of school-age children suddenly attending to their learning at home. University classes moved onto Zoom alongside many other activities. But for the Glee Club, as for all other choruses, the pandemic meant a total cessation of activities during the long spring. Evidence mounted that the COVID-19 virus was spread aerially via aerosols, such as those produced by talking or singing, and a widely publicized super-spreader chorus rehearsal in Washington State that resulted in the infection of up to fifty-three people and two deaths made it abundantly clear that in-person rehearsals were out of the picture.[12] The limitations of Zoom and other video conferencing technology meant that traditional choir rehearsals at a distance would be difficult as well; each participant in a Zoom call experienced a slight delay in receiving audio from the others on a call, with the result that attempts to sing together disintegrated into chaos.

The Glee Club did not give up easily, however. Newly elected president

James Wilusz announced plans in May to record a virtual choir performance of "Virginia, Hail, All Hail" and "The Good Old Song" and recruited alumni to join. Over fifty singers participated in the performance. In the fall, the students were able to return to the University in person, albeit with significant restrictions: no in-person performances by any performing arts groups, especially singing, and restrictions on student gatherings in groups larger than five people. The restrictions removed any hope that the Glee Club would be able to have a normal season, and some of the big events planned for the year, which marked the 150th anniversary of the announcement of the Cabell House Men, including an international tour and the reunion weekend already being planned for April 2021, had to be postponed.

Still, Wilusz and his officers soldiered on. Unable to have in-person rehearsals, they embraced Zoom rehearsals, in which Albinder led the group while each member sang on mute. Unable to have in-person performances, they embarked on planning and executing a virtual Christmas concert. The 80th Annual Virginia Glee Club Christmas Concert, with videography, a guest appearance from the Virginia Gentlemen, and alumni joining on "Winter Song" and "The Twelve Days of Christmas," was released on December 18 on one of the Glee Club's YouTube channels.[13] (In typical student group fashion, the group had had to start multiple channels, as they sometimes forgot to transition administration rights on their YouTube, Facebook, and Twitter pages when members graduated.) And fundraising was strong, with the group more than quadrupling their fundraising efforts from the prior year. They were even able to audition and accept three new members, all virtually.

As the Glee Club turned the pages on the end of 2020, the new year ahead, their 150th, bore a mixture of promise and challenge. Although vaccines against COVID-19 from Moderna and Pfizer had been approved and were being distributed to first-line responders, the supply was severely constrained, and all felt it was likely to be another year before enough people were vaccinated for anything like a return to normal. However, the Virginia Glee Club had weathered the storm. Thanks to the foresight of Thomas Deal and the other members of the AFA and to an energized alumni base, the group had survived the cessation of all its normal activities, and the energies of Wilusz and his executive officers meant that the group embraced the challenges and accomplished a transformation, however temporarily, into a virtual choir. The Glee Club has a foundation that it can continue to build upon. As the light of hope from the vaccines dawned ahead, it could look forward to continuing to give shape and hope to the ten thousand voices of its members and alumni.

1   Jean Price, "Muslim Song Disappointing at Annual Christmas Concert," *Daily Progress*, December 18, 2010.

2   Frank Albinder, "Concert Not Only About Christmas," *Daily Progress*, January 1, 2011.

3   Frank Albinder, "The End . . .," *Tour of the West* [blog], March 11, 2012, http://virginiagleeclubtourofthewest.blogspot.com/2012/03/end.html.

4   D. R. Tyler Magill, "'The White Nationalists Were Allowed to Take the University': A Letter to U-Va.'s President," *Washington Post*, October 4, 2017.

5   Siva Vaidhyanathan, quoted in Graham Moomaw, "Thousands Crowd Lawn in Support of Sullivan," *Daily Progress*, June 18, 2012.

6   Paul Schwartzmann, Daniel de Vise, Anita Kumar, and Jenna Johnson, "U-Va. Upheaval: 18 Days of Leadership Crisis," *Washington Post*, June 30, 2012.

7   Andrew D'Amato, "Size Matters," *Notes from the Path*, Fall 2014, 3.

8   Thomas Deal, "The Season of Endings and Beginnings," *Notes from the Path*, Fall 2015.

9   Magill, "'The White Nationalists.'"

10   Jack Stripling and Nell Gluckman, "UVA Employee Suffers Stroke after Clash with White Supremacists," *Chronicle of Higher Education*, August 16, 2017.

11   Brian Coy, "Latest Updates on UVA's Response to the Coronavirus," *UVA Today*, March 19, 2020.

12   Sarah Al-Arshani, "A Washington State Choir Rehearsal Was Deemed a 'Super Spreader' Event after 45 People Were Infected with the Coronavirus and 2 Died," *Business Insider*, March 30, 2020.

13   "The 80th Annual Virginia Glee Club Christmas Concert," YouTube, December 18, 2020.

APPENDICES

LIST OF CONDUCTORS

STARTING SEASON	CONDUCTOR	TOTAL SEASONS SERVED
1879–1880	John Duncan Emmet	1
1887–1888	Joseph Reid Anderson Hobson	1
1889–1890	Zelotes Wood Coombs	1
1891–1892	James Stuart Doubleday	1
1892–1893	Harrison Randolph	3
1895–1896	Frederick G. Rathbun	1
1897–1898	George Latham Fletcher	1
1898–1899	Francis Harris Abbot	1
1902–1903	Burnley Lankford	1
1904–1905	Robert B. Crawford	2
1905–1906	Cyril Dadswell	1
1905–1906	John A. Shishmanian	1
1910–1911	Martin S. Remsburg	1
1914–1915	Alfred Lawrence Hall-Quest	3
1917–1918	Erwin Schneider	1
1917–1918	Kirk Payne	2
1920–1921	Nevil Henshaw	1
1921–1922	Arthur Fickénscher	12

STARTING SEASON	CONDUCTOR	TOTAL SEASONS SERVED
1933–1934	Harry Rogers Pratt	10
1942–1943	Randall Thompson	1
1943–1944	Stephen Tuttle	8
1948–1949	Henry Morgan	1
1952–1953	Donald MacInnis	6
1957–1958	David Davis	7
1964–1965	Donald Loach	25
1966–1967	Frederic H. Ford	1
1973–1974	James Dearing	1
1989–1990	Cheryl Brown-West	1
1989–1990	Michael Butterman	2
1991–1992	John Liepold	5
1995–1996	J. Craig Fennell	1
1996–1997	Bruce Tammen	5
2001–2002	Burke Morton	1
2002–2003	Michael Slon	1
2003–2004	Frank Albinder	18 (to date)

LIST OF PRESIDENTS

SEASON	PRESIDENT
1870s	
1880s	
Glee Club 1880–1881 season	Unknown
Glee Club 1881–1882 season	Unknown
Glee Club 1882–1883 season	Unknown
Glee Club 1883–1884 season	Unknown
Glee Club 1884–1885 season	Unknown
Glee Club 1885–1886 season	Unknown
Glee Club 1886–1887 season	Sterling Galt
Glee Club 1887–1888 season	J.R.A. Hobson
Glee Club 1888–1889 season	No president
Glee Club 1889–1890 season	Charles Shirley Carter
1890s	
Glee Club 1890–1891 season	Fallow season
Glee Club 1891–1892 season	William H. Sweeney
Glee Club 1892–1893 season	Charles Behan Thorn
Glee Club 1893–1894 season	Bernard W. Moore
Glee Club 1894–1895 season	Micajah W. Pope

SEASON	PRESIDENT
Glee Club 1895–1896 season	McLane Tilton, Jr.
Glee Club 1896–1897 season	Rockwell Smith Brank
Glee Club 1897–1898 season	John Lawrence Vick Bonney
Glee Club 1898–1899 season	Edmund Bradford Burwell
Glee Club 1899–1900 season	Unknown
1900s	
Glee Club 1900–1901 season	Fallow season
Glee Club 1901–1902 season	Fallow season
Glee Club 1902–1903 season	Albert Lonsdale Roper
Glee Club 1903–1904 season	Edward H. Miller
Glee Club 1904–1905 season	Thomas Pinckney Bryan
Glee Club 1905–1906 season	James Tappan Hornor
Glee Club 1906–1907 season	Fallow season
Glee Club 1907–1908 season	Fallow season
Glee Club 1908–1909 season	Fallow season
Glee Club 1909–1910 season	Fallow season
1910s	
Glee Club 1910–1911 season	Malcolm W. Gannaway
Glee Club 1911–1912 season	Arthur F. Triplett
Glee Club 1912–1913 season	Roger M. Bone
Glee Club 1913–1914 season	Fallow season
Glee Club 1914–1915 season	Robert V. Funsten
Glee Club 1915–1916 season	Malcolm W. Gannaway
Glee Club 1916–1917 season	Robert Gilliam Butcher
Glee Club 1917–1918 season	William S. Thomas
Glee Club 1918–1919 season	William S. Thomas
Glee Club 1919–1920 season	William S. Thomas
1920s	
Glee Club 1920–1921 season	John Koch
Glee Club 1921–1922 season	Frederick R. Westcott

SEASON	PRESIDENT
Glee Club 1922–1923 season	Harry Glenn Kaminer
Glee Club 1923–1924 season	Randolph Conroy
Glee Club 1924–1925 season	Randolph Conroy
Glee Club 1925–1926 season	E. Lacy Gibson
Glee Club 1926–1927 season	E. Lacy Gibson
Glee Club 1927–1928 season	L. Reyner Samet
Glee Club 1928–1929 season	E. D. Brooke
Glee Club 1929–1930 season	James Lindell Ellis
1930S	
Glee Club 1930–1931 season	Unknown
Glee Club 1931–1932 season	Herbert L. Morgenroth
Glee Club 1932–1933 season	Charles W. Gasque
Glee Club 1933–1934 season	James M. Berry
Glee Club 1934–1935 season	Guy Hope
Glee Club 1935–1936 season	Rial Rose
Glee Club 1936–1937 season	McDonald Wellford
Glee Club 1937–1938 season	Clement Manly Wade, Jr.
Glee Club 1938–1939 season	Frantz Hershey
Glee Club 1939–1940 season	Thomas P. Bryan
1940S	
Glee Club 1940–1941 season	Albert Kirven Cocke
Glee Club 1941–1942 season	Joe Tucker
Glee Club 1942–1943 season	Charles Edwin Butterworth, Jr.
Glee Club 1943–1944 season	Daniel G. Wheeler
Glee Club 1944–1945 season	Walter H. Beaman, Jr.
Glee Club 1945–1946 season	Charles H. Goodrich, II
Glee Club 1945–1946 season	Charles Stevens Russell
Glee Club 1946–1947 season	George L. Jones, Jr.
Glee Club 1947–1948 season	J. Robert Winstead, Jr.
Glee Club 1948–1949 season	George A. Van Pelt

SEASON	PRESIDENT
Glee Club 1949–1950 season	John C. Hall, Jr.
1950S	
Glee Club 1950–1951 season	Thomas Jefferson Smith, III
Glee Club 1951–1952 season	John A. Warwick, Jr.
Glee Club 1952–1953 season	Charles Bell, Jr.
Glee Club 1953–1954 season	T. Walley Williams, III
Glee Club 1954–1955 season	Frederick Emerson
Glee Club 1955–1956 season	Alvin L. Pritchard, Jr.
Glee Club 1956–1957 season	Dan Moore
Glee Club 1957–1958 season	Palmer Rutherford
Glee Club 1958–1959 season	Robert Velle
Glee Club 1959–1960 season	Ben Fulton
1960S	
Glee Club 1960–1961 season	Jim Brewbaker
Glee Club 1961–1962 season	Michael Stillman
Glee Club 1962–1963 season	Kenneth Moorman
Glee Club 1963–1964 season	Frank McLeod
Glee Club 1964–1965 season	Douglas Miller
Glee Club 1965–1966 season	Peter Zwanzig
Glee Club 1966–1967 season	Douglas Dixon
Glee Club 1967–1968 season	William R. Anderson
Glee Club 1968–1969 season	Craig Caputo
Glee Club 1969–1970 season	Harvey Bryan Mitchell
1970S	
Glee Club 1970–1971 season	Michael A. McCallister
Glee Club 1971–1972 season	John R. Wood
Glee Club 1972–1973 season	Stephen C. Yowell
Glee Club 1973–1974 season	W. Steven Martin
Glee Club 1974–1975 season	Laird Boles
Glee Club 1975–1976 season	Kirk Cordell

SEASON	PRESIDENT
Glee Club 1976–1977 season	Douglass List
Glee Club 1977–1978 season	Nicholas Cooke
Glee Club 1978–1979 season	Eric Sall
Glee Club 1979–1980 season	Matthew Koch
1980S	
Glee Club 1980–1981 season	Charles Kipps Purcell
Glee Club 1981–1982 season	Matthew Freeman
Glee Club 1982–1983 season	Rafe Madan
Glee Club 1983–1984 season	Tucker Echols
Glee Club 1984–1985 season	Dan Vincent
Glee Club 1985–1986 season	Thad Polk
Glee Club 1986–1987 season	Charles P. Wise, Jr.
Glee Club 1987–1988 season	Wade Wilson
Glee Club 1988–1989 season	Bruce Kothmann
Glee Club 1989–1990 season	Steve Billcheck
1990S	
Glee Club 1990–1991 season	Stephen Sweeney
Glee Club 1991–1992 season	Michael McCullough
Glee Club 1992–1993 season	Jim Heaney
Glee Club 1993–1994 season	Donald C. Webb
Glee Club 1994–1995 season	Jonathan Finn
Glee Club 1995–1996 season	Andrew Breen
Glee Club 1996–1997 season	George Shirley
Glee Club 1997–1998 season	Drew Cogswell
Glee Club 1998–1999 season	Dan Shomaker
Glee Club 1999–2000 season	Brad Dakake
2000S	
Glee Club 2000–2001 season	Bert Steindorff
Glee Club 2001–2002 season	Thomas Deal
Glee Club 2002–2003 season	Thomas Deal

SEASON	PRESIDENT
Glee Club 2003–2004 season	Tristan van Tine
Glee Club 2004–2005 season	Kevin Ross Davis
Glee Club 2005–2006 season	David Faulkner
Glee Club 2006–2007 season	Chris Tuggey
Glee Club 2007–2008 season	Matthew Young
Glee Club 2008–2009 season	Jack McQuarrie
Glee Club 2009–2010 season	Jeff McKenzie
2010S	
Glee Club 2010–2011 season	Patrick LeDuc
Glee Club 2011–2012 season	Jacob Friedmann
Glee Club 2012–2013 season	Aki Ko
Glee Club 2013–2014 season	Jordan Stillman
Glee Club 2014–2015 season	Zachary Seid
Glee Club 2015–2016 season	Andrew D'Amato
Glee Club 2016–2017 season	Joseph Marchese-Schmitt
Glee Club 2017–2018 season	William Wheaton
Glee Club 2018–2019 season	Colin Sullivan
Glee Club 2019–2020 season	Denny Jeong
2020S	
Glee Club 2020–2021 season	James Wilusz
Glee Club 2021–2022 season	Noah McIntire

LIST OF MEMBERS

This is a listing of all the known members of the Virginia Glee Club, based on historical records. Members are listed in alphabetical order, grouped by the first decade in which they were a member.

1870S
John W.G. Blackstone · Samuel W. Budd · George Pierce DuBose · Alexander Barclay Guigon · Charles William Kent · George I. Lyell · Archibald W. Patterson · William Kimsey Seago · Charles Steele · Sylvanus Stokes · William Brooke Tunstall · Woodrow Wilson

1880S
Harry S. Bailey · W.N. Berkeley · William H. Blair · Wilhelm P. Brickell · M. André Burthe · Charles Shirley Carter · William B. Coles · Zelotes Wood Coombs · Montgomery Beverley Corse · Thomas L. Dabney · Frank B. Dallam · Sterling Galt · Charles P. Garland · Guy C.M. Godfrey · Thomas H. Haden · Edwin Forest Hill · Joseph Reid Anderson Hobson · David W. Houston · Thomas J. Kirkpatrick · Joseph U. Larrabee · Albert Latady · Thomas Blanks Lytle · Ernest H. McClintic · Harry L. Myers · George H. Norton · Marshall Olds · J.B. Pace · Joseph Bryan Page · Thomas Pinckney Jr. · Jonathan Adams Saunders · Howard Sheild · George Tucker Smith · Ernest Milmore Stires · Robert Cary Stribling · William E. Stringfellow · Beverley Tucker · Edward C. Tucker · George Keesee Vanderslice · Robert F. Williams · John R.C. Wrenshall

1890S
Francis Harris Abbot · George Ainslie · James H. Aldrich · Lewis M. Allen · John T. Alsop · Walter Meade Antrim · William H. Beadles · John Lawrence Vick Bonney · Rockwell Smith Brank · Gustave A. Breaux, Jr. · William R. Bright · Samuel Miles Brinkley · William N. Bronaugh · John William Brown · Franklin Madison Bullwinkel

· Edward Callahill Burks · Edmund Bradford Burwell · Oliver W. Catchings · William Robert Chapin · John Henry Chapman · Malvern B. Clopton · Charles Archibald Clunet · Preston D. Cockrell · Everette H. Coleman · William L. Cooke · Edward A. Craighill, Jr. · Thomas Graham Dabney · William Edgar Darnell · John Graham Davidson · Benjamin C. Day · Charles L. DeMott · James Harry Deyerle · William B. Eagles · Joseph P. Eastwood · Henry R. Elliott · Edgar Howard Farrar · Thomas Clinton Firebaugh · Henry C. Ford · Thomas · Gardner Foster · Clyde Chew Glascock · William W. Glass · Fergus A. Goodridge · William Douglas Gordon · Alfred L. Gray · Ernest Alphonso Gray · Henry Waldo Greenough · Duncan Lawrence Groner · Charles Hancock · Walter Hullihen · Horace Barton Kane · Marshall L. King · Wythe Leigh Kinsolving · Mency Moyd Krise · Frank O. Landis · Burnley Lankford · Cleveland C. Lansing · David Harris Leake · R. Eugene Lockett · James Adair Lyon, Jr. · Joseph G. Maloy · Robert Edward Lee Marshall · Robert F. Mason · Frank L. McCaleb · Douglass McCormick · Briggs McLemore · Bernard W. Moore · Charles W. Moorman · Herbert Rollo Morgan · Owen C. Morris · Charles Mullikin · Thomas H. Neel · Marshall Lee Nininger · Herbert Old · John Randolph Page, Jr. · Hugh F. Parrish · James H. Paxton · William Allen Perkins · Arthur Peter · Paul Pettit · Micajah W. Pope · John D. Potts · J.P. Powers · Norborne Robinson, Jr. · Edward Reinhold Rogers · William Walter Rose · Lawrence Thomas Royster · William H. Saunders · Harry Howard Shelton · William P. Shelton · Joseph Stebbins, Jr. · Joseph Clay Stiles · William S. Stuart · William H. Sweeney · Eugene Lanier Sykes · Richard B. Taylor · Clarence Allison Templeton · C.H. Thompson · Charles Behan Thorn · McLane Tilton, Jr. · Gideon Timberlake · Elbert Lee Trinkle · William Peyton Tucker · Joseph Augustine Turner · Roger Atkinson Walke · William James Way · David Irving White · Luke Mathews White · William Young White · Joseph P. Winston · John Whiton Woodworth · Philip H. Worman

1900S

Larmour G. Adams · George Harold Atkisson · Nathan Bachman · Samuel McGowan Benet · Charles Hamrick Biddle · Frank Dunham Boyd · Thomas Bryan · Eugene Callaway · Osmon Beverly Campbell · Robert Richard Carman · Lavillon Dupuy Cole · Charles C. Crawford · James Keene Daingerfield · Roland Herman Darnell · James Livingston Davis · Aldrich Dudley · Frederick Garner Duvall · George Pomeroy Edgar · John Pierpont Fletcher · John Wesley Gaines · William Walter Gaunt · LeRoy B. Giles · Emerson Jason Griffith · Lewis Routt Hampton · Franklin Collins Harris · Perry Hilleary · Jacob Chaplain Hodges · James Tappan Hornor · Frederick Grey Hudson Jr. · Robert Howard Hudson · Howard Hume · John Edmund Norris Hume · William McCulley James · Henry Grant Lind · John Janney Lloyd · John Jennings Luck · Hugh McIlhany · Charles S. McVeigh · Emmett A. Meeks · Clark Flickner Miller · Edward H. Miller · William Cline Moomaw · Ephraim R. Mulford · Sigourney F. Nininger · Julian Osborne · Karl Osterhaus · Hugh N. Page · William Nelson Page · John Beverly Pollard · Archibald Cary Randolph · Paul E. Rauschenbach · James Taylor Robertson · Frank Roswell Rogers · Albert Lonsdale Roper · Frank Morse Rummel · Marmaduke Parr Sale · Alexander Mitchell Shoemaker · John McG.

Stucky · Thomas Randolph Turner · Irving Miller Walker · George Wendling · Garland Wiley · Robert Williams · Harold L.A. Williamson · Stanley Wimbish · Samuel W. Zimmer

1910S

Edward Clifford Anderson · James Ervin Anderson · Percy Rudolph Ashby · John DuBose Barnwell · Laurence Scott Barringer · William Smith Bean · Claude Swanson Betts · Wade Blackard · Donald Peabody Blagden · Roger M. Bone · Bodley Booker · William H.K. Booth · Robert Iverson Boswell · Stephen Elkins Bowers · Edwin Thurman Boyd · Horace Thompson Brettelle · Richard Bridges · Charles Rowland Brooks · Andrew J.T. Brown · Thomas Moore Bruce · Theodore Robert Bunting · Lorenzo Grady Burton · Robert Gilliam Butcher · W. Wymond Cabell · Vaughan Camp · William McCutcheon Camp · Charles Claude Carroll · Thomas Fitzgerald Carroll · Burr Noland Carter · Henry Ward Chittenden · George Gordon Cook · George Daniel Cooper · William F. Cox · Mortimer Park Crane · Frank Battle Dancy, Jr. · Arthur Kyle Davis, Jr. · Robert Evans Denney · Sheffey Lewis Devier · Thomas Claude Durham · Charles Morris Durrance · J.B. Earnest Jr. · Jesse Rudolph Ewell · William E. Ewers · Isaac S.D. Farrar · Robert V. Funsten · Malcolm W. Gannaway · Ernest Cleon Gill · Charles Crum Gillican · John W. Hamilton · Edgar J. Hecht · George O.H. Hinkle · Hugh Maury Hite · Charles Otto Hodges · Harry Randall Van Horne · James Manney Howard Jr. · William White Howard · William Barrington Hubbard · Seward William Jabaut · Micah Jenkins · Laurence Carpenter Jones · Edward White Kearns · James Arthur Kennedy · Barrington King · James Joshua King · David Lamon · James Archibald Leach · William Prescott Lecky · James K.M. Lee · William Dovel LeSage · Frank Nelson Lewis · Zachary Robert Lewis · Fred Spencer Loar · Marshall Hancock Lynn · William Roderick Mallan · Hunter Marshall · Laurance Clifford Martin · Matthew Scovell Martin · James Allen McAllister · Samuel Overton McCue · John Franklin McDowall · William Albert McGregor · John Garret McHugh · William Baird McIllwaine · Charles Alexander McKeand · Henry Edward McWane · Victor Metcalf · Arthur Irvine Miller · Barnes Thompson Moore · John A. Morrow · John Hugh Murphy · Marion Wetmore Niedringhaus · Charles Mallen O'Connor · Adolph Shelby Ochs · Allison Everhart Palmer · Alexander Wilson Parker · John Crump Parker · John Rice Patterson · Holland Evant Persinger · Charles Cazenove Plummer · Samuel Ferdinand Poindexter · Archibald Robinson Randolph · George Coleman Reedy · Frederick C. Rinker · Albert Northrop Roberts · Mason Romaine · Walter Rompel · Howard Calvin Ross · Peter Whitman Rowland · Warwick Inman Rowland · Christopher Winfree Ryan · Richard B. Saunders · Samuel Saunders · John Jacob Schaefer · Richard Eppes Shands · Keating Lewis Simons · Beverly Chew Smith · Cecil L.R. Smith · Walter Gillespie Sprinkel · Alfred Louis Stern · Claude Emmett Stump · Oscar Arthur Stumpe · Claudius Terrell · DeLos Thomas, Jr. · William S. Thomas · Howard Clark Thompson · Byron Henry Tichenor · Arthur F. Triplett · Russell Ashby Walker · George P. Waller · Frederick W.C. Webb · Kenneth Taylor Wegner · John Ellington White · William Charles Wilkes · H. Reid Wilkins · Charles Shipley Wilson · Allen Whitney Wright · John Wesley Wright

1920S

Hampton Parton Abney · Thomas Gibbs Akeley · John Wilson Ames · Ronald Ames · James Francis Anderson · Charles Greene Andrews · David Burton Andrews · Howard Hicks Ashbury · William Everett Atkinson · John W. Avirett · Henry Ayers · Robert Edward Aylor · Charles H. Ballard · Harry Barsky · Horace Greeley Bass · Frederick Edwin Beachley · Allen Murray Beard · William Donald Beard · John Howard Beebe · Jesse Cox Beesley · Emanuel Victor Benjamin · Carlysle A. Bethel · Howard William Richard Biers · Richard A. Billups · Morgan Birge · David Louden Black · John Arthur Bloss · Thomas Munford Boyd · William Orlando Bristow · Edgar D. Brooke · William Alexander Bryson · Fred Burnett · William Daniel Cabell · Charles Walker Cammack · Joseph Hazard Campbell · Ezekiel Samuel Candler · Willis Todd Carey · Randolph Fitzhugh Carroll · Bernard Peyton Chamberlain · Charlie Thomas Chapman · Samuel Cheek · William Morgan Chew · Frank Mason Chubb · John Herbert Claiborne · Randolph Royall Claiborne · Thomas Sterling Claiborne · Walter William Clem · Pierre Dey Collins · Charles O. Conrad · Randolph Conroy · William F. Cox · William Radford Coyle · David Rice Creecy · Carol Lamar Cunningham · James R.V. Daniel · Harris Davenport · William Forrest Davenport · Bernard Solbert Davis · John Maxwell Davis · Daniel Marcus Dean · Richard Gibson Deane · Launcelot Dent · Lucian Minor Dent · John Arrel Detchon · Charles William Dowden · Alfred Kemper Eagle · Malcolm Bennett Easterlin · James Lindell Ellis · Seger Pillot Ellis · John Dymock Entenza · Solomon Sidney Feuerman · Horace Fisher · Louis Miller Fisher · Gerald Flaum · Gordon Edward Fogg · Frederick Forman · John Conway Fox · Edwin Francis Fredericks · Alvin Friedlander · Richard Whitaker Gamble · Samuel Howard Garst · Fred B. Gentry · Robert Allen Gibbons · John Emerson Gibbs · E. Lacy Gibson · Francis Farquhar Gibson · Milton Goldstein · Robert Gorham · Joseph Brown Graham · Leslie Belfield Gray · Fred B. Greear · John Dismukes Green · George Russell Gunn · Louis Hager · F. Hammond · Louis Machen Hammond · Clifford Graham Harriz · Benjamin Franklin Hart · Albert Allen Hayes · James Elliott Heath · William Hardy Hendren · James Hannan Hennelly · Frederick Stuart Hilder · Leonard Ogden Hilder · Robert Lee Hinds · Frank Arthur Hobson · Alan Jerome Hofheimer · Theodore Witter Holmes · Wendell Ray Holmes · Daniel E. Huger · Nolan Hussey · Richard Lee Hyde · Samuel Spencer Jackson · James W. Jervey · James Chappelle Justice · Elijah Fletcher Kahle · Harry Glenn Kaminer · Richard Keith · Lester Grafton Knibb · Daniel Delehanty Kobbe · John Hosack Koch · John Dominique LaMothe · Henry Van Bergen Larom · Henry Jefferson Lawrence · John Raymond Leatherbury · Charles H. Lewis · Fulton Lewis, Jr. · Howard Marshall Lloyd · William Emmons Lloyd · Charles Marion Love · William D.C. Lucy · Frederick Garland Madara · Wilbur Lee Mahaney · Robert Thornton Marsh · McAlister Marshall · Lewis Charles Mattison · Robert Grice Maverick · Harry Colton McKee, Jr. · George Robert McMahon · Jesse Milton McNeil · Rodgers Meyer · Edwin G. Michelian · Elmer Miller · C. Venable Minor · Eldred L. Minor · Allan C.G. Mitchell · Charles Arthur Mone · Lambeth Raymond Montfort · Robert Ward Moore · Herbert Leslie Morganroth · John James Morris · Joseph Lewis Mulford · Paul Grosclose Mustard · R. Myers · Timothy John Nash · Richard Newman · Robert Allen Newman · Norman Coleman Nicholson

· James Joseph O'Donnell · Charles O'Farrell · Charles B. Manley O'Kelley · Freyhan Odenheimer · Fred N. Ogden · Arthur James Ogle · Fred Shank Palmer · Francis Harcourt Parrish · John Cromwell Parrott · Richard Peard · Giles Albert Penick · Whitmel Stringfellow Peoples · John Ormond Randolph Perry · John Minnich Pfautz · Winston Phelps · Leroy Moore Piser · William Samuel Potter · Elwood Alexander Powell · Albert William Powers · Harry Borum Price · Merrill M. Pye · Middleton Elliott Randolph · David Phillip Reese · Arthur Murray Reeside · Raymond Owen Reilly · Arch John Riggal · Cary Robertson · John Pier Roemer · Edward Roll · Edgar H. Rowe · William Kable Russell · Edmund R. Rutledge · Robert Watson Sadler · L. Reyner Samet · George C. Saunders · Walter Saunders · Edward David Seerie · Charles Dannelly Shaw · James Edwin Shaw · Kingman Cody Shelburne · Preston Runyon Sherwood · Francis Lewis Shrady · Harold Matthews Shuff · Raymond Simon · Frank Willis Smith · Andrew Broadus Smither · Gerald Corwin Speidel · Clarence Whittington Staten · Walter G. Stephenson · William C. Stephenson · Robert Francis Stone · Virgil Van Street · Edward Marshall Sturhahn · John Vandergrift Summerlin · Oscar Swineford · Thomas Austin Sydnor · Robert Wall Taylor · Frank Porter Temple · Carrel Ingersoll Tod · John Robinson Treganza · Edward Donald Tunis · Eugene Welford Turner · Samuel Roger Tyler, Jr. · Lyttleton Waddell · Albert Wilson Walker · Absalom Nelson Waller · Solomon Barth Weinberg · Green Peyton Wertenbaker · Frederick R. Westcott · Chase Stuart Wheatley · James Clifford White · Lawson Moore Wilhoite · Milton Paul William · Felix Williams · Thomas Leigh Williams · Robert Allen Williamson · Jere Malcolm Harris Willis · William Lawrence Wilson · Edward Wellford Withers · Wright Yount

1930S

John Martial Ackerson · Charles L. Anger · Alan Arensberg · Fontaine C. Armistead · John Grant Armistead · Macon Arthur · Thomas James Ashley · William Brockliss Atkinson · Robert Lee Auldridge · Ira Lewis Avery · Theodore A. Ayers · Andrew Bird Babb · Howard Bailey · William Ludwell Baldwin · Sylvan Hyman Bank · John B. Bayer · Robert Massie Beers · William Noland Berkeley Jr. · Gerald A. Berlin · Irving Berlin · James M. Berry · William Black · S.J. Blair · Bruce Bode · George Boone · James Borden · Carroll Preston Bradford · David Brewster · James S.K. Briggs · Donald Bruce · William F. Brunner · Thomas P. Bryan Jr. · D.P. Bryon · Samuel Gillett Buck · R.K. Burke · George Edward Burnett · Nathan Bushnell · Henry Meade Cadot · Charles Callery · Lloyd George Carr · George C. Carrington · John Hill Carruth · Harold Crasswell Chamberlain · Hollis Chenery · J.A. Cocke · C.W. Coleman · William James Condon · Thomas A. Conlon, Jr. · Thomas Poultney Cook · E.T. Coons · Francis M. Cooper · Randolph S. Copeland III · Walter Francis Cornnell · Monroe Couper · Martin Cowen · Joseph Ball Crallé · Thomas Bigelow Crumpler · Walter M. Cushman · Howland Staige Davis · J.Vernon Davis · George M. Dawes · Albert Maynard Deekens · Ralph O. Deininger · John Rensealor Dekle · Louis Delman · George Denison · James Bernard Desberg · Betram Diener · Bernard James Diggs · Joseph Ellis Dill · Fred Thomas Dove · Frank Simms Dudley, Jr. · Thomas Marshall Duer · Frank R. Dunham · Grosvenor Brune Van Dusen · Edward Ryant Dyer, Jr. ·

Bruce G. Eberwein · Howard Berryman Edwards · John E. Egan · Henry Tobias Egger · Alexander R. Ehrbar · Marx Eisenman · Charles Chilton Epes, Jr. · Joseph Gilbert Faatz · Charles James Faulkner · Henry Bard Field · Robert Webb Fine · Saul Ira Firtel · Robert Fitzgerald · Paul W. Fitzpatrick · Monroe Philip Flaster · Herman Westinghouse Fletcher · Charles W. Gasque · Thomas S. George · J. Gerber · William Nathan Gillison · Vincent Gerald Gilmore · Kenneth Seaman Giniger · Eric B. Graham · Robert Gravatte · Arthur P. Gray · John Greenleaf · Edward W. Gregory · Alton Alexander Gulkis · Charles Tilden Hagan · James Patteson Hancock · James Waddell Hancock · Francis Gilkeson Harper · James E. Harper · Joseph Harvey Harris · Edward T. Harrison · Aubrey Eaton Harvey · Ray E. Hawkins · Frantz Hershey · Frederick Hicks · Arthur W. Higgins · Richard P. Hilder · Thomas O'Neal Hindman · Francis C. Hoare · Peyton H. Hoge · Norman Holland · Guy Hope · Winston Hope · Hugh Horne · Estes Vaughan Howard · John Hines Howard · Maurice G. Jackson · Lewis D. Jacobson · Werner Lutz Janney · Julian C. Jaynes · Daniel A. Jenkins · George Booker Jenkins · William Ferdinand Jensen · Beverly Jones · Robert C.W. Jones · William Whitmore Jones · Jacob Epstein Katz · Frank Keppelmann · Joseph Kessler · William Whitfield Kirk · S.J. Kirsten · Thomas John Klinedinst · Gunther Kenneth Klose · William Wilder Westbury Knight · Fred Fry Knobloch · Herman William Kuehn · Lansing B. Lee · Oscar Arthur Levy · W. Terry Lewis · Heath Licklider · Henry Leonard Lieberman · Charles F. Lloyd · Robert Frederick Loomis · Edmund Groff Lorenz · Girard R. Lowrey · Alfred Marshall Luttrell · Edward Lyman · Carl Halford Madden · John Kendrick Mallard · Edmund Lucien Malone · John Marshall · Max R. Marston · Philip P. Marvin · Edward Francis McCarthy · Charles A. McCarty · James Bruce McClelland · Donald Ray McGoldrick · Robert McKim · C.E. McKinley · Ernest Mead · Howard E. Medinets · Harold Lewis Meisel · Elwood F. Melson · Fielding Mercer · Daniel Tatum Merritt · Alphonse H. Meyer · Louis Michaels · Ross S. Mickey · Lyddane S. Miller · Howard C. Mirmelstein · Ross E. Mohney · William M. Moore · Roger W. Morrison · Robert Morse · Mandeville Mullally · Richard W. Murdoch · Edwin Robson Nelson · Frank P. Nichols · Frederic Ernest Nolting · Ernest Edward Northen · Alexis Obolensky · William F. Ogburn · Gasper R. Pacheco · James E. Palmer · Littleton Walke Parks · Carl D. Paternostro · Daniel H. Payne · Raymond D. Pearce, Jr. · William Herndon Pearson, Jr. · John M. Perry · Marvin Perry · John B. Petter · Vincent Stockton Petter · Alfred Pew · Armistead Peyton · Harry E. Phillips · Randolph P. Pillow · Moss Plunkett · Robert B. Posnick · Edmund Logan Pratt · William Thomas Purdum · Elmer Wharton Ramsey · Menger Milton Ramsey · Hubbard Mansfield Rattle · Charles Rawolle · Bernard Harold Raymond · Bernard Westerman Recknagel · R. Gardner Reed · Richard H. Reimers · Eugene J. Reiner · Walker Reynolds · Francis Bayard Rhein · Clarence K. Rhodes, Jr. · Chester Harris Robbins · William Thomas Roberts · Harrison Robertson · Howell Allison Robinson · John Lenzie Rogers · Carl Martin Rohmann · Edwin B. Roller · Leighton Parks Roper · Rial Rose · Julius Frank Rosenbaum · James R. Ross · Robert R. Ross · Donald G. Russell · Hugh E. Russell · Robert C. Rutledge · Arthur D. Sale · Frederick Robert Schwartz · Richard Sellman Scott · Clement B. Sharpe · Peter Kyle Sheffield · William Louis Sherman · Kenneth Silver · Edwin Clement Silvers · Thomas Porter Simpson · Lewis A. Slutsky · Edward

Samuel Smith · Rufus Wilson Smith · Marshall J. Snapp · Lawrence Snoddy · George Waterbury Snyder · Kendrick Anderson Sparrow · Louis Thanter Stableford · James R. Stanton · Allen Watts Staples · Edward Donald Steinbrugge · William Robert Stephenson · Henry Eugene Stevens · Arthur C. Stever · Albert H. Stoddard · David Farnham Stoddard · John Bispham Stokes · Melvin Jack Storz · William Gerhard Suhling · Luther L. Sullivan · Timothy John Sullivan · Andrew R. Summers · Windsor Langborne Taliaferro · William Howard Terry · Armstrong Thomas · Thomas M. Thornhill · John Bradford Tillison · Duane L. Tower · Anthony G. Tramonte · Vincent Tramonte · Joseph B. Tucker · David MacAllister Turner · Richard Dickens Vermillion · Clement Manly Wade · Donald Gardner Wallace · John William Walters · Ronald Sinclair Warburton · John Goebel Watson · Melvin Ray Watson · Donald R. Webb · William Eldridge Weber · Robert Welch · McDonald Wellford · Kenneth W. Whitaker · Thomas Newby White · George Stanhope Wiedemann · Louis T. Wilds · Alfred Graham Williams · Carrington Williams · Hadley Bernard Williams · James Lawrence Williams · Samuel Williams · Virgil Floyd Williams · Francis Folliard Wilshin · Maxwell Kenneth Woltz · Peter Wood · Lester G. Woody · B.C. Worthington · Cecil Johnston Wright · William P. Youngquist · Robert Ziegler

1940S

John H. Aberle · Robert Andrew Abernathy · Gordon Able · Norman N. Adler · Robert D. Albrecht · William H. Albrecht, Jr · Ernest H. Alderman, Jr. · Pedro Juan Alfaro · Harry D. Allen, Jr. · William R. Allen · Albert Amsterdam · N.C. Anderson · Thomas Robert Anderson · Thomas Martin Ansbro · J.L. Arnold · Robert Poland Atkinson · James C. Austin · Robert W. Ayers · Edwin P. Bailey · John S. Ballentine · W.M. Balson · William W. Banks · Jon Barker · Edward Barksdale · James W. Barksdale · John O. Barksdale · Arthur E. Barnard · Bennie E. Barnett · Robert Tupper Barrett, Jr. · David M. Barry · John J. Barry · James H. Bash · Barkley DeRoy Beale · Walter H. Beaman, Jr. · Jesse Beeghley · Francis Bell III · John Almon Belmeur Jr. · Leslie O. Belton, Jr. · Carl W. Randolph Benson · James E. Berdahl · Edward Berry · Kenneth F. Bevan · Carl Beyer · Livingston L. Biddle · Joseph Birdsall · Gerald Black · Francis W. Blankner · Charles Boatwright · Donald Jules Boday · Elmer Bryan Kyle Boeger, Jr. · Chester Bolen · R.S. Booth · Benjamin Franklin Borden · Paul Webb Bourjaily · F. Lewis Bowman · Sidney S. Bowman · Eugene D. Brand · Richard Martin Brandt · Robert D. Brandt · Randolph Brent · Thomas Brierly, Jr. · Richard Brooke Jr. · Arville H. Browder · William Horner Brown · Donald Bruce · Robert A. Buckingham · Joseph C. Buntin · Thomas Burchett, Jr. · Arthur W. Burke, Jr. · Quinter Milton Burnett · Charles Edwin Butterworth, Jr. · Robert C. Cahoon · Gilbert Campbell · Robert E. Canfield · Benjamin Lee Carleton · John Carr · Robert Edouard Carrigan Jr. · Philip Joseph Caruso · Irby Cauthen · Robert Thomas Cauthorne · Ralph van Sickler Chamblin, Jr. · Ralph Chandler · Duncan Dunbar Chaplin · Edward N. Cheek · Alan G. Cherry Jr. · Charles A. Chilton · H. Louis Chodosh · Sanford Chodosh · John T. Clark · Myrick Canfield Clark · John R. Clarke · Julian W. Clarkson · Lyell Buffington Clay · Robert Clemons · Joseph Haney Cochran · Peyton Cochran · Albert Kirven Cocke · James I. Collier, Jr. · Paul Connair · Erskine Conrad · H.B. Cooke · Thomas

M. Cooney · Albert B. Cooper, Jr. · Robert E. Cooper · Wilbur Russell Copeland · James Cory · J.W. Cotton · R.Mc. Coupland · Charles W. Cover · Tread Covington, Jr. · Mark W. Cowell · Martin Boyd Coyner, Jr. · Harvey Craig · W.N. Craigue · Alan H. Crosby · Charles Crowder · Fred Cruser · Eugene Carl Culbertson · John Moncure Daniel, Jr. · Herbert Dann · Edgar B. Darden · David A. Dashiell · Nicholas E. Davies · A.J. Davis · John B. Davis · John G. Davis · Robert L. Davis · W.D. Davis · Henry M. DeButts · William Raymond DeValinger · Daniel Wesley DeVilbiss · John D. Divers · D.P. Dixon · Ernest M. Dixon · Murray T. Donolio · Herbert A. Donovan, Jr. · Barclay M. Dorset · Leon E. Dostert · Cyrus H. Doub · William R. Dougherty · Herbert A. Dozier · John B. Dragoo · David B. Drewry · Alfred Hall Drummond · John C. DuBois · Oliver Witcher Dudley · William Duke · Albert Williams Eastburn · Charles Eastland · Charles R. Eastwood · William C. Eaton · Lloyd Edwards · J.R. Eggleston · Herschel Elliott · Mahlon Elliott · David H. Ellsworth · Robert Elmer · Daniel Stebbins Ely · William Embry · William Portwood Erwin · John Estes · Frank L. Evans · Richard Everson · George Newlin Ewing · Robert R. Fair · Henry Farmer · Cyrus Creston Farrow · Robert J. Field · Roger H. Fitch · John Fitzgerald · Kenneth P. Fitzgerald · D.M. Fletcher · Robert C. Forbes · George E. Foresman · William A. Forrest · John J. Forst · Wilson F. Fowle, Jr. · Ira Chester Fox · Roger Fraley · Calvin Hunter Frazier · Harold H. Freeland · Dan Freeman · Thomas Brandt Furcron · Morton Gallub · Edward Gamble · Robert Gamble · Robert H. Gammon · Frederick Ellington Garbee · Bruce Garden · Lewis Gardner · Philip Lincoln Garland Jr. · Omer Allan Gianniny · William C. Gibbons · Cass Gilbert · William H. Giles · Frank Gilliland · David Gleason · Joseph E. Godridge · Eugene Goetchius · Charles H. Goodrich, II · Charles Wilson Gordon · John Gordon · Kelsey Goss · Clinton Gould · Clyde Gould · Erl C.B. Gould, Jr. · William Gram · John Gravely III · Robert Von Grimm · Edwin Guernsey · Anthony Guggenheimer · Irlwin Gumley · David W. Gurney · James A. Hageman · William Homer Hale · John C. Hall, Jr. · Sonny Hall · Charles E. Hamm · Gene Paige Hamman · Euclid Murden Hanbury · Stuart B. Hanckel · John Hankins · Frederick H. Hanny · Philip Hardy · Martin L. Harkey · William D. Hart · Winfield S. Harvin · John D. Haxall · Charles E. Haymaker · Kenneth A. Hedlund · Lawrence G. Heinrich · L. Hendricks · Charles M. Herbeck Jr. · Guy C. Heyl, Jr. · Reuben P. Hines Jr. · Don Hoenstein · Fred C. Holler · George D. Hopper · Robert G. Van Horn · Hoke I. Horne II · D. Horner · J.H. Huffman Jr. · John L. Huffman · Arthur D. Hughes · Robert A. Humphreys · Alfred C. Hunt · Walter F. Hutcheson · David M. Hutchinson · William Irvin Huyett · Charles L. Hyser · Jerry A. Isear, Jr. · Richard B. Isenhour · John R. Jackson · Joseph H. James, Jr. · Philip James · John Janowsky · Alfred B. Jarden · Harold S. Jeans · Jack P. Jefferies · Charles T. Jenkins · Felix Jenkins · H.E. Jenkins · Daniel C. Jensen · William Francis Jensen · Joseph C. Jerdee · Frederick W. Johns, Jr. · Richard L. Johnson · Robert Lewis Johnson · William Johnson · Greenhow Johnston · George L. Jones, Jr. · J. Roddey Jones · Ronald Gilbert Jones · Harvey D. Karkus · Jack Nelson Kegley · Robert A. Kehres · Murl Tucker Keiser · John Kirsten Kelly · Richard S. Kephart · William Byron Kerner · Robert Samuel Key · Joseph F. Kiningham · Edward Snyder Kline · John W. Knight · F. Koch · John D. Kreis · John Frederick Read Kuck · W.H. Lacey · Robert T. Lamkin · Munson H. Lane Jr. · Dillard Chappell Laughlin · F.S. Leake · Benjamin C. Lee · Mallon Lemaire · August W. Lentz · Harry N. Lewis · Ira Clair Liebrand · Richard R. Lilliefors · Arthur S. Lloyd · Norman Elbert Lloyd · Bradford B. Locke, Jr. · Thomas S. Lodge · Robert Paul Long · Joseph B. Loughran · Moses Richardson Lovell · Martin J. Lowenkopf · Paul Lyday · Raymond S. Lyons · Warren Maas · Colin Henry MacAdam · John P. MacBean · Robert Magill · Jim Mallory · J. Fred Manneschmidt · Robert F. Mapes · John Allen Marfleet · George Marko · Joseph H. Marko · Wirt P. Marks III · Robert A. Marshall · William C. Marshall · Gilbert Drew Martin · J.R. Matthews, Jr. · Vernon Mattox · William Charles Mayer, Jr. · Thomas G. Mays, Jr. · William Arthur Evelyn McBryde · John W. McCarthy, Jr. · John McCloskey · John McConnell · Robert E. McConnell, Jr. · Robert McCormack · Conrad Grove McCown · John McCown · Harrison L. McCoy · Marvin E. McCoy · John McDonald · E.P. McElgunn, Jr. · Samuel Edgar McFadden · Hunter H. McGuire Jr. · Malcolm S. McKenney · William H. McLarin · James E. McTamany · John W. McTigue · Edward C. Melton · Owen Meredith · Beverly V. Michel Jr. · Addinell Hewson Michie · Robert M. Milford · Brinton Marshall Miller · Ridgely D. Miller · Warren Miller · Charles L. Minor · Frank Malcolm Minor · Lloyd A. B. Mitchell · Charles M. Moon, Jr. · Charles Moore · George Lacy Moore · Hiram Wayland Moore · Price Mosher · Samuel Munson · Walter Munster · James Myatt · Edward M. Myers · Peter Van S. Myers · David J. Nagle · Henry F. Neighbors · Walter Draper Neighbors · Bruce Nelson · Robert Nelson · Willoughby Newton · William T. Nichols · William Henry Nicholson · Walter G. Noble · James Nottingham · Frank Harrison Nye · Ernest H. O'Bannon, Jr. · Charles F. O'Connor · Ralph E. O'Dette · James A. O'Lone · Thomas Joseph O'Reilly · Samuel P. Oast · Robert E. Offenbacker · Kenneth H. Okkerse · Warren Okkerse · Gordon C. Page · John L. Palmer · Donald Paschal · Theodore Patterson · J. Payne · Lee M. Payne · Philip Marshall Payne · George A. Van Pelt · Carleton Penn · John Peters · George T. Petsche · James Pfahl · Charles Robert Phillips · Jack B. Phillips · William H. Pigg · Charles Platt, III · William C. Plummer · James H. Powell · Wallace Power · Harvey Baker Powers II · David Dorrance Preston · William Ballard Preston · Robert D. Provost Jr. · Carl Donald Quarforth · James Sidney Quarles · William Quattrocchi · William Quinn · James H. Ransone · Donald J. Raven · J.F. Reed · Robert Reese · Bill Reisinger · Thurman B. Reynolds · William Richardson · F.W. Riel · Paul M. Robbins · John R. Roberson · Beverly Ford Roberts · Calvin H. Roberts · Edgar Roberts · Lon E. Roberts, II · Dana Robertson · Gilbert Rodli · Bart Rogers · W.L. Rogers · Frank Rolston III · Jason Rome · Stephen N. Root · Malcolm L. Rosenblatt · Richard William Rosenfeld · Frederick Cruser Rowland · Charles Rucker · Charles Stevens Russell · William H. Russell, Jr. · Rodham T. Rust · William Stuart Rust · Joseph Ruvane · John Rybolt · George F. Rykman · Marvin M. Sager · Carlos Salgado · Frank Salisbury · Thomas Raysor Salley · Victor Salvatore · J. Edward Sandridge · Charles R. Sanford · Charles Garland Saunders · Bruce Geoffrey Saville · Albert Scafuro · Joseph Scannell · Henry C. Schultz · John R. Schultz · Charles R. Scott · Hobart L. Scott, Jr. · Phil P. Scroggs, Jr. · Leslie Eugene Seaward · George G. Shackelford · David Shane · John Sharrett · Louis Shell · Burton Sherman · Marion Moore Sherman · Nick Shively · Julien Shoemaker · Robert Paschal Shook · William Langley Sibley III · Frederick Theodore Sickert · Albert Siewers · Harold

D. Sill · Maurice L. Sill · Lester F. Simmons · Garced Sketchley · K.E. Smallridge · Jamie Mecklin Smith · John A. Smith · Joseph H. Smith · Lester Smith · Louis Smith · Thomas Jefferson Smith, III · Timothy Smith · Ward H. Speer · William Courtney Spence · William Russell Spence · Philip Hamilton Spencer · Robert Lee St. Clair Jr. · Val H. Steiglitz Jr. · George Louis Stein · Sigmund Charles Stein · Harold Daniel Stetson · Edward J. Stoll · Kenneth H. Stoll · Alvah F. Stone · Robert Stone · Putnam T. Stowe · Frederick Lee Strasser · Robert D. Stratton · Luther Warren Strickler · William Stull · Jack Sturman · Columbus Downing Tait · Philip Talbot · Stuart Talbot · Edmund M. Talley · Bruce A. Talmadge · John Philip Talmage · Charles S. Taylor, Jr. · Henry P. Taylor · Robert T. Taylor · Victor Taylor · William A. Taylor · William W. Temple · Robert B. Thomas · John N. Thomasson · James R. Thorne · Warren I. Titus · Albert R. Tobe, Jr. · Francis Gwynn Townes · John F. Townsend · Charles N. Trader · DeForest Trimingham · David Turner · Robert Turner · Robert T. Tuttle · Bob Tyler · Franklin S. Tyng · Allan Murray Unger · Edmund John Van Valkenburg · Lemuel W. Vaughan · George B. Vest, Jr. · John Marshall Vivian · Martin Votaw · George Walker · Tony Walker · William W.A. Walker · Charles R. Wallace · Ray R. Waln · Robert Walter · Samuel L. Walton, Jr. · Wesley Ward · William C. Ward · Edward van Stan Ware · Richmond A. Ware · R.C. Warthan · Frederick D. Watts · James S. Weaver · J.H. Welch · Robert Welch · Frederick U. Wells · Daniel G. Wheeler · Sherman Whipple · John B. White · Peter W. White · James H. Whiting · Alan C. Whitlock · Robert F. Whitmore · C. Gooch Whitworth · Harold Wibberley · Ned H. Wiebenga · T.D. Wilkerson · Louis A. Wilkinson Jr. · Berkley E. Williams · Frederick Mosby Williams · George W. Williams · James Williams · Lucius A. Williams Mason Williams · Allen Willis · John H. Willis, Jr. · William Scott Willis · David Wilson · Edwin Laird Wilson, Jr. · Joseph Robert Winstead, Jr. · Charles Parmele Wise · Frederick Starr Wood · Roy A. Wood · Stanley Wood · Frederick Worcester · Kenneth Wright, Jr. · Russell Alton Wright · John W. Wyatt · Jacob Bernard Wyckoff · George M. Wysor · John D. Wysor, Jr. · Henry Park Xanders · Harold Yarbro · David S. Yates · William Lassiter Yost · Edward Earle Zehmer · Ephraim E. Zeitz · A. di Zenega · John Paul Zirpel

1950S

Arnold Abrams · William Albert Alesker · Charles Altmann, III · Wells Anderson · F. Mather Archer · George Armstrong · Charles Lewis Arnold · William Byron Babcock · Hilton M. Bailey, Jr. · Robert Bair · Stanley C. Baker · James Barlow · James Clifton Barlow · John A. Barnes · John H. Barnes · Robert Harrold Bayne · Robert Livermore Beal · Robert von Beck · Robert Russell Beers · Charles Bell, Jr. · Edwin Bennett · James D. Benson · Frederic Berry · Paul Ruyter Berryman · Robert Bersch · C.E. Bingham · R.W. Birch · Lloyd Lawrence Bird · Winfrey Blackburn · F.W. Blankemeyer · Richard A. Bodkin · Dane R. Boggs · Francis Bondurant · Kenneth L. Bonner · Hendrik Booraem, V · Ralph Bowden · Stevenson Bowes · Peyton G. Bowman · Morton Boyd, Jr. · Richard A. Brand · John M. Brandt · Francis J. Breazeale · Patrick John Brill · Richard Garland Brockwell · Daniel F. Brown · Francis Wilson Brown · Jack R. Brown · Wilson Brown · Robert Brubaker · Warren Brubaker · William Bruce · Thomas Gibbes Buist · Richard C. Bull · William Bunge · William

Burdick · William H. Burgess · Thomas Cantieri · Russell Carew · Robert J. Carlson · John A. Carter · William H. Carter · William L. P. Carter · Miles Cary, Jr. · Robert Caven · Derwood S. Chase, Jr. · Thomas Chase · Roy Clark · Harold Cloutier · T.L.R. Cole, Jr. · Warren Coleman · Harold Leroy Collier · Christopher Taylor Collins · Charles White Conklin · John Edward Connelly · Robert L. Cooley · Louis C. Cornick, Jr. · Rene Coudert · Charles Cowley · Philip Paul Cox · K. Cravens · Peter Cressman · C.E. Crider · Claude Crockett, Jr. · Alexander C. Crosman · Jimmie K. Crowder · William Cudlipp, III · William Czechanski · David Damewood · Julian Hawes Dancy · Neil Davis · Philip Davis · Robert M. Davis, Jr. · Russell H. Davis · Robert Dawson · Robert Deas · E.P. Denigen · Clarence Rich Diffenderffer, Jr. · Malcolm Douglas · T. Hoyt Drake · Leonard K. Drumheller · G.L. Dudley · J.S. Dudley · Norman B. Duey · Roger Dunne · James K. Dunton · Charles DuPuy · Benjamin Duval · Louis Dvorsky · Newton G. Edwards · Frederick Emerson · Robert Enslin · William Johnson Evans · Morris Everett · Howard Earl Fauver · James W. Feeley · Eugene P. Feinour · John Henry Neff Fernald · Tim Ferneyhough · James P. Finch · Woody Fitzgerald · George Fleshman · Jack Flowers, Jr. · William Foulkes · Richard Fowler · Andrew Francis · Benjamin Ira Franklin · Bruce French · Leslie Friedman · John Frothingham · Melvin E. Fuller · Steven Fullerton · Benjamin E. Fulton · John V.M. Gibson · Peter Gilbert · P.J. Glasener · Roy Glassberg · M. Harris Goodman · Cooper Graham · Ernest Greene · Charles R. Greer · Thomas Campbell Grier · Phillip Groves · Robert Ellis Guilford · Cyrus Guynn · Louis Busch Hager · D.B. Hall · Philip H. Hancock · W.R. Hancock · Wallace Neil Harding · Russell Harley · A.L. Harlow · Howard O. Haverty · William T. Hawkins · William Hazen · E.B. Heflin Jr. · Walter Hellmut · John Highfill · Kilby S. Hodges · Robert L. Hoffman · Bernard Peabody Holland · Buell Hollister · John Holmgren · William A. Holton · Eugene Troy Horn · William Horton · John M. Hotchner · Calhoun Howard · Charles D. Howell · William Carl Howell · David G. Hubby · Ray Hudnall · Eugene Hughes · Joseph Hughes · James Wadsworth Hulfish Jr. · Jerry Hulsizer · James Sterling Hutcheson · Barry Hutchings · Mark Jander · Owen H. Jander · J.A. Jennings · Edward Darrell Jervey · Evans B. Jessee · Edwin Gordon Johns · Merwyn Johnson · Paul Johnson · Paul Mooring Johnson · Thomas F. Johnson · Ken Jones · Robert H. Kaufman · Dana L. Kelder · David A. Keller · Gene Ryland Kelley · Peter Kennedy · Donald John Kenneweg · Lytton W. Kernan · William G. Key · Samir Khalidy · Peter M. Kilcullen · J.W. Kincaid, Jr. · H.N. King · William Knight · Victor Lawson · Laird Leeder · Nicholas Frederick Lenssen · Thomas Middleton Lewis · R.S. Lizars, Jr. · Eric Loges · John B. Longman · DeWitt H. Loomis · Herbert Lord · William M. Lovell · Ed Lovern · Alvah Low · Kermit Lowry, Jr. · Charles Kelly Lunt · Philip Lutz · John Theodore Lyman · Peter Houston Lynch · Robert A. Lyne · Charles Mabon · Henry J. MacDonald · Jerry MacDonald · Malcolm MacLeod · Harrison Ray Magee · Owen Robert Mahan · Alexander J. Mallis · Martin Gray Mand · Roger Lewis Manshel · Dominick Charles Marino · Samuel Marney · David Marsee · Roger Massey, Jr. · David W. Maupin · John Mayo · Richard W. McBride · R.C. McCahan · James Richard McCarren · Lawrence L. McEvoy, Jr. · William McGonegal · Hugh M. McIlhany · A.O. McLane Jr. · Frank McLaughlin · W. McLovell · William McSween · George Wythe Michael ·

Edward Miller · George Miller · David Mitchell · Jacques Mitchell · Charles Withers Moncure · James Moody · D. Moore · Dan Moore · Thomas Moore · Douglas E. Mooreside · George E. Morse · Henry Moyer · William B. Murdaugh · Joseph Murrie · Charles Nichols · Edward Nichols · Robert W. Nuckles · John Nunn · Marshall Paine · Lydon Parent · Calvin W. Parker · Russell Paul · Vito A. Perriello, Jr. · James Piper III · Graham L. Platt · Orland Edward Pollock · William Clarence Poole · James N. Pope · Thomas B. Porter · J. William Powers · Alvin L. Pritchard, Jr. · Ralph Proctor · Richard A. Pschirrer · Leonard Pullen · Robert Randall · E.O. Rapp · Thomas Ratcliffe · David A. Reinach · David Ridgely · Wingfield Roberts · Alexander F. Robertson · Charles Robertson · Barry Rogers · Edward Sidney Rogers · George McKinley Rogers, III · Douglas Roller · Ralph M. Rudolph · Peter Runkle · Eugene F. Russell, III · Palmer Rutherford · Leon H. Sample, Jr. · Edwin Sanders · John P. Sawyers · Paul Scarborough · Howard Schuster · Glenn Sedam · John Seltzer · George Sempeles · Roland Thayer Sheets · Charles Shook · George Russell Silvernell · Spiros Basil Skenderis · J.R. Smals · Donald Smith · Eugene T. Smith · Godfrey Smith · Loran Robert Smith · Quentin C. Smith · S. Jerrard Smith · John Smuck · Fred L. Somers · Kenny Sothern · Irvin Norman Sporn · Wilford Spradlin · Frederick H. Stabler · Daniel V. Stapleton · Maurice Leroy Starkey, Jr. · Clark Stearns · Robert Steffey · George Edward Stevens · Andrew Stewart · Michael Stillman · Meredith Dickinson Stoever · W. Arthur Stone · John Stonhouse · John C. Straton Jr. · Harold J. Stroehman · Benjamin W. Sublett · John Sutton · James E. Swenarton · Robert H. Swindell, Jr. · Joseph Talbot · Charles H. Tall · Ryo Tanaka · Grant Howard Tankersley · Charles C. Tarkenton · Wayne Taylor · Sam Rountree Telford · Burns Tichenor · Fred W. Tims · J.R. Tinkelpaugh Jr. · Paul Tipton · Leif Oscar Torkelson · Tom Towle, Jr. · Howard Townsend · David C. Tribby · Charles Tunstall · Malcolm E. Turnbull · Richard W. Turner · Robert H. Turner · Stephen F. Turner · Charles Twining, Jr. · James D. Vaughan, Jr. · Robert Nicholas Velle · Phillip J. Walker · Garvin Walter · Philip Walter · Thomas A. Warburton · G.W. Ward Jr. · Arthur Ward · Donald Ward · John A. Warwick, Jr. · John A. Washington · Eliot Chambers Wells · William Thorne Wessels · Beverly West · William Whalen · William Stansbury Wheatley · David White · L.E. White Jr. · Arnold J. Wiener · Francis B. Williams · T. Walley Williams, III · Jesse Wilson III · William Myers Wilson · Williard Winn · Mack Wood · James Woods · Robert Lewis Wright · Edward Malcolm Wyatt · G.M. Wyatt · Albert Thompson York · Philip Young

1960S

Dominic E. Amadio · William A. Andersen ·William R. Anderson · Maximilian Aue · Scott Bachelor · Geoffrey R. Baer · Robert Dixon Bartlett · Henry Baskerville · William Baxter, Jr. · John S. Baymiller · James Beckley · Robert Mason Beecher · James L. Bell, II · Richard Bennett · Jack Douglas Bilby · Robert L. Borum · Raymond Lee Bowers, Jr. · Patton L. Boyle · James W. Bradshaw · Robert F. Brady, Jr. · John Ford Brent · James M. Brewbaker · Gregory K. Brewer · Thomas Brittingham · Stephen H. Brod · Bradley Brooks · Randall Victor Brungart · Kenneth Buckingham · Walter Bundy III · Karl Bunkelman, Jr. · John A. Burrows · W. Madison Burton · Jeffrey Busby · Craig Caputo · William D. Carleton, Jr. · Philip Carpenter · Jerry P. Carr · Timothy C. Carwhile · M. Campbell Cawood · Lance Cerny · Ralph Jennings Chambers, Jr. · Richard Chandler · Don Michael Cheadle · Mark Choate · Gary Chorney · Kevin Clark · Raymond W. Clements · Jerry Lee Coffey · Roy Collins · Steel H. Colony · John W. Conway · Elbert Gary Cook · Carlton C. Coolidge · Richard Covington · Bob Crawford · Robert F. Darby, Jr. · William H. Dassler · David H. Davis · James W. Davis, Jr. · Dean J. DeBuck · Frederick H. Dennis · C. Jeffery Dickinson · M. Thomas Diklich · Douglas Dixon · William Dodge · Christopher W. Douglass · Wilmont Drake · Dwight Douglass Duncan · Harold R. Dutton · David W. Dyer · Richard T. Edwards · Thomas Lee Emerson · Andrew J. Falconio · Gary S. Farr · Brian Fatzinger · Thomas G. Faulkner · Dallam Goss Ferneyhough · Robert C. Field · Stephen Fisher · John Fizer · T. Ford · Dale I. Foreman · Robert B. Foster III · Arthur Fox · George Martin Franck · John Albert Franklin · Richard Fredenburg · Carroll Pittman Freeman · A. Fulton · Peter Furbush · James Gacek · Patrick Lynn Garner · Wesley Garvin · John J. Gaughan · Joseph Gibson · Barrie A. Gillis · Lee Gilman · Stanley Goldstein · Roger D. Gough · Keith Gordon Graham · Lance Charles Graham · Robert Edward Graham · Gary Paul Gross · R. Lee Groves · William Butler Guffey · Anthony F. Guida · Clay G. Guthridge · Thomas Jackson Hall · Daniel F. Hanson · James Harney · Haw W. Harper · Byron E. Harris · Michael E. Harris · Richard Harris · William David Hasty, Jr. · Charles Roger Hill · Robert Hobbs · Alan Hollenbeck · B. Krik Holman · H. Alexander Holmes · John McClure Hotchner · S. Hoye · Lawrence R. Hudnall · Richard W. Hughes · D. Hume · Christopher W. Hutchinson · Paul Ikerman · Roger Israelson · Gregory M. Ivy · David H. Johnson · James F. Jones · John Vernon Jones · Charles Thornton Keene · Frederick E. King, II · Thomas W. Klingelhoefer · George Marshall Kraus · James A. Kruchko · Stephen Lane · Joseph Roosevelt LeBlanc · Claude Lee · Tom Lefler · John Lert · Markham VanFossen Lewis Jr. · Randall G. Lewis · Stuart F. Lewis · Steven A. Linas · Jan Peter Linke · John Leland Loder · Bruce MacDougal · Malcolm MacGregor · Walter Mallory · Peter March · John M. Martinez · Randolph D. Mason · David Mathers · David Baughn Matthews · Thomas Virgil Matthews · John C. McCall Jr. · Robert McCullough · John Hunter McDaniel · Frank McLeod · David R. McWilliams · Thomas David Mercurio · Paul K. Merrel · Alfred T. Merritt · John Wesley Merritt · Douglas L. Miller · Douglas Miller · Gordon D. Miller · James E. Miller · Harvey Bryan Mitchell · Robert N. Moody · Wallace Mook · Delmas Moore · William H. Moorhouse · John Kenneth Moorman · David D. Mukai · Francis I. Mullin III · Woodie Munday · John C. Murden · Roger Newton · Edward P. Nolde · Joseph Herbert Norton III · John Wilson O'Neill · Guy B. Oldaker · Stephen Olin · Leonard Olschner · Jan G. Owen · Harold Van Patten · Kenneth S. Patterson · Thomas L. Pearce · Cedric Eugene Pearson · Samuel H. Pettway · John Geoffrey Pflaumer · James E. Pirkle · Andrew F. Pitas · Ralph Pitman · Carlos Polit · Stephen Preas · Eccles V. Pridgen · Jonathon Reed · Mitchell Reese · Robert Hunt Riegel · Ruste Righton · Robert B. Roberson · Alan Roberts · Lewis J. Roberts Jr. · James Rogers · William R. Rogers · Edwin B. Roller Jr. · Robert K. Rose · Martin Rothenberg · Richard A. Rubin · John N. Rust · John William Ryland · James L. Sanders · Thomas S. Saunders · John Scarborough · Steve Scarbrough · Christopher Schooley · Thomas O. Schricker · Peter Selove · Edgar McDowell Shawen · Ralph N.

Shuler · David Sinkler · Thomas Smidt · Bruce Smith · James P. Smith · Thomas F. Smith · Steven B. Sorkin · Jacob Sprouse · Frank Stegall · Richard Steinman · Robert Stenson, II · John Scott Stephens · Brad Stillman · James Peter Stillman · Lynn Paul Stockberger · James Stone · Christopher Swenson · Agnew Swineford · Edward Tappe · David L. Temple, Jr. · Horace B. Thompson, Jr. · Mark A. Thompson · Guy K. Tower · Richard F. Tuck · Wayne Tuggle · Nicolas Tulou · Alexander Tunstall · James E. Turner, Jr. · Douglas Uhlig · H. Ryland Vest · William N. Wade · G. Scott Walker · Jon G. Walker · Kenneth W. Waller · Alan B. Wambold · James L. Wamsley · Steven Watson · Thomas P. Watson · Frederick L. Wedel · Henry Bartlett Weir · Randall G. Wert · Edwin S. Williams · James E. Wintermeyer · David B. Witt · G. Bradford Wolcott · Karl Woodard · Herbert R. Woodel · Winston L. Wright · Richard L. Yoder · Wayland Yoder · Dale Van Zant · Peter Zwanzig · Robert Zyromski

1970S

· Gary J. Aichele · Jorge Amador · Gerald Archer · H. Clarke Ashbrook III · Richard Michael Austin · James T. Babb · James Ballowe · James Barden · Mark Bateman · Charles W. Batten · Harold Bayar · Roy William Bayliss · Scott Bayliss · Benjamin C. Beach · Douglas Bennett · James P. Bennette · Jack S. Blevins · Gary Blunt · Laird Boles · Joseph Bourdow · William Bowron · Lawrence E. Bradley · Peter Brehm · David Brewton · Stephen Briggs · Matthew Brown · Jeffrey Browning · Carter Bryan · Charles F. Burch, Jr. · Louis Burkot · Douglas Burnor · Glenn Butterworth · Michael Caddell · Ronald Campbell · Gary Chandler · Michael Checknoff · Peter T. Clarke · Theodore R. Clemons Jr. · Wayne G. Coates · Nicholas Cooke · Gary S. Copenhaver · Kirk Cordell · Michael Crickenberger · Michael W. Culbertson · John Thomas Darbyshire · Jonathan Davies · Scott T. Davis · Mark Delcuse · Magruder Dent · Claudie E. Denton · Stuart Diamond · Charles W. Dixon · Stephen Donahue · James Dunton · Derek Preston Dutcher · Robert Ellis · Paul N. Evans · Wyatt Ewell · Christopher Faith · John Fargo · Gary S. Farr · David Ferretti · Stephen E. Fischer · Allen Fitzpatrick · John Flack · John Fornaro · David M. Foster · James R. Fotter · David Fredenburg · Mark Freese · Elliot Freier · David Freneaux · Kenneth Friedman · Randall S. Frye · Randolph Frye · Anthony Gal · Robert Gehlmeyer · Gerard Geier · Charles Gentry · George Gerachis · Jack Gerard · Barry Germany · Jackson Gibbs · Jay Gibbs · Christopher Gibson · John Gibson · Steven Gifford · Richard Lenwood Gillette Jr. · Richard L. Goldberg · Harold Goodman · Croxton Gordon · James Christian Gordon · Donald Grasberger · Gary J. Gray · Richard Habel · Kerry Haber · Peter Hackes · Robert Ridley Hagan, Jr. · Angus Hagins · Mack Hagins · Benjamin A. Hagood · Christian Halstead · Richard S. Hanger · Stephen Hanna · Andre Harlfinger · Philip Hart · James Hartigan · Charles Haskins · Robert Helms · Stephen Herr · Brian R. Higgins · Jonathan Hill · Thomas Hill · Ellis B. Hilton · William Hinkle · Charles Hobson · Randall Hoeflein · John Hoffacker · Joseph Hogan · David Holaday · Paul Houghton · Richard Stevenson Howell · Joel Hulett · Patrick Hurst · Steven James · Jonathan M. Jay · William H. Jeschke · Kenneth Johnson · Robert Jones · Michael Julius · Stephen Kain · Frederick M. Kaspick · Thomas Kern · Carroll Kinsey · Worth Kirkman · Daniel Couch Klein · Edward Kloberdanz · Matthew Koch · Mark Kupke

· Robert Lacey · Norris Lackore · Christopher Lahr · John Lamb · Douglas Lasky · Lawrence M. Lavin · Kenneth Lawless · Mark Lawson · Peter Lawthers · Stephen R. Ledford · John Craig Leiby · Clark Lewis · David Lingerfelt · Douglass List · Daniel Listrom · Randall Lord · Christopher Loye · Robert W. Lyon · Andrew W. Mackey · Rafe Madan · John Madden · David Makel · Rea Marshall · William Steven Martin · Chris Massey · Charles Matthews · Charles Cain Mayhew · Michael A. McCallister · Douglas McCallum · Michael McCalmont · Kenneth McCaskill · Duncan J. McCrea · Terrance McGovern · Timothy McLaughlin · Daniel McLearen · James A. McLendon, Jr. · David Meiselman · Kevin Meiser · Paul A. Meyer · Mark Milby · Robert Miller · Aubrey Mitchell · Gregory J. Molner · Blake Morant · Jeffrey Morrison · Dennis Moulton · William Shaw Mulherin · Scott Myhre · Christopher Nelson · Kim Nelson · James A. Niederberger · Sean O'Neil · William Old · DeCourcy W. Orrick · Stanley Parchman · Jeffrey D. Peterson · Steven Peterson · Richard Petty · John R. Pherson · William Piper · Frank Poole · Richard Poole · James Pope · Paul A. Pope · Thomas Potter · Mark Powers · Charles Kipps Purcell · David Quittmeyer · Stephen Read · James A. Recktenwald, Jr. · Steven Redding · Jeffrey Lynn Reider · James Richardson · John Rickard · Charles Romine · Gary Rosenzweig · John Rouse · Gordon M. Ruef · Steven Russell · Eric Sall · Omar Sbitani · David Schumaker · Charles Scott · Daniel B. Shelly · Kim C. Shelton · Thomas Shricker · Edward Alexander Silver · Peter Simmons · Darrell Simpson · Robert C. Simpson · Leigh M. Smith · Mitchell Smith · Jeffrey A. Snyder · Russell Speidel · Lloyd F. Stamy, Jr. · Craig Stern · Fred B. Stillman · William M. Stone · Kirk Story · William Story · Charles Surber · Thomas C. Sutton · Mark Talley · John Thompson · William Thompson · Norris Tollefson · John Torrence · Dennis Tosh · Nelson Turner · John Vance · Thomas I. Viar · Richard C. Viohl · Robert Viol · John Voelker · Robert Vorperian · Robert Wagner · David Waller · John Wampler · Matthew Warren · Norman M. Warren · Steven Wellner · Peter Williams · Terence Wilson · Richard Wingo · John R. Wood · Dale Edward Wright · Mark Wright · Christopher Wronsky · John V. Yenchko · Stephen C. Yowell · Dennis Zakas · Wayne M. Zell · Richard Zenith

1980S

Mark Adams · John Armstrong · Michael Armstrong · Stephen Bailey · Ruben Basantes · Michael Beatty · Patrick Bell · David Belmonte · David Belote · Terry Bergey · Steve Billcheck · Wayne Boley · Martin Boo · Mark Boodée · Cleve Bosher · John Bratsch · Mike Braun · David Breen · Richard Brown · Ellis Butler · Scott Butler · Phil Byers · Chi young Chung · Darryl Churchill · Hywyn Churchill · Lee Coghlan · Thomas Cook · Joseph Costa · Dyron Dabney · Vertram Darrell Dabney · Dennis Dannel · Jeffrey Davis · Douglas DeGenaro · Gregory Demme · Phillip Dennis · David Detweiller · David Dokken · Sean Drumheller · Kevin Dwyer · Lawrence Ebert · Tucker Echols · Kurt Elam · Andrew Erickson · Todd Etter · Stephen Farlow · William Farquhar · Lehman Ford · Chris Foster · David Foster · Bradford Fox · Matthew Freeman · David Garland · John Gereski · Jay Gibbs · James Gibson · Marshall Ginn · Richard Glass · Michael Goggin · Thomas Goodrich · Dean Goodwin · Michael Green · Laurence Greenberg · Thomas Grexa · Trevon Gross · Richard Hammerly ·

Seung Jo Han · Stephen Harrison · Mason Harrup · Michael Hayes · Timothy Hefferon · Eric Heinsohn · Michael Hirsch · Nicholas Hoffman · Charles Hoggatt · Charles Douglas House · David Hughes · David Hyatt · David Jensen · Fielding Johnson · Stephen N. Jones · Wayne Jones · F. Burton Kann · Andrew Kaufman · Robert Keenan · Sean Kelbley · Kevin F. Kelley · Thomas Kelly · David Kenney · Robert Kesler · Andrew Kopser · Martin Kopser · Bruce Kothmann · Daniel Kothmann · Benjamin Lane · Michael Lane · Thomas Larus · Michael Laurenson · Lawrence M. Lavin · Thomas Leckey · Barry Lee · Deron Lovaas · Brady Lum · Mark Lyons · Rafe Madan · Bradley Marino · Forrest R. Marshall · Ernest Mathews · Vernon Melton · Scott Messner · Larry Mueller · Parker Myers · William Nelson · William Nichols · John Paul Nicolaides · Aaron Nir · Christopher North · Gilbert Pearman · Guido Peñaranda · John Perry · Keith Perry · John Plemmons · Thad Polk · Timothy Polk · Jeffrey Pool · Lester G. Pretlow · Jeffrey Prevenost · Jamie Richards · Tim Riggs · Jamie Rim · Jay Robards · Jeff Rogers · Christopher Rossbach · Thomas Rowe · David Ryan · Mark Salyer · Jeff Saunders · Morton Saunders · Bill Schmitz · Thomas Jay Sheffler · Anthony Shin · William Simson · Edward Smith · Lewis Smith · David Snouffer · Steven M. Sokoll · Jeffrey Stark · James Starr · Thomas Stluka · Todd Stone · Brogan Sullivan · Halsted Sullivan · Gregory Swaluk · Todd Takken · James Tavenner · Bryce Taylor · Hugh Teller · Christopher Tickle · Donald Toet · Aven Tsai · Theodore Turnau · John Vick · Dan Vincent · Spencer Vining · Nicholas D. Vlissides · John Wadlington · Brian Wagstaff · Pierce Walmsley · John Webber · Daniel Weigand · Stephen R. Welke · Brian White · Jonathan Wiening · Andrew Wilder · Jeffrey Willmore · Wade Wilson · Charles P. Wise, Jr. · Charles Wolfe · Paul Wolfe · Robert Worst · Xuemeng Xia · Andrew Youkilis · Neal Young

1990S

Drew Adelman · David J. Almquist · Curt Alt · Chris Ambrose · Chris Anderson · Rich Arnold · Michael Arthur · Jason Baker · Matthew Ballenger · Chris Baltimore · Scott Barker · Aaron Bartley · Michael Belinkie · Matthew Benko · David Bennett · Joseph Bernier-Rodriguez · Lars Bjorn · Patrick Blake · Steven Block · Tim Boda · Steve Bognaski · Matthew Bosher · Jon Brandt · Matt Breaks · Andrew Breen · Adam Bronstein · Brent Brown · Nathan K. Brown · Dave Buck · Eric Buechner · Andrew Burdick · Phil Byers · Frank Cardillo · David Cary · Kelly Caylor · Gerald Cephas · Don Chesworth · Donald Childress III · Eugene Chung · Drew Cogswell · Alexander Cohn · Nick Comerford · Tom Cook · Christopher Corr · Bradley Dakake · Jason Dandridge · Kurt Daniel · Thomas Deal · Chris DiBiagio-Wood · Chris Dillon · Robbie Dillon · Len Discenza · Kevin Dixon · Greg Dodson · John Duncan · Dave Eisenstadt · Kevin Elliott · Warren Ellsworth · Tom Ellwood · Tim Estes · Todd Feagans · Shawn Felton · J. Craig Fennell · Jonathan Finn · Matt Fischer · John-Paul La Fleur · Chris Foster · Mark Foster · David Fouché · Elliott Garber · Andrew Garibaldi · Chris Goldberg · Andrew Goldman · Austin Graham · Adam Greene · D.J. Gregory · Doran Gresham · Kai Groennings · Benjamin Grosz · Peter Habib · Marcus Hagegård · James Haley · Jeff Hall · Mitch Harris · Adam Hatcher · Jason Hathaway · Christopher Hawkins · Jim Heaney · Andrew Heffernan · C.J. Higley · Erik Hirsch · Chris

Holly · Jim Holmberg · Jared Hood · Charles Hornbostel · Jonathan Howse · Parker Hudnut · David Irby · Joel Peter Iverson · Archimedes Jao · H. Mitchell Jarrett · Tim Jarrett · Benjamin Johnson · Scott Johnson · Scott Johnston · Dave Keller · Farrell Kelly · Hyun Kim · Scott Kirkpatrick · Bobby Koo · Jun Koo · David Lattimore · J. Todd Lawrence · Ben Levin · Stephen Liang · Jared Q. Libet · John Lin · William Luckert · Karl Lugo · Mitchell Maddox · D.R. Tyler Magill · Jason Maier · Jason Malec · Kapil Malshet · Eric Martin · Stockton Mayer · Michael McCullough · Hall McGee · John McLaughlin · Denis McNamara · Kyle McNiff · Eric Meade · Brian Menard · Wren Miller · Douglas Min · Nathan Moore · Rudy Morgan · Tariq Moustapha · Walker Muncy · Sean Murray · Neil Nagraj · Tom Nassif · John Navarrete · Christopher Newman · Scott Norris · Tim O'Brien · Dixon Oates · Andrew Oh · John Edgar Park · Jeff Pavlovic · Tien-I Peng · Matthew Pierson · Brett Posten · Jonathan E. Provan · Derek Ramsey · Poulson Reed · Charles Repp · Sam Retzer · Robert Rhodes · Todd Rich · Kevin Ritz · Dan Roche · Scott Rohrbaugh · Justin Rosolino · Eric Rothwell · Justin F. Rousseau · Hugh Scott · Ronald A. Secrist · Willis Shawver · Alex Shin · George Shirley · Dan Shomaker · Todd Simkin · James Skinner · Jimmy Skinner · Jeff Slutzky · Jared Smith · Norman Smith · Sean Smith · Andrew Snyder · John Stanzione · James P. Steichen · Brett Stein · Bert Steindorff · Christopher Strain · Bryan Strickland · Matt Svoboda · Stephen Sweeney · Jeffrey Alan Taylor · Joseph Thibodeau · Benjamin Thompson · Jayson Throckmorton · Jeff Tucker · Daniel Twining · Matt Vanderzalm · Herbert Verr · Cabell Vest · Kris Walker · Blaise Warren · Donald C. Webb · Francis Thornton West · Francis West · T. Scott White · Morgan Whitfield · John Williamson · Rob Wise · Luke Wiseman · Jim Wiser · Seth Wispelwey · David Witkowski · Carter Wood · Derek Woodley · Evan Wooten · Andrew Wright · John Wright · Jason Wynn · Thomas Yang · Matt Zalubowski · Van Zeiler

2000S

Jasper Adams · Stephen Alexander · Matt Amodio · Jalil Andraos · Erik Arvidson · Matt Baer · Mike Belote · Frank Block III · Frank Block Jr. · Richard Block · Charles Blundon · Daniel Brown · Kevin Brown · Michael Del Bueno · Matthew Burnham · Sean Carlton · Aeryk Carr · Clay Carter · Greg Chafuen · Wo Chan · Michael Chen · Raheem Choudry · Jonathan Chung · Kevin Comer · Ryan Conley · Ynigo Daniel Coronacion · Olen Crane · David Crouch · Jonathan Damron · Lance DaSilva · Amos Davis · Kevin Ross Davis · Ben DiBiagio-Wood · Jonathan Duey · David Duxbury · Daniel Eckstein · Daniel Eichelberger · Juan Esteves · David Faulkner · Evan Fay · Matthew Floyd · Michael Galdo · Xiang Gao · George Gardenier · Franklin Geho · Chris Gercke · Michael Gifford · George Glass · Nathan Glass · Daniel Gomez · Eliott Grabill · Stephen Grant · Mark Grey-Mendes · Eric Grube · Nicholas Gunter · Thomas Hale-Kuipec · Ben Hamlin · Sean Happel · Ben Hassan · Michael Heiligenstein · Matt Heim · T.J. Henderson · Matthew Herbeck · Dan Herbst · Ray Hervandi · Jack Higgins · Daniel Hine · Wes Hockaday · William Hodges · Matthew Hogancamp · Erick Hong · Will van Hook · Blake Hunter · Harris Ipock · Ben Israel · Prakash Jayanthi · Michael Jefferson · John Jesus · Yuchen Jin · Adam Johnson · Chris Johnson · Tae Uck Kang · Jared Kassebaum · Alex Kast · Andrew Keller · Steven Kern ·

Tad Knier · Jimmy Ko · Jonah Lampkin · Hoo Lee · Leo Lee · Taki Lee · David Leon · Yong-Bee Lim · Giorgio Litt · Andrew Lockhart · Erik Loken · Marton Lonart · Ian Macdonald · Rob Marney · Robert Martinson · Gordon Marx · Jeff McKenzie · John McMahon · Lewis McNeel · Jack McQuarrie · Scott Meadows · Jake Mello · Burke Morton · Thomas Tuen Muk · Yojiro Murai · Winston Noel · Patrick O'Kelly · Hyung Joon Ohoe · Gerie Palanca · Sang-Ha Park · Alex Patton · Madhu Ravi · Rollin Reeder · Bart Renner · Won-Suk Rhee· Phillipp Risseeuw · Jay Robertson · Breier Scheetz · Adam Schulz · Mitch Seipt · Michael Shenefelt · Darin Showalter · David Sibert · David Simpson · Daniel Singer · Matt Smith · David Solomon · Varun Srirangarajan · Richard Staines · Garrick Suemith · Benjamin A. Sutphen · Nathan Swayne · Tommy Sweets · Sam Thienemann · Keith Thomas · Paul Tiffany · Tristan van Tine · Nick Trzcinski · Brendan Tufts · Chris Tuggey · Blake Tysinger · Jaime Vasquez · Ted Ke Wang · Matt Waring · Matt Wells · Trevor Wesolowski · Colin Whitlow · Christoph Wilhelm · Robert Wingfield · Han Gyul Yi · Matthew Young · Steven Young · Jonathan Yu

2010S – 2020S

Aaqil Abdullah · Siddarth Ajith · Miguel Alt · Brian Ammer · Seamus Anderson · Perrin Arnold · Charles Arthur · Nick Baldi · Brent Baumgartner · Richard Becker · Alex Boland · Matthew Bond · Scott Boulineaux · Forrest Brown · Alex Bryant · Nathan Burns · Andrew Burrill · Walter Buzzini V · Connor Campbell · Chris Cantone · Michael Capps · Michael Carmone · John Castillo · David Chang · Michael Chang · Timothy Chaplin · Todd Chatlos · Joey Chavez · Jerry Chen · Kevin Chen · Kai Cheng · Philip Collender · Ian Coombs · Nathaniel Coombs · John Costello · Jon Cottrell · Max Craft · Evan Craighead · Aidan Cronin · Dan Culbertson · Ben Cunningham · Tyler Curran · Andrew D'Amato · Adrian Dan · Daniel DeBord · William DeBord · Matthew Doyle · Ryan Duffin · Alden Duquette · Matthew Fay · Joseph Franco · Max Freedman · Jacob Friedmann · Bill Fuchs · Jonathan Garber · Jack Gereski · Benjamin Gonzalez · Cameron Goss · Chris Hall · Duke Hallman · Joey Hamilton · Charles Hancock (II) · Matthew Harris · Erik Haukenes · Michael Hawes · Tianyang He · Brian Henriquez · Marvin Hicks · Jacob Higgins · Ryan Hoak · Henry Hollandsworth · Javad Jarrahi · Denny Jeong · Damian Jessup · Nathan Johnson · Nick Juan · Artemie Jurgenson · Tong Kang · Jeremy Kemp · Mustafa Khan · Daniel Kim · Grant Kim · Edwin Kimko · CJ Kling · Aki Ko · Ryan Koontz · Matthew Korbon · Ho Shin "Andrew" Kwag · Chun-Ju Lai · Tass Lai · Kevin Lambert · Zack Larrabee · Patrick LeDuc · Justin Lee · Yongjin Lee · Kevin Lewis · Zach Lingle · Eric Liu · Travis Lively · Ting Cheong Lo · Trygve Loken · Melvin Lopez · Drew Lytle · Nick Lytle · Duane Macatangay · Joseph Marchese-Schmitt· Ned Martin · Jashan Matharoo · Sina Mazaheri · Seth McChesney · John McClorey · Mark McDonnell · Matthew McDonnell · Ben McGriff · Noah McIntire · Jacob McLaughlin · Scott McQuiddy · Rob Merrera · Luke Merrick · Jacob Mirpanah · Chuck Moran · Martin Moro · Andrew Morton · Chris Morton · Yangfan Mu · Mike Muldoon · Michael Mullins · Philip Munck · Matt Nicklas · Tong Niu · Jamar Nixon · Richard Ohr · Andrew Orvedahl · David Orvedahl · Christian Osborne · Austin Owen · Josh Palmer · Jonathan Park · John Perez · Wilson Pillow · Ameer Pretty · Ryan Pugh · Arjun Pundarika · Jimmy Qing · William Rainey · Jonathan Ramirez · Paul Redling · Connor Reilly · Marcus Rini · Daniel Roberson · Logan Romberger · Zachary Seid · Caleb Selph · Patrick Semesky · Varun Sharma · Tom Shaw · Michael Conor Sheehey · Jason Sheridan · Shayne Shiflett · Sean Shih · Thomas Short · Hriday Singh · Geoffrey Skelley · Matthew Slomka · Matthew Smith · Varun Srirangarajan · Jason Steckler · Jordan Stillman · Antonio Stoakley · Colin Sullivan · Steve Sun · Ravi Suresh · Kelin Swayne · William Talbot · Richard Tan · Mayank Tandon · Kyle Thornburgh · Pierce Tickle · Rafael Tiongco · Callen Toscano · Tu-an Truong · Rice Tyler · Brian Uosseph · Theo Voudouris · Ram Vuppaladadiyam · Luke Waddell · Jimmy Wang · Ben Warrick · Eric Weitzner · Chris Welsh · Will Wheaton · Kevin Willcox · Nick Williams · James Wilusz · Jay Windsor · Christopher Wong · George Wu · Eric Wuerschmidt · Keith Yacko · Haoran Yan · Kris Yorke · Sung Bae Yun · Tony Zeto · Bill Zhang · Victor Zheng · Yufei Zheng · Michael Ziegler · Alex Zorychta

INHABITANTS OF 5 WEST LAWN

Charles Hancock (1897-1898)
Walter F. Cornnell (1938-1939)
John B. Davis (1942-1943)
Thomas Jefferson Smith, III (1945-1946)
James Nottingham (1946-1947)
Myrick Canfield Clark (1950-1951)
Claude Crockett, Jr. (1957-1958)
Richard Harris (1968-1969)
Croxton Gordon (1973-1974)
David M. Foster (1974-1975)
Douglass List (1976-1977)
Eric Sall (1978-1979)
Matthew Koch (1979-1980)
Charles Kipps Purcell (1980-1981)
Leigh M. Smith (1981-1982)
Scott Myhre (1982-1983)
Thad Polk (1985-1986)
Michael Butterman (1987-1988)
Ellis Butler (1988-1989)
Andrew Youkilis (1989-1990)
Daniel Weigand (1990-1991)
Brogan Sullivan (1991-1992)
Matthew Benko (1992-1993)
Donald C. Webb (1993-1994)

RECIPIENTS OF THE GILBERT J. SULLIVAN AWARD

Bonnie J. Ford, 2006
Laurence G. Mueller, 2009
Donald G. Loach, 2010
Ernest Campbell Mead, Jr., 2010
Thomas M. Deal, 2016
Douglass Wm. List, 2016

LIST OF MAJOR SOURCES

Ballowe, James. "A History of the University Glee Club."
   Published in the *Glee Club 1980 Annual Report,* 1977.

Bruce, Philip Alexander. *History of the University of Virginia.*
   New York: MacMillan, 1921.

Dabney, Virginius. *Mr. Jefferson's University.*
   Charlottesville: University of Virginia Press, 1981.

College Topics / Cavalier Daily, various issues, 1890 to present.
Corks and Curls, 1888–present.
Virginia University Magazine (also known as the *University of Virginia Magazine* and the *Virginia Spectator*).

Concert programs from 1964 to 1989. Collection of Donald Loach.
Concert programs from 1993 to 1999. Collection of Jeff Slutzky.
Glee Club scrapbook, 1934–1940s. Small Special Collections Library
   of the University of Virginia
      This volume captured concert programs, newspaper clippings, cor-
      respondence, and other memorabilia from the Harry Rogers Pratt
      years, preserving some of the earliest existing programs of the Glee
      Club despite its twenty-five year sojourn in various forgotten (and
      no doubt damp) corners of the Glee Club House at 505 Valley Road.

INDEX

Founder's Day concerts, 105, 132, 220; at Gonzaga College High School, 212, 217; at the Jefferson Hotel, 183, 187; at the Jefferson Memorial, 182, 184, 186, *187*; at Kennedy Center, 131; at Monticello, 182, 185–86, *185*; at Old South Church in Boston, 191; at Quigley Seminary, 203; spring concerts, 93–94, 103, 113–15, 118, 127, 130, 140, 150, 153, 166, 179, 184–85, 194, 199, 201, 210, 214, 218, 232–34; at the Yale Club, 210, 220; at the Washington National Cathedral, 114, 125, 152

Virginia Glee Club, touring, 97, 125, 142, 150, 152, 171n15, 233–34; in the 1890s, 29, 31–32, 41–42; in the early 1900s, 44–45, 52, 55, 57; in the 1920s–1930s, 68–70; in the 1960s–1970s, 107, 126, 131–32, 138; in the 1990s, 200, 202–205, 210; in the 2000s and 2010s, 217, 222, 232; in 2020, 238–239; international, 106, 121–25, *124*, 127–30, *128*, *129*, 138–39, *139*, 143–46, *144*, *145*, 150, 152–53, 165, 212–15, *213*, *214*, 232, 240; to New York City, 75, 77, 79–81, *80*, 83, 86–87; spring break tours, 123, 150, 177, 203, 230, 237; Tour of the Northeast, 190–95, 201, 222; Tour of the South (1992), 175–80, *179*, *180*, 182, 194; Tour of the West Coast, 229–30

Virginia Glee Club, works performed (*see also songs by title*): "All the Things You Are," Jerome Kern, 209–10, 213; "Alle psallite," 178; "Alleluia," Randall Thompson, 210; *Alto Rhapsody*, Brahms, 96, 155, 217; "Ascendit Deus," Jacob Handl, 189, 210; "Ave Maria," Biebl, 138–39, 150, 177–78, 184, 188, 192–93, 210, 220, 228; "Ave Maria," Bruckner, 210; "Ave Maria," Adam Gumpelzhaimer, 188–89; "Ave Maria," Mark Keller, 188–90; "Ave Maria," Moore, 184; "Ave Maria," Alice Parker, 188,

190; "Ave Maria," various settings, 184, 189, 205; "Ave Maris Stella," Grieg, 209–10; "Ave Verum Corpus," Byrd, 166; "Avinu Malkeynu," Max Janowski, 209; *The Ballad of Little Musgrave and Lady Barnard*, Britten, 160; "Behold, I build an house," Lukas Foss, 201, 207n8; "Betelehemu," Wendell Whalum and Via Olatunji, 190; "Bogoroditse," Devo, 199; "Break Forth, O Beauteous Heavenly Light," Bach, 211; *Broken Glass*, David Davis and Michael Stillman, 128, 131; *Cantate Domino*, Hans Leo Hassler, 127; *Cantate Domino*, Dieterich Buxtehude, 122; "Cantique de Jean Racine," Fauré, 209, 212; *Carmina Burana*, Carl Orff, 153–54, 188; *Chichester Psalms*, 183; "Chorus of the Returning Pilgrims," Wagner, 210; "Christ lag in Todesbanden," Bach, 179; "Christus factus est," Bruckner, 189; "Clapping Music," Steve Reich, 190; "Come Again, Sweet Love," Dowland, 228; "Come, Heavy Sleep," Benjamin Broening, 173, 175, 178; *Concerto Grosso*, Handel, 198; *Crucifixus*, Lotti, 199; David set (Josquin, Thomas Tomkins, William Billings, Benjamin Broening), 183–85; *Defense of Corinth*, Carter, 131; "De Profundis," Arvo Pärt, 175, 190, 197–98; "De Profundis," Lassus, 136; *Dettingen Te Deum*, Handel, 114, 153; *Deutsches Magnificat*, Heinrich Schütz, 132; "Deux Motets," Maurice Duruflé, 173; *Die erste Walpurgisnacht*, Mendelssohn, 151; *Die Meistersinger*, 86, 127; *Dixit Dominus*, Handel, 197–98; "Dona nobis pacem," Ralph Vaughan Williams, 234; "Drink to Me Only with Thine Eyes," Colonel Mellish, 209; "Duo seraphim," Victoria, 212; "The Elegy of Spring," Shawn Felton, 200; "El yivneh hagalil," 201; *Emblems*, Carter,